$\mathcal{O}$UR GRATITUDE TO

Josh & Dottie McDowell for taking us under their wings, believing in the project, and standing with us.

We are also deeply grateful to the two following people and the organizations they represent for sharing with us dozens of scholarly, sensitive and scriptural articles for the Appendices in this book:

Marilyn Adamson, leader within Cru and the founder and director of Everystudent.com.

S. Michael Houdmann, Founder, President, and CEO of Got Questions Ministries.

We are grateful to Need Him Global for agreeing to allow us to refer people to their ministry, thereby offering people a safe place to ask questions about Jesus and be able to talk to someone live.

We are grateful to Sonia Armour and Joel Craig for their invaluable insight in the beginning stages in the manuscript of this book and to Jeanne Cadeau for her superb proofreading.

*L*IGHT IN ACTION THANKS

The hundreds of volunteers who have acted, assisted, and translated,

Along with our beloved families & our churches,

Together with countless others, spread across the planet, who have courageously

Stood with us, mentored us, and gone to battle on their knees

So that *Tetelestai* could become a reality.

TETELESTAI

FACILITATOR GUIDE

Produced by: Light in Action INC.
1104 El Sonoro Dr.
Sierra Vista, Az, 85635

Cover & Interior Design: Light in Action INC.

ISBN-13: 978-1718731691
ISBN-10: 1718731698

TETELESTAI

FACILITATOR GUIDE

ARLEN & CYNTHIA ISAAK

LIGHT IN ACTION
PRODUCE - TRAIN - EQUIP
www.lightinaction.org

To Him who loved us

and has freed us from our sins by His blood...

TO HIM BE GLORY...FOREVER

Revelation 1:5,6

CONTENTS

Dates You Will Be Meeting

Fill out the dates you will be meeting to study each chapter.
Have each participant fill this chart out in their own Study Guide as well.

CHAPTER	DATE & TIME
1- In the Beginning	
2 - The Promise	
3 - Provision	
4 - Deliverance	
5 - The Law	
6 - Atonement	
7 - Lamb of God	
8 - Messiah	
9 - Salvation	
10 - It is Finished	
11- Eternal Life	
12 - What do You Believe?	

BEFORE YOU BEGIN

Falling in Love with the Hero

"He gave me a link where I could read the Gospels in Arabic." I[1] sat spellbound listening to Margaret[2], a former Muslim from Saudi Arabia, as she told her story. Margaret shared how she had a growing disillusionment with Islam. In despair, she had stumbled onto a forum where someone online gave her a link to where she could read the New Testament.

"Margaret, what was your reaction to reading the Gospels?" I asked. Her eyes came alive,
"I fell in love with Jesus."

Whether or not your testimony is as dramatic as Margaret's, if you have had the privilege of hearing the Gospel, you know it is unlike any other story in the world. It is the Story of how the God of the Universe sent His only Son to die in our place in order to give us Eternal Life. Together with Margaret and millions of others around the world, we too have fallen in love with the Hero of this Story.

Fiercely Poetic

The beauty of the Story of Jesus is that it actually begins in the book of Genesis. From cover to cover the Bible contains one stunning plot: Redemption. When we worked on the transcripts for *Tetelestai,* we were repeatedly overcome by the harmony of the Scriptures. In awe, we would say to each other, "The Bible is fiercely poetic!" Our prayer is that the episodes of *Tetelestai* will help *you* trace the Eternal Story of Redemption from the Garden of Eden to the risen Christ.[3] As we unfold the Scriptures together, we pray that you also will stand in awe at a fresh glimpse of the God who passionately loves humanity and paid the ultimate price for our rescue.

What we can't do... but you can!

Over a thousand volunteers from over 150 different churches worked together with the *Light in Action* team for the filming of *Tetelestai.* Motivated by a love for Jesus and a desire to make Him known, we poured ourselves into this series. We dreamed of the day when *Tetelestai* could assist men and women around the world in

---

[1] Margaret shared this story with Cynthia Isaak; Arlen didn't get to meet her.

[2] Margaret is her English name.

[3] The *entire* Bible's intricate symmetry is breathtaking. *Tetelestai* does not cover the entire Bible, however. Because we are limiting this series to only eleven episodes, we have had to be selective in which stories we covered. We have chosen to highlight 24 key Biblical narratives. We trust these stories will paint a vibrant Big Picture of the Story of Redemption.

sharing Christ with others, whether in evangelism or discipleship. Now that *Tetelestai* is in your hands, the last and most important step is up to *you*. It's the most crucial step, and it's something we cannot do.

We can't sit beside people as they watch an episode and answer their questions. We can't hang out with them afterward and engage in stimulating discussions that draw them closer to God. We can't offer to take them out for coffee if they want to talk one-on-one.

We cannot do any of those things, but *you can!* That's why your role as the Facilitator for *Tetelestai* is so crucial! We hope this book will assist you in making each episode applicable and personal so that God can bring about true transformation through His Word.

Pointers for Truly Connecting:

1. **Take a roll call.**
   This doesn't have to be out loud, but we encourage you to keep track of who is coming to your Bible Study. This will help you learn names, track progress and be intentional about pursuing follow up with these individuals.

2. **Pray for each person by name.**
   Using your roll call list you can pray for each person regularly. Remember, there is a real battle for the souls of people, both unsaved and saved. Satan wants to keep unbelievers far from Christ, and believers in a state of uselessness. The antidote for both of these is prayer along with meaningful and intentional interaction with the Word of God.

3. **Follow up with those who miss a study.**
   Don't let it slide! If you've noticed someone didn't come, give them a call! Let them know they were missed and set up a time to make up the missed lesson. I know many people who are grounded in the Word of God today due to people who were passionate about mentoring them. Don't give up on people easily!

4. **Be honest:**
   Have you ever noticed how everyone sits up and pays closer attention when the leader says something like, "I struggle with this, too," or "I've messed up."? The beauty of the Gospel is that there's only One Star: it's Jesus! We don't ever have to be afraid of telling people we need Him; it makes them realize how much they do, too.

5. **Show genuine interest in people:**
   The best way to make people want to come back is by truly loving them and helping them realize you

truly care about them. Jesus said, "*By this everyone will know that you are my disciples, if you love one another.*" (John 15:35)

Who are you doing *Tetelestai* with?

A Group of Believers

I have a friend in Cambodia who is getting ready to use *Tetelestai* in her leadership training. Strong believers will be equipped in evangelism using *Tetelestai*. Perhaps you also are planning to use *Tetelestai* with a group of solid Christians. These tips will help:

Pointers for a Believer's Bible Study:

1. **Personal growth:**
   Watching God's Redemption Story progressively unfold from Genesis through to the resurrection of Christ is a breathtaking journey that will deepen each person's walk with God.

2. **Training for outreach:**
   From the first day of the Bible Study to the last, encourage every single person in the group to see this series as a time of training, getting them ready to also lead a Bible Study…. but with an unbeliever.
   It is crucial for your group to be faithfully memorizing the verses and learning where to find the various passages in their own Bibles so that someday they also can be confidently reaching out to others.

   During the discussion time encourage them to think of how an unsaved person would be reacting to those very same questions. The other day, Qwon, a Vietnamese college student who is a new believer, watched a few episodes of *Tetelestai* with us. During the discussion time, he tried to envision the questions or hurdles that he would have had as an atheist.

A Group of Seekers

From beginning to end, the *Tetelestai* Bible Study was designed for evangelism. You won't have to tweak anything in your Bible Study if you're reaching out to non-believers.. The *Facilitator's Guide* you hold in your hands will walk you through this Bible Study step by step, assisting you in leading an unbeliever to Christ. You will find more helpful pointers throughout this chapter as well.

A Mixed Group:

If you have both believers and seekers in the same group, *Tetelestai* will be an easy tool for you to use. It will give a solid foundation to the believers and help lead the seeker to Christ.

Pointers for a Mixed Group Bible Study:

1. ***Keep the Focus on Evangelism***
   This will be easy to do because the series was written with this focus in mind.

2. ***Recruit Prayer***
   Sometimes a youth group might decide to host an outreach where each person brings a buddy to the Bible Study. Before starting the series, recruit each believer in the group to not only bring their friend but help you by faithfully praying for their salvation.

What Size is Your Group?

This Facilitator Guide was designed with a group Bible Study in mind, but can easily be adapted to be used one-on-one as well! In fact, our first test group involved a friend of ours doing a *Tetelestai* Bible Study with a Muslim co-worker. She would watch an episode and then later they would meet online to discuss the questions.

What changes in a one-on-one context? Well, in a group Bible Study, during the discussion time, the topics are divided up. In a one-on-one Bible Study you won't have to divide up any topics. Simply read and discuss all of them.

Equipping You with Answers. Say What?!

We hope your Bible Study Group asks a lot of good questions. Don't let that thought scare you! We've gathered some incredible supplementary materials to help you along the way. We have compiled a list of the possible questions your group might have and prayerfully provided you with brief answers. These questions and answers are located at the end of each Chapter under the heading, "Questions your group might have."

The Appendices of this Book:

What if a brief answer is not enough, though? Someone in your Bible Study may have a question that is so complex or weighty that further discussion is required in order to adequately answer their question.

For example, you may have someone in your Bible Study who, like Margaret from Saudi Arabia, comes from an Islamic background. The thought of God having a Son, or the Bible being the trustworthy and uncorrupted Word of God are only two topics that will be giant hurdles!

With anticipation to questions (like these!) that might arise during this series, we have gathered specific articles to address these various topics. We have placed these articles in the Appendix of this book. Each article is sensitive, scholarly and biblical, and will equip you with the tools necessary to help each member of your Bible

Study navigate the tricky waters of these weighty issues. From archaeological discoveries to discussions on homosexuality, each article will help you deal with these questions in light of the Scriptures.

FAQs about the Appendices:

Q: Where did the articles come from?

A: Two incredible ministries, EveryStudent.com and GotQuestions.org have graciously shared their articles with us for the Appendices.

> "**Got Questions Ministries** seeks to glorify the Lord Jesus Christ by providing biblical, applicable, and timely answers…to point you to what the Bible says concerning your question.[4]"

> **EveryStudent.com** was founded by Marilyn Adamson, a leader in Cru. Marilyn is a former atheist whose life was transformed by Jesus Christ. Her life is now centered on helping others come to know Him. [5]

Q: Can I make copies of these articles for those in my Bible Study Group?

A: Both GotQuestions.org and EveryStudent.com allow you to print their articles for the sake of allowing people to read them (never for the purpose of sale). Copy them in their entirety and give each article the proper credit to the respective ministry.

Q: Are the articles in different languages?

A: Both GotQuestions.org and EveryStudent.com are international ministries that work in 40+ languages with an ever-growing reach. This is very valuable information if you are reaching out to people in your group who speak English as a second language! Consider directing them to the respective websites for certain articles. For example, this link: https://www.gotquestions.org/Arabic/Arabic-Bible-God-Word.html takes you to the article, *"Is the Bible God's Word?"* in Arabic from GotQuestions.

Q: Why are there two Appendices?

A: This book you hold in your hands contains both the Appendix from the Study Guide (which is the "student book" to accompany *Tetelestai*) as well as the Appendix for you, the facilitator.

> **Study Guide Appendix:** Because you have an exact copy of Study Guide Appendix, you can read the very same articles that are being recommended to your students. We feel this is important so that you know what they are reading and can better encourage them or answer their questions.

---

[4] https://www.gotquestions.org/about.html

[5] https://www.everystudent.com/menus/marilyn.html

Facilitator Guide Appendix: These articles are only in your book but you may make copies of them if you feel your students would benefit from them. They are all articles we felt were helpful in equipping you to face some of the different questions that you will face throughout this series.

Q: What is the difference between the two Appendices?

A: The Appendix to the Study Guide (student book) covers the general questions that most people face as they begin to study God's Word. The Facilitator Guide Appendix (the teacher book) however, contains articles that we believe will help equip you as the facilitator in answering *specific questions from people of various socio-religious backgrounds.*

Pointers on Answering Questions:

1. *Encourage them to take notes:*
   We don't expect people to take notes while the actual episode is playing, but after watching it you will have a brief discussion time. Encourage your group to jot down any references, questions or thoughts they may have during this time.

2. *Don't bring up unnecessary questions:*
   We have tried to anticipate questions that people from a wide range of worldviews might have. These are *not* questions you should introduce however, in the discussion time! In other words, if the question doesn't come up naturally, there's no need to discuss it. Sometimes bringing up an unnecessary question will cause more harm than good. For example, there's no reason to go into a discussion on the fact that the trinity is biblical if no one in your group even questions that[6].

3. *Affirm the questioner:*
   Always: 1) Affirm the question. You might say something like, "That's an interesting question; I'm glad you asked that." 2) Always answer with respect. If the person is rude or arrogant, don't let that change the way you respond. Never mock or belittle. Never raise your voice or get angry.

4. *Encourage questions:*
   My mother always said that when someone has a counterfeit they hope no one examines it too closely. However, when someone knows they have the genuine article they enthusiastically and unreservedly encourage people to investigate. They know they have nothing to be afraid of and nothing to hide. One

---

[6] Obviously this is a principle not a hard fast rule! The Holy Spirit needs to be your Guide! If you're aware of the fact that a large number of people in your group struggle with a certain question, you might want to pray about bringing it up yourself during the discussion time. Another reason you may have for bringing up questions is if you are using *Tetelestai* to train leaders. Talking about specific questions they will need to prepare for, will be your prerogative.

of the best things you can do when mentoring anyone who is studying the Word of God is to encourage them to dig deeper and have the freedom to ask questions. We have nothing to fear, friends. We hold the Truth!

5. ***Don't be afraid to say "I don't know."***
Some of the professors I most admired were those who could admit, "I don't know, but I'll help you find the answers." This type of honesty actually builds people's confidence. Rest assured that no one knows everything or expects anyone else to! Don't leave people hanging, however. The answers are out there; help them find them.

6. ***Keep to the main point:***
Encouraging people to feel that they can ask questions does NOT mean you need to discuss each topic *right then*. Your goal is to help people go away with the main theme of the Bible Study pulsing through their hearts. It's your job to keep the discussions from getting derailed onto a side road.

7. ***Offer to talk one-on-one:***
Be available to talk with students one-on-one after the study. At times, certain students are too shy or feel uncomfortable speaking during group discussions, but have questions they would still like addressed. Other times, students who feel very free to give an opinion can end up dominating the discussion time. In both of these cases, your best move may be to offer to engage with the student after the study is over. This will allow all students a rich and comfortable environment in which to learn and share.

8. ***Sometimes, "Wait and see" is the best answer:***
If you are studying the Bible with someone who comes from a completely different worldview from the one given in Scripture, each episode is going to bring new hurdles for them. The Word of God is powerful and will continue to work in the heart of a sincere seeker. Sometimes (especially early on in the series) the best answer is: "You know, I love your question. It shows that you're really wrestling with this. There's still a lot of ground to cover in this series. Please hang tight, and keep listening and give the Bible a chance. Things will start to fall into place and make more sense as we go. Think of it this way, if we were building a house now, we would be down working on the foundations or the walls. But the answer to your question is up on the roof! If you wait just a little while longer I think you'll receive the answer to your question. "

9. ***Point them to the "Dig Deeper" Section in their Study Guide:***
The *Dig Deeper* section points them to the articles in their Appendix that are relevant to that chapter.

Where the Real Power Is

We could not be more proud of the *Light in Action* team and the incredible talents God poured out upon each one making this series. From the costumes, make-up, acting, and photography to the editing and special FX, it still blows my mind when I see what each member on our team did to make *Tetelestai* a reality. We're pretty stoked about the whole thing.

Not for a minute, however, do we lose sight of where the real power in the *Tetelestai* series lies. We know lives will be changed because of the power of *God's Spirit using His Word.* The Bible is sharper than a two-edged sword; it penetrates right to someone's heart and judges their thoughts and attitudes. (**Hebrews 4:12**)

Hostile, Hardened or Apathetic?

I don't think a month goes by when I don't hear an amazing story about someone coming to faith when they studied God's Word. The Bible has the power to disarm the hostile attacker, soften the mind of the hardened skeptic, and grip the heart of the apathetic mocker.

Recently I read the story of a young Confucianist scholar named Li-Show-Ting. When Li-Show-Ting's uncle became a follower of Christ, Li-Show-Ting was horrified. He decided the best way to help his uncle come back to his senses and return to ancestor worship, was to show him how ridiculous and inconsistent the Bible was. He decided to read the New Testament out loud to his illiterate uncle in order to reveal the New Testament's mistakes to him.

"However, Li-Show-Ting was in for a surprise. As he read aloud he was held spellbound by what he read. It made so much sense to him...[7]" Li-Show-Ting eventually surrendered His life to Christ and became an amazing evangelist leading over ten thousand people to the Lord in his lifetime!

An Open Bible

A few years ago, we had the privilege of meeting Abdu Murray, a former Muslim. I love his story! As a Muslim, Abdu took great pride in starting arguments with Christians in order to "knock the faith out of them[8]" and sway them towards Islam. One day Abdu decided to read the New Testament in order to find more fuel for his arguments. He did this with no intention of believing a word of the Bible but solely for the purpose of criticizing it.

As Abdu read, however, he was convicted and God began to work in his heart. Abdu, a brilliant man who has been named in *Best Lawyers in America,* did not take his quest for the truth lightly. Eventually, after tireless

---

[7] Janet and Geoff Benge. *Lottie Moon: Giving Her All for China;* YWAM Publishing; 2001, pg. 145 and 146

[8] These are his own words for describing his arguments.

investigation, Abdu became a passionate follower of Jesus Christ. Today, Abdu Murray is an author, apologist and international speaker[9]. His challenge to all those who seek to win others to Christ is this: "May we never have lofty words and a closed Bible.[10]"

God is Already at Work!

As the facilitator of this Bible Study, there's one last truth of which you must never lose sight. This truth will always fill your heart with courage and anticipation. When you look into the faces of the ones you will lead in this Study Group, you can rest assured that God is at work within them and something radical (albeit invisible to our human eyes) is happening. God tells us that His Spirit is *already* convicting them of their need for Him. (**John 16:8**) When we study the Word of God with someone else, we are partnering with what God is already doing in their hearts!

Pointers for Trusting in the Bible's Power:

1. ***Have Bibles on hand:***
   Each episode contains the references for the verses read in that episode. While we don't expect people to be able to follow along or read these verses while watching the episode (it's too fast for that) we do expect you to open up the Bible during the discussion time. It's a good idea to have a couple extra Bibles on hand.

2. ***Encourage people to get Bibles of their own:***
   If someone doesn't have a Bible, you may consider giving them one or helping them download a Bible App for their cell phones. Having their own Bible is critical for understanding and growth.

3. ***Teach them how to use the Bible:***
   It can seem tedious or bothersome to teach someone how to navigate the Bible. It is absolutely crucial, however, and worth every extra minute you patiently wait for someone to figure out how to find the verses in their own Bible.

4. ***Have each person follow along in their own Bible:***
   Seeing the truth of the Word of God with their own eyes during the discussion time, makes a world of difference. This also ensures that, down the road, that person will be able to find the verses again and show others the same truths! You are sowing seeds that will reap a great harvest!

---

[9] Abdu Murray is the North American director with Ravi Zacharias International Ministries (RZIM) www.rzim.org

[10] You can read his bio on RZIM: http://rzim.org/bio/abdu-murray/ or watch his testimony: https://www.youtube.com/watch?v=ENrCDKf5geQ

5. ***Encourage them to read the Bible during the week:***

In the *Study Guide* designed for each participant to use, there are two different lists of Biblical references. The first is entitled: *Read it for Yourself.* It's a list of the passages that were taught in the Episode. The second is entitled *Dig Deeper.* This list often contains more verses that will give further information to what was taught. At the end of each Bible Study, encourage your group to read the Bible on their own during the week.

You also have a copy of Read if for Yourself and Dig Deeper in each chapter so you know exactly what the students are looking at in their Study Guide and can better encourage them in their reading.

6. ***Encourage them to memorize verses from the Bible:***

I love the late Dawson Trotman's story[11]. He was the founder of the mission organization *Navigators*[12]. Dawson tells of a verse memorization competition held at a youth group he was invited to attend. Dawson memorized each verse. He was not a believer and did this only to get points for his team. These verses, however, kept coming back to his mind during the week and started stirring his soul, eventually convicting Dawson of his need for the Savior!

In the *Study Guide,* a verse is given to memorize for each episode. Be sure to make this an integral part of your Bible Study. Encourage each person to memorize the verse. We suggest giving a small token prize for those who do memorize it. Make it fun. I have seen time after time, a room full of sophisticated adults really getting into this! Many of them will memorize the verse only because they know it will please you, and they'll get a chocolate out of the deal. You and I both know however, that the true prize is the fact that God's precious truths are being sown in their hearts.

Independently of whether your group is made up of Christians or seekers, this memorization is important. These verses will help ground believers in their faith and prepare them for sharing it with others. These same Scriptures will begin to work within the hearts of those who do not yet believe. God's Word brings conviction in ways you and I cannot measure... just as they did for Dawson Trotman.

A Life-Changing Journey

Know that as you embark on this adventure of being the facilitator for the *Tetelestai* series, that the *Light in Action* team has been praying for you! Our prayer is that this resource will serve you in engaging the hearts and minds of those you will be leading. Over the next few weeks, as you trace God's hand through the pages of biblical history, may this study infuse your group with a renewed boldness and confidence for sharing the

---

[11] http://turret2.discipleshiplibrary.com/1B.mp3 Listen to an audio recording of Dawson telling his incredible testimony.

[12] You can read more about the Navigators on their website: https://www.navigators.org/

Gospel with others. As you unpack key biblical narratives and watch foundational truths come to life, may the power of God's Word presented in a fresh way draw each of you closer to Him.

Above all, may you fall more deeply in love with the Hero of the Story. For some in your group, it will be falling in love for the very first time as they discover God's stunning plan for our Redemption and are introduced to the One we were created for. For them, this will truly be a life-changing journey. *One that brings Eternal Life.*

*"..Whoever hears my Word and believes in Him who sent Me has Eternal Life and will not be judged but has crossed over from death to life." (**John 5:24**)*

Arlen & Cynthia Isaak
along with all the beloved
Light in Action Team

CHAPTER 1

IN THE BEGINNING

Pre Bible Study Checklist:

- ❏ Choose the dates for this 12 session Bible Study.
- ❏ Gather everyone's name and contact information.
- ❏ Have extra Bibles and pens on hand.
- ❏ Pray for each participant to come and be open to God's Word and His Spirit.
- ❏ Be familiar with the Introduction you will give to this Bible Study series.
- ❏ Be familiar with the Synopsis.
- ❏ Be familiar with the questions and dynamics of how the Group Discussion will flow.
- ❏ Glance through the *"Questions Your Group Might Have"* located at the end of this lesson.

Synopsis of the Episode:

In the Beginning describes how the restless search for fulfillment within the heart of every human reveals a soul thirst placed there by God to draw us to Himself. With archaeological discoveries and astounding fulfillment of prophecies, *In the Beginning* presents a fast-paced solid apologetic for the accuracy and trustworthiness of the Bible. As you delve into **Genesis 1:1** you will discover the attributes of this God you were created to know.

Facilitator's Introduction to share with the Group:

Thirty Seconds:

Have you ever caught only 30 seconds of an action movie right in the thick of the most dramatic scene? Although the music is intense and the action is fast-paced, you don't know who all the characters are and you're unaware of the intricate plot. While those around you may be moved to tears when the hero gives his life to save someone, you find yourself disconnected and confused.

How could things have been different? Well, watching the movie from the beginning would have helped, wouldn't you say? For many people, their exposure to the Bible is similar to this example. If you could compare the Bible to a movie, then they've watched thirty seconds of most famous scenes…. but without understanding the plot.

Tetelestai:

In the most famous passage of the Bible, the Hero dies. Moments before He breathes His last breath, however, He proclaims a word: "Tetelestai." The word "*Tetelestai*" (Teh-TELL-eh-sty) is Greek for "It is Finished." *What* exactly had Jesus finished…? *Why* does this phrase have the potential to change human destiny? In order to find these answers, we're going to start the Story of the Bible from the beginning, study several key narratives and unfold the plot. As we do, I hope the message of the Bible comes to life for you. It reveals the Story of a God who passionately loves humanity and will pay the ultimate price for their rescue.

What does this have to do with you?

Seeking Answers?

If you are spiritually curious, we want to walk this journey with you. We want you to feel comfortable as you ask questions, investigate, and wrestle with what the Bible has to say. We pray this Study will put the pieces of the Bible together in a way that will allow you to catch a breathtaking glimpse of God's love, and how much He desires to have a relationship with you.

Going Deeper?

If you already have a relationship with God, we pray that throughout this Bible Study two things will happen:

First, we pray the beautiful truths of God's Word will soak into every part of your soul. Our desire is that you fall more deeply in love with God as you take a fresh look at the depths of what He has done for you.

Second, we pray that today you will already begin to think about who you are going to share His life with. Perhaps a neighbor, a relative, a classmate or co-worker? As you grapple and engage with His Word, please see this as a valuable training time that will equip you to effectively share God's Eternal Story of Redemption with those who have never heard.

Watch Episode 1 - *In the Beginning*

Only the Eternal God can Truly Satisfy Us:

There is a longing within every human heart. A hunger in the soul. A thirst that can't be satisfied. Deep inside, we long for something more, more than what is in our world. These longings cannot be satisfied by pursuing knowledge, pleasure, wealth and possessions. They are amplified as we search for meaning and purpose during the few days of our lives. There is only One who can bring meaning, fulfillment, joy and peace to your life. He is the only One who can fill the void and quench the thirst within our souls.

Until we find Him there is a restless yearning, a longing that He put in our hearts. Just as thirst is necessary to draw someone to water, these longings within our heart were meant to call us to God. Within the heart of every human being, He has placed eternity. Because of this, nothing but the Eternal God can truly satisfy us.

You can Know God Through the Bible:

It is through the Bible that you will be introduced to the Eternal God. The Bible is a collection of 66 individual writings called books. Even the name "Bible" comes from a Greek word that means "books" The Bible has been divided into two sections called the Old and New Testaments. To make reading easier, each book was divided up into chapters and verses. In the first few pages of your Bible you will usually find a list of these books. Follow along in your Bible to verify the accuracy of everything that you hear, so that your confidence will be in what God says!

God is the True Author of the Bible:

The Bible is the world's best seller! It is the most quoted, read and printed book in all of history. It has been translated into almost 2,500 languages. It has influenced and transformed lives throughout the ages. The Bible was written through 40 different men, over a period of 1,600 years, across 3 continents, and in 3 languages. Even though these authors came from a wide range of professions and lived in various locations during different time periods, the diverse manuscripts came together perfectly. **2 Timothy 3:16** and **2 Peter 1:21** affirm that God told these men what they should write. Over 3,800 times in the Bible you will find phrases emphasizing that God is the Author of the Bible, phrases such as **Jeremiah 1:2**, *"And the word of the LORD came to him…"*.

The Bible is Historically Accurate:

Throughout the ages, archeology has confirmed the accuracy of the Bible. Even the most minute details of little-known passages have proven to be historically sound. Take **Isaiah 20:1** for example. Historians questioned the veracity of the events described in the passage. In 1843, however, in northern Iraq, archaeologist Paul Émile Botta unearthed the palace of King Sargon. Astonishingly, engraved on the palace walls was a description of the very same events being described in **Isaiah 20:1**! With the Bible's help, renowned archaeologist Dr. Nelson Glueck discovered more than a thousand ancient sites in the Transjordan area, and another 500 in the Negev. In his book, *Rivers in the Desert,* Dr. Nelson Glueck stated that there has never been an archaeological discovery that has contradicted the Bible! Dr. William Ramsay, a Scottish professor and archeologist, concluded that because of the Bible's historical accuracy, it had to be the very words of God Himself.

Prophecies Confirm the Bible's Divine Authorship:

The Bible contains hundreds of prophecies foretelling future events. In **Psalm 22,** King David described crucifixion 400 years before it was used as a form of capital punishment. **(Isaiah 44:28)** Isaiah mentioned King Cyrus by name 150 years before his reign. **(Isaiah 39:5-7)** Isaiah also foretold the fall of Jerusalem 100 years before it was taken over by the Babylonians. In **Daniel 11** there are 135 prophecies so precise that they describe major alliances, battles, marriages and even murder. This same book, Daniel, foretold the rise and fall of the Babylonian, Medo-Persian, Grecian and Roman empires.

The Bible Tells One Eternal Story:

The Bible has one running plot that connects all the details and events together. Throughout all the drama and descriptions, there is one theme that makes the whole Story make sense. It is this central plot that we are going to watch unfold as we study this Book. So what is the "Eternal story of the Bible"? What better place to start than the beginning!

God is Eternal:

In the very first verse of the Bible, **Genesis 1:1**, we see that before time began, God already existed. God never had a beginning, nor will He have an end. That's hard for our minds to grasp because we humans are confined by time. We can talk about the past as we remember days that have gone by, but we cannot go back in time. We can make plans for tomorrow as we dream about the future, but we cannot go ahead in time even one minute! God, however is not like that! God is *outside* of time. God is present in the past, the present, and the future, all at the same time! **(Psalm 90:2)** He never changes. He never gets tired. He never diminishes. God is eternal!

God is All-Present:

Not only is God not limited by time, God is not limited by space. We humans are completely limited by space. No matter how much we would like to be in more than one place at a time, we cannot. No matter how fast we travel, or how much our schedule demands of us, we can only be in one place at a time. God is not like we are! The Bible says that God is all-present, or in other words: God is everywhere at the same time. **(Psalm 139:4,7-10)**

God is Triune:

There is something else we discover about God in the first four words of the Bible. The book of Genesis was written in Hebrew. The word for "God" in Hebrew is Elohim. In Hebrew, when you see an "im" on the end of the word, that usually signifies it is plural. Why then does the word for God, "Elohim", have an "im" on the end of it? This plural ending on the name for God is the first indication that we have in the Bible that the One God reveals Himself in three Persons.

Dr. Arnold Fruchtenbaum wrote that the Hebrew Scriptures portray God to be One in three Persons. The New Testament sheds even more light on the subject, revealing Him to be Father, Son, and Holy Spirit. Each One being eternal, equal, and distinct.

The truth is that God is infinite. For us humans, who are finite, to fully comprehend God would be like expecting little ants to be able to learn how to read! Just as it would be impossible for them to grasp even the most basic concepts of our language, it would be impossible for *us* to fully comprehend an infinite God! God has told us many things about His nature in the Bible that we must believe even without fully understanding.

God is All-Powerful; the Creator and Sustainer:

In **Genesis 1:1** we see that God is the Designer and Creator of everything that exists. By the power of His word He created everything. **(Genesis 1:3)** God sustains the universe in all of its vastness. **(Hebrews 1:3)** What then could be impossible for God? More than 50 times in the Bible God is described as being all-powerful. When you face a serious problem or when your future seems to offer you no hope, with whom do you seek counsel? Where do you go for help? The all-powerful God of the Bible says to you: "Come to me! Trust in me. I care for you."

God is All-Knowing:

Have you ever considered how much knowledge it would take to design the heavens and the earth? Whether looking through a telescope at our vast galaxy or peering through a microscope at finely tuned biological organisms, we will never fully understand the complexities and intricacies of our universe. The Designer of the universe does, however! The Bible says that God is all-knowing. **(Psalm 147:5)**

Far more amazing is the fact that this incredible God chose to know you and me personally! So many times we feel so alone wondering, "Does anyone even care that I exist?" It is through this Book, the Bible, that you will be introduced to Someone who not only knows your name, but chooses to know every single thing about you. **(Psalm 139:1,2,4,13,16)**

You Were Created for this Relationship:

You were created by this Wonderful God. He is the One your heart longs for! This is why God has given us His Word: the Bible. Knowing Him is the reason for this life. He offers you a relationship that goes beyond this life and lasts forever. Today could be just …*the Beginning.*

Group Discussion Time: Personal & Relevant

1. Divide into groups of 3-5 people.
2. Distribute the topics listed below, giving a topic to each group to discuss. *(If you have more than 3 groups, just repeat the topics.)*
3. Allow the groups ten minutes to discuss their topic and record their answer in their Study Guide.
4. After ten minutes, have everyone come back together again.
5. Ask each group to choose a representative to read their group's answer. Encourage everyone to take notes in their Study Guide as the other groups share the answers to their topics.
6. After "Topic One's" answers are shared, read the "Summary" for Topic One before moving on to Topic Two and so on.

Topic One: Brevity of life & the search for fulfillment.

Question: What events or instances have reminded you of how short or fragile life is?

Have you ever been shocked at how much someone has aged when you haven't seen them in awhile? What are some other examples you can think of?

_____

_____

Question: Because people innately know life is short, they are constantly searching for fulfillment and meaning in their life. From constantly switching phones to constantly switching boyfriends, what examples of the restless search for fulfillment can you think of? Do those things ever satisfy?

> **Facilitator's Summary:** Whether it's coming across old photographs, visiting older relatives, or hearing an ambulance go by, we're constantly reminded of the brevity of life. In this short life, people around the world are searching for meaning and fulfillment. God has told us that our hearts were made for Him and that only He can truly satisfy us.

Topic Two: The Bible

Question: What was the evidence presented for the Bible being God's Word? Which two facts did you find the most compelling?

You can refresh your memory by glancing through some of the notes provided.

> **Facilitator's Summary:** The facts surrounding the Bible's authorship, authenticity and accuracy are truly astounding! Take time out to further investigate this topic. In your Study Guide, you'll find more articles about the Bible with archaeological discoveries, manuscript evidence and more. Remember, the very words of this Book were written by God for you.

Topic Three: Relationship with God

Question: How do you get to know someone and how do these same principles apply to getting to know God? *Whether it's on a social media page or in person, how someone expresses themself shows what they care about and what they think. How do we know what God thinks and what He has to say?*

> **Facilitator's Summary:** A relationship requires spending time with someone and listening to what they have to say. As you take time out to read the Bible you will get to know God better. If you've never read the Bible, I'd like to encourage you to begin this week! In your Study Guide you'll find a list of some of the verses that were mentioned today. As you read the Bible, ask God to show Himself to you. This is the reason He gave us His Word, that we might know Him.

Watch Episode 1 - "What does this mean for you?"

1. Only God can truly satisfy:

"There is a longing within the heart of every human being. This week, take time out to notice the brevity of life and the restlessness that drives people everywhere to pursue the satisfaction of the thirst within their souls. Remember that these longings in your heart were meant to call you to God, the only One who can truly satisfy you."

2. The Bible was written for you:

"To record the words of the Bible, God used forty different authors, living in different time periods, in different places, writing in three different languages. Yet, amazingly from these diverse manuscripts, one eternal story emerges. You too, can examine the thousands of archaeological discoveries that verify the Bible's accuracy and the astounding prophecies foretelling future events. As you do, remember that the very words of this Book were written by God for you."

3. God cares for you:

"In Genesis 1:1, we saw how God is eternal and triune. We also saw how He is all-powerful, creating the world by simply speaking! The Challenges you face in your life may seem impossible, but they are not impossible for this Almighty God who says, "Come to Me! I care for you!""

4. God desires a relationship with you:

"We saw God is all-present and all-knowing. As the Designer of this universe, He understands its every single intricate detail and function. You may feel alone, thinking no one even knows you exist. But this same God chooses to know you personally and already knows everything about you. Now you have an opportunity to get to know Him through His Word, the Bible."

Closing Checklist:

- ❏ "Does anyone have any questions?" (Either as a group or one on one.)
- ❏ Encourage them to jot down any questions or comments during the week.
- ❏ Encourage them to read the Bible and articles contained in their Study Guide. See list below:

Read it for yourself:

Ecclesiastes 2	A snapshot of King Solomon's search for meaning.
Ecclesiastes 12:13,14	King Solomon's conclusion.
II Peter 1:20-21 & II Timothy 3:16	The authors of the Bible were told by God what to write.
Genesis 1	God created the world; He is eternal, triune, all-powerful, all-knowing and all-present.
Psalm 139:1-16	God not only knows everything about you but cares deeply for you.
Isaiah 55:1-11	God's invitation for all who are thirsty to come to Him for satisfaction.

Dig Deeper:

Why You Can Believe the Bible:	**Pg. 185** (Study Guide 117)
Exciting archaeological discoveries:	**Pg. 197** (Study Guide 129)

*Ask someone to read the verse out loud from their Study Guide:

Memorize this:

"You have searched me, LORD, and you know me." **Psalm 139:1**

Facilitator's Comment on Verse:

This verse describes how intimately God knows us and loves us. I want to challenge each one of you to memorize this short verse before we meet next time!

Optional: offer a small prize such a chocolate for those who memorize the verse.

Facilitator's Closing Comment:

Next time we get together, we're going to cover topics such as: What is the purpose of our existence? Where did all the suffering and evil in the world come from? Is there hope? We'll explore this and more next time!

Questions your group *might* have:

Remember: *Keep your group on track! If you find a question is more disruptive than beneficial, graciously thank them for their question and tell them you look forward to talking about it one on one.*

1. **I don't believe God exists.**	**Pg. 31**
2. **I don't believe God wrote the Bible.**	**Pg. 32**
3. **Hasn't the Bible been corrupted?**	**Pg. 32**
4. **Did God create the universe in a literal 6 days?**	**Pg. 33**
5. **Atheistic Evolution?**	**Pg. 33**
6. **Trinity**	**Pg. 33**

1. "I don't believe God exists."

Encourage the honest seeker to:

1. **Continue studying the Bible.**

   Give the Bible an honest evaluation, read it, and investigate its truth claims.

2. **Ask God to reveal Himself to him or her.**

   You can encourage him or her by saying, "Talk to God and be honest with Him. (He already knows how you feel!) Tell Him, 'I don't know if you really exist, but if You do, please show me and help me to understand your Word.' "

4. **Keep asking questions!**

   Never be afraid to ask questions! There are answers. Keep pursuing the truth.

5. **Check out the following resource:**

Recommended Resource:

Is there a God? Pg. 255

2. "I don't believe God wrote the Bible."

Encourage the honest seeker to:

1. **Continue studying the Bible.**

   The true story is told of two men playing golf. As they played, the first man began a conversation about God. The second man said he was an atheist and did not believe in God. "Really?" the first man asked, "Have you ever read the Bible?" When the second man said he had not, the first man calmly said, "Well, then you're not an atheist; you're just lazy."

   The fact is that an honest seeker of truth will be willing to look into the facts before coming to a decision.

2. **Pray.**

   Encourage him or her to pray and ask God to make the Bible make sense to them, even if they are unsure of God's existence. Encourage them to pray, "If you exist God, please help me understand the Bible."

3. **Investigate.**

   Recommend the article below:

Recommended Resource:

Why You Can Believe the Bible. [13] Pg. 185

3. "Hasn't the Bible been corrupted?"

This is an argument that many Muslims have been taught. (Although most cultists or skeptics have also been conditioned to respond in this way.)

1. Calmly ask, "<u>When</u> was the Bible corrupted and <u>where</u> in the Bible has it been changed? Can you show me the places it has been altered?" (Most people will have nothing to say at this point.)

2. Recommend he or she take time out to investigate further the incredible reliability of the copies we have of the Bible, and the wealth of manuscript evidence.

3. In addition to the resources mentioned above (question #2), recommend also:

Recommended Resource:

Has the Bible Been Corrupted? (for Muslims) Pg. 252

---

[13] This article is also included in the Study Guide, the book that the participants use.

4. "Did God create the universe in a Literal 6 days?"

The Bible clearly teaches that the eternal, all-powerful, all-knowing, all-present God created the Heavens and the Earth. While the authors of *Tetelestai, the Eternal Story of Redemption* hold to a literal 6 day view of the Creation account in Genesis, there are Bible-believing Christians who believe the six days represent ages. This is not something that we believe is worth arguing about in this type of Bible Study. The important issue to focus on is that God created the world (not exactly *how* long it took Him to do it!) and that this loving God desires a relationship with you and me!

5. Atheistic Evolution?

The view that the universe came into existence by chance, or in other words, that everything randomly came about from nothing is in direct contradiction to the Bible. There are many astounding proofs for special creation, evidence that a Designer deliberately and intelligently created the universe. Many organizations are devoted to educating the public in regard to the amazing evidence that God created the universe.

Recommended Resource:

Is there a God? Pg. 255

6. Trinity

The trinity is not an easy concept for anyone to understand. Just as it was articulated in, *In the Beginning,* the truth is, "God is infinite…. We cannot fully comprehend God."

Think of trying to explain a difficult concept to a small child. There are many things that are difficult or even impossible to explain to my youngest son, Joshua. He simply does not have the maturity or comprehension to be able to understand them. He does trust me, however, and if I tell Joshua something he believes me. The gap between my understanding and Joshua's understanding is nothing compared to the gap between the mind of God and the mind of man!

The fact is that the Bible clearly states that God is One in three Persons; each One being equal yet distinct. We may not understand this, but we face the fact that God has revealed Himself in that way to us.

People in your group with the following worldviews will struggle with the concept of the trinity:

1. Muslims

Muslims are taught to believe that Christians believe in three gods. Let your Muslim friend express his or her questions and confusion about the trinity, and help show them what the Bible teaches.

Point him or her to any resource by former Muslims Abdu Murray or Sasan Travassoli. Both of these scholars show Muslims how God is Love and perfectly loves. God demonstrated perfect love before He ever made the world because perfect love existed in the trinitarian relationship between God the Father, God the Son and God the Holy Spirit.

2. Jehovah's Witnesses

Jehovah's Witnesses believe that the concept of the trinity is of the devil. Keep encouraging your Jehovah's Witness friend to examine what the Bible says in context. Many verses that are used against the trinity are taken out of context. Above all, don't pick a fight or get angry. Continue encouraging them to read and ask questions. It might be helpful for you to read the article, *"Why the Jehovah's Witnesses' Bible is Not Accurate."* (It may not be the right time to recommend your friend read this article or fully go into all these reasons with them just yet.)

Ask the Holy Spirit for wisdom and keep encouraging them to study the Bible. As someone sincerely and openly examines the Scriptures, it is impossible to not see the trinity even reading from the Jehovah's Witness, *New World Translation*[14].

If you realize that your Jehovah's Witness friend is open and wants to discuss this further, then you may want to refer to one of the articles in the Appendix on the deity of Christ. See also Revelation 4 and 5. God the Father and God the Son given equal worship as they are given throughout all of Scripture. **Revelation 22:13** - Jesus is referred to as the Alpha and the Omega, the Beginning and the End.

---

[14] The *New World Translation* is the Jehovah's Witness Bible that has been incorrectly translated and deliberately altered to match their doctrine.

5. **Jews**

> The concept of the trinity it absurd and blasphemous to Jews.
>
> Check out any resource (article, video, or book) on the trinity by Messianic Jew, Dr. Arnold Fruchtenbaum for excellent explanations on seeing the trinity in the the Torah, the Old Testament.

Recommended Resources:

Trinity Explained Pg. 262

Trinity (for Muslims) Pg. 265

How could God, being One, have a Son? (For Muslims) Pg. 266

What does the Bible Teach about the Trinity? Pg. 270

Why the Jehovah's Witnesses' Bible is not Accurate Pg. 273

 **TELESTAI**

CHAPTER 2

THE PROMISE

Pre Bible Study Checklist:

- ❏ Have extra Bibles and pens on hand.
- ❏ Have chocolates for prizes for anyone who memorized the verse.
- ❏ Pray for each participant to come and be open to God's Word and His Spirit.
- ❏ Be familiar with the Synopsis.
- ❏ Be familiar with the questions and dynamics of how the Group Discussion will flow.
- ❏ Glance through the *"Questions Your Group Might Have"* located at the end of this lesson.

Synopsis of the Episode:

In The Promise, God creates the first man and woman to have a loving relationship with Him. When Satan appears in the Garden to deceive Adam and Eve, you will learn of Satan's origin and final destiny. Adam and Eve's relationship with God is broken when they make a devastating choice to listen to Satan's lies and disobey God. As God proclaims a judgment upon Satan, a mysterious Promise is given to Adam and Eve, alluding to a future Deliverer who will restore the broken relationship between God and man. Right there in the Garden, an innocent one is slain in order to cover Adam and Eve, a shocking picture of the ultimate price God will one day pay to rescue humanity. A loving relationship with God is broken when Adam and Eve sin. God, however, promises to send a Deliverer who will pay the ultimate price to restore the broken relationship between God and mankind.

Greeting

- ❏ Note the attendance.
- ❏ Verse and chocolates.
- ❏ Brief open discussion of their Bible reading or articles.

Watch Episode 2 - *The Promise*

We were Created for a Relationship with God:

God wants you to know Him. In Genesis, the first book of the Bible, we read that this relationship was God's plan from the very beginning of time. Unlike the rest of His creation, the man and woman were created in the image of God. (**Genesis 1:26-27**) They would not merely be physical beings, for God created humans with a spiritual side capable of knowing and loving Him. God Himself walked and talked with Adam and Eve in the Garden of Eden.

God Gave Adam and Eve a Choice:

God did not force Adam and Eve to love and obey Him. He wanted them to choose to love Him; for real love is only love if it is a choice. God gave Adam and Eve this choice by commanding them not to eat the fruit from the Tree of the Knowledge of Good and Evil. (**Genesis 2:16-17**) God gave them a simple command with clear consequences: if they ate the fruit of that tree they would die. God is the author of life. To reject God, is to reject life. If you reject life, then you are choosing death.

Satan came to the Garden as a serpent:

(**Genesis 3:1**) While this passage in Genesis does not reveal the serpent's identity, several other passages in the Bible provide us with the answer. God created a multitude of spirit beings called angels. They were made to worship and serve God alone. **Isaiah 14:12** tell us of an important angel named Lucifer. At some point in time, this good angel became wicked (**Ezekiel 28:15,17**) Lucifer, consumed with pride, desired to usurp God's throne. (**Isaiah 14:14**) Because God is holy, completely pure with nothing evil in Him, He will not allow anyone evil to remain in His presence. Lucifer and the angels who joined him in this rebellion were expelled from Heaven. (**Ezekiel 28:16**)

From that point on, the Bible refers to Lucifer as Satan, and the rebellious angels are known today as demons or unclean spirits. The Bible tells us that one day they will be thrown into a horrible place called the Lake of Fire, to be punished for the rest of eternity. Today, Satan knows his time on earth is limited and seeks to destroy God's creation by enticing them to rebel against God.

Satan Tempted Adam and Eve:

In the Garden of Eden, Satan accused God of lying to Adam and Eve. Satan told them they would not die if they ate the fruit from the Tree of the Knowledge of Good and Evil. (**Genesis 3:1-4**) Satan wanted them to doubt

God's *word*. (**Genesis 3:5**) By trying to convince Adam and Eve that God could not be trusted and was trying to keep something good away from them, Satan sought to cause Adam and Eve to doubt God's *love*. (**Genesis 3:6**) Adam and Eve listened to Satan's lies and chose to disobey God. **Romans 5:12** says that at that moment, sin entered the world. Sin is anything that goes against the perfect character of God.

Sin Broke their Relationship with God:

When Adam and Eve sinned they were filled with the feelings that sin brings: shame, guilt and fear. (**Genesis 3:7**) Trying to make coverings out of leaves was a desperate attempt to deal with these feelings, but the shame they felt went down to their very soul. Before sinning, they had walked and talked with God, but now they were running away from Him! (**Genesis 3:8**) Despite the fact that Adam and Eve had disobeyed God and rejected Him, God did not give up on them. Instead, God reached out to them. (**Genesis 3:9**)

Sin Affected the Entire Earth:

When God gave Adam and Eve a chance to confess their sin, (**Genesis 3:10-13**) neither Adam nor Eve admitted that what they had done was wrong. Regardless, they stood completely guilty before a holy God. Their sin would now have consequences that affected the entire earth. (**Genesis 3:14-19**) Their once-perfect world would now produce thorns and thistles. Their day-to-day life would be one of hard work and sweat. All animal life would suffer. Hardship, pain, tears and sorrow would now be a part of human existence. Harmony and peace would be disrupted by evil. All would suffer because of sin.

The Payment for Sin is Death:

Romans 6:23 states that the wages, or payment for sin is death. From that day forward, all people would age and die, returning to the same ground from which Adam had been made. (**Genesis 3:19**) After physical death, the Bible says each person will be judged by God. (**Hebrews 9:27**) If someone were to die with the condemnation of their sins upon them, they would be separated from God forever. Adam and Eve had chosen to obey Satan. Because of this, they were in danger of facing the same destiny as Satan: eternal death in the Lake of Fire.

The Promise of a coming Deliverer:

Instead of instantly sentencing Adam and Eve to eternal condemnation, however, God chose at that moment to give a stunning promise. (**Genesis 3:15**) God promised that one day a Son would be born who would not have a human father. This Son would one day crush Satan's head, but in the process, the Son himself would be hurt. In this promise to Adam and Eve, God not only foretold the destruction of their enemy, but the deliverance of humanity. This promised Son would liberate humanity from their slavery to sin and death.

He would restore the broken relationship between God and man. This was the first promise of the coming Deliverer.

An Innocent One Died to Cover them:

Adam and Eve had tried desperately to deal with the shame they felt because of their sin. God Himself, in His love and mercy, covered Adam and Eve with animal skins. (**Genesis 3:21**) In order to make garments of skin an animal had to die! Think about it: That day in the Garden, who disobeyed God? Who deserved to die? Did that animal deserve to die? No! Adam and Eve were the ones who disobeyed God. Even though they deserved to die, God provided an innocent one to die in order to cover them.

Adam and Eve could not resolve the problem of their sin, only God could. Unlike the clothing made from leaves, these garments of skin were *God's* plan done in *God's* way. God covered their shame by clothing them in the one who had died for them. God was beginning to reveal more of His plan and the ultimate price that would be one day be paid in order to rescue humanity.

Group discussion time: Personal & Relevant

1. Divide into groups of 3-5 people.
2. Distribute the topics listed below, giving a topic to each group to discuss. *(If you have more than 3 groups, just repeat the topics.)*
3. Allow the groups ten minutes to discuss their topic and record their answer in their Study Guide.
4. After ten minutes, have everyone come back together again.
5. Ask each group to choose a representative to read their group's answer. Encourage everyone to take notes in their Study Guide as the other groups share the answers to their topics.
6. After "Topic One's" answers are shared, read the "Summary" for Topic One before moving on to Topic Two and so on.

Topic One: Real love must be a choice

Question: How did God give Adam and Eve a choice in the Garden instead of programming them to automatically obey Him?

Question: What does that say about the type of relationship that God desires to have with humanity?

_____

_____

> **Facilitator's Summary:** You were made in God's image, created to interact with God, love Him and be loved by Him. We saw in the episode _In the Beginning_, that only a relationship with God can bring true satisfaction and fill the longings in our hearts. God, however, does not force us into this relationship. God gives us the opportunity to trust Him and what He says in His Word, the Bible. Real love is only love if it is a choice.

Topic Two: Tactics of the enemy

Question: We saw how Satan tempted Adam and Eve to doubt God's love and God's Word. How do we see Satan influencing people in those two areas today? How have you experienced this in your own life?

_____

_____

> **Facilitator's Summary:** Satan didn't put a gun to their heads. Instead he planted seeds of doubt: "You can't trust what God says" and "God doesn't love you." Be aware that Satan is still using the same tactics today: he wants people to doubt God's word and doubt His love.
>
> We usually think an evil messenger would be obvious, but it seemed like just a harmless conversation to Adam and Eve. **II Corinthians 11:4** says that Satan can masquerade as an angel of light, which makes his tactics all the more sinister!

Topic Three: Clothing made from leaves

Question: Driven by shame, guilt and fear, Adam and Eve tried to make clothing out of leaves. What type of things do people do today in an attempt to make things right or to alleviate their consciences?
What versions of "leaf clothes" do you see in our culture?

_____

_____

> **Facilitator's Summary:** Our natural impulse when we've done something wrong is to try to make it right again. Whether it's giving money to the poor, making promises or saying prayers, somehow we hope to make up for what we've done wrong. However, just as Adam and Eve's leaf clothes were inadequate to fix the broken relationship between them and God, our good works will never be enough. We *cannot* pay for our sins through our own efforts. Only God can resolve the problem of our sin.
>
> That's what makes this story so beautiful! God reached out to Adam and Eve even when they had rejected Him. That day, an innocent one died in order to cover their shame. This event pointed to the future and the ultimate price that would one day be paid to restore their broken relationship with God. God also gave them a promise that He would one day send Someone who would rescue humanity.

Watch Episode 2 -"What does this mean for you?"

1.God's plan is for a relationship with you.

"God's plan from the beginning of time was for a special relationship with humanity. God also desires a relationship with you! Like Adam and Eve, God made you in His image, with a spiritual side capable of knowing and loving Him. God wants you to trust Him and to believe in His Word."

2. Satan's tactics are the same with you.

"We often think that a message from Satan would be overtly evil. But when Satan came to talk to Adam and Eve he seemed harmless and simply started a conversation with them. Be aware that Satan will use the same tactics with you. Often he will use methods that appear harmless or even attractive. He will do whatever it takes to get you to doubt God's Word and to doubt God's love."

3. Only God can resolve the problem of your sin.

"When Adam and Eve disobeyed God, their relationship with Him was broken. In desperation, they tried to cover themselves with leaves. Just as Adam and Eve's leaf clothes were completely inadequate to take away the shame and guilt of their sin, your good works will never be enough. You cannot pay for your sins through your own efforts. Only God can resolve the problem of your sin."

4. God is calling you.

"Even though Adam and Eve had disobeyed God and run away from Him, because of His love, God Himself reached out to them. This is the same God who is searching after you. He loves you and is also calling your name. God promised Adam and Eve He would one day send a Deliverer who would rescue humanity. This was a promise for all people. It was a Promise for you."

Closing Checklist:

❏ "Does anyone have any questions?" (Either as a group or one on one.)

❏ Encourage them to jot down any questions or comments during the week.

❏ Encourage them to read the Bible and articles contained in their Study Guide.

Read it for yourself:	
Genesis 1&2	God creates the world.
Ezekiel 38: 12-17	Satan rebels against God.
Genesis 3	Adam and Eve disobey God.
Genesis 1	God created the world; He is eternal, triune, all-powerful, all-knowing and all-present.
Romans 5:12	Adam's sin was passed down.
Romans 6:23	The payment for sin death.
Genesis 3:15	The promise of the Deliverer

Dig Deeper	
Who is the Devil and is he a threat?	**Pg. 200** (Study Guide 132)
Satan is our enemy	**I Peter 5:8**
We love God because He first loved us.	**I John 4:19**

*Ask someone to read the verse out loud from their Study Guide:

Memorize this:

"For all have sinned and fall short of the glory of God." **Romans 3:23**

Facilitator's Comment on Verse:

We've all sinned and fallen short of God's standards. In the same way that Adam and Eve's sin broke their relationship with God, our sin separates us from God as well. As we continue to study God's Word, we'll find out more about how God resolves the problem of our sin, and how He restores this broken relationship.

Facilitator's Closing Comment:

Don't miss next week. We're going to find out what happened to Adam and Eve's descendants! And as history progresses, we'll meet two key people whose lives and choices impact our world to this very day.

Questions your group *might* have:

Remember: *Keep your group on track! If you find a question is more disruptive than beneficial, graciously thank them for their question and tell them you look forward to talking about it one on one.*

1. **Was God cruel to threaten Adam and Eve with death if they disobeyed?**	Pg. 45
2. **Why did God create Lucifer if He knew he would become evil?**	Pg. 45
3. **Who is Satan?**	Pg. 46
4. **I thought the first sin was sex?**	Pg. 46
5. **Why do you think Genesis 3:15 means born without a human father?**	Pg. 47
6. **Wasn't it cruel of God to kill that animal?**	Pg. 47

1. Was God cruel to threaten Adam and Eve with death if they disobeyed?

If we went scuba diving and I told you, "Do not take this breathing equipment off your face or you will drown," would that be a threat? Would you say, "Oh they're so cruel to threaten me like that saying that they're going to kill me if I disobey their orders," ?

No, it's not a threat; it's a command. I'm telling you exactly what to do because the command brings life. I'm warning you of real consequences. It's simply reality. Below the surface of the water there is no oxygen for you to breathe. If you remove yourself from the source of oxygen you will drown in a matter of minutes. It's simply a fact.

In the same way, God is the source of life. To reject God is to reject life. To reject life is to choose death.

2. Why did God create Lucifer if He knew he would become evil?

God is completely all-knowing. There is no doubt that God knew that Lucifer would rebel against Him. God did not cause Lucifer to sin; Lucifer chose to rebel. God ultimately used Lucifer's rebellion in His plan to reveal God's love to humanity and for His glory. As we keep on studying, even though we'll never fully understand all of the "whys" when it comes to God, I think once you see this whole story come together, you'll understand a lot better.

Recommended Reading

Why did God create Lucifer if He knew He would sin? Pg. 276

3. Who is Satan?

The Bible is very clear on Satan's identity. Just as Episode 2 *The Promise* explains, Satan was a good angel who rebelled against God, and instead of worshipping God wanted to take God's place. (**Isaiah 14:12-15; Ezekiel 28:12-17**) He is a liar and a deceiver. (**Revelation 12:9**) He seeks to draw people away from God and is known as our enemy (**I Peter 5:8**) His final destination is the Lake of Fire; he is currently not there. (**Revelation 20:10**)

The late C.S. Lewis in his book *The Screwtape Letters* said that people often fall into two unhealthy extremes in regards to the Devil, either to disbelieve his existence, or to become obsessed with him. Either way, Satan is pleased.

Recommended Reading
Who is the Devil and is he a threat? Pg. 200

4. I thought the first sin was sex.

(See also Pg. 293 for "Why does God say you can't have sex outside of marriage?")
The first sin was not sex. It was disobedience to God's command to not eat the fruit from the Tree of the Knowledge of Good and Evil.

God created sex. It is beautiful, wonderful, good and part of His perfect design for marriage. Sex is part of the intimacy God planned for between a husband and a wife. In fact, Songs of Solomon is an entire book of the Bible celebrating this relationship in marriage. Not only did God create Adam and Eve with the ability to have sex, He blessed them and told them to "be fruitful and multiply!" (**Genesis 1:28**) God repeats this blessing on sex within marriage in many places. (See **Proverbs 5:15-19**)

Never let anyone convince you the Devil came up with sex or that God is against sex. God is against the *abuse* and *misuse* of sex.

5. Why do you think Genesis 3:15 means "born without a human father"?

This is only the first hint we have in the Bible of this promised Deliverer. As you keep studying, you'll find the Bible will give us more and more information of this promised One who would rescue humanity, defeat Satan, and restore the broken relationship between God and man. **Isaiah 7:14** repeats this promise more clearly, and is later quoted in the New Testament where we see its fulfillment. While Adam and Eve only heard this mysterious promise that alluded to the future, we can look back in history and see the whole Story put together.

6. Wasn't it cruel of God to kill that animal?

Sin and the consequences of sin are equally horrible. It must have been a very shocking event for Adam and Eve to see the death of that first animal in the Garden. They had never seen death before. God chose this graphic event to portray to Adam and Eve how serious sin is, and the price God would one day pay in order to rescue all of humanity.

 **CHAPTER 3**

PROVISION

Pre Bible Study Checklist:

- ❏ Have extra Bibles and pens on hand.
- ❏ Have chocolates for prizes for anyone who memorized the verse.
- ❏ Pray for each participant to come and be open to God's Word and His Spirit.
- ❏ Be familiar with the Synopsis.
- ❏ Be familiar with the questions and dynamics of how the Group Discussion will flow.
- ❏ Glance through the *"Questions Your Group Might Have"* located at the end of this lesson.

Synopsis of the Episode:

Provision begins with the vast majority of Adam and Eve's descendants turning their backs on God and thus becoming increasingly violent and corrupt. Only Noah's family chooses to follow God. God sends a cataclysmic global judgment upon the earth, while graciously providing a single way of escape. All who reject this one way to be saved, perish. When the world once again re-populates, God chooses Abraham to be the father of a unique nation through whom the promised Deliverer will come. In a divine test involving Abraham's son, a substitute dies in Isaac's place, providing a striking illustration of God's future Plan for humanity's Redemption.

Greeting

- ❏ Note the attendance.
- ❏ Verse and chocolates.
- ❏ Brief open discussion of their Bible reading or articles.

Watch Episode 3 - *Provision*

All People are Born Sinners:

Because of Adam and Eve's sin, all people in the world are born sinners, separated from God. (**Romans 5:12**) Yet God's desire was still for a relationship with all people. God provided a way that they could approach Him and be His friend. Each person, however, would have to *choose* for themself, whether or not, they wanted a relationship with God.

The Majority of Humanity had Rejected God:

Genesis 4 and 5 give us details of a highly advanced civilization with agriculture, the raising of livestock, the building of great cities, the development of iron working, the forging of tools and the invention of musical instruments. Tragically, however, by chapter 6, the vast majority of humanity had chosen to turn their backs on God. (**Genesis 6:5-6**) There was one man, Noah, who had chosen to walk with God. (**Genesis 6:9**) Like all people, Noah was a sinner. Yet because He believed what God said, he was declared righteous: having all his sins forgiven and being fully accepted by God. He would no longer be treated as a sinner, but as a friend. What a contrast to the people who surrounded Noah. The world had become horrifically evil and violent as they vehemently rejected God.

Noah built the Ark by Faith:

Because God is holy and must punish sin, He told Noah He would send a judgment of floodwaters to destroy all life upon the earth. (**Genesis 6:13-14**) God gave Noah detailed instructions on how to build an ark in order to save all those who would believe, from the coming judgment. (**Genesis 6:14-16,22**) **Hebrews 11:7** explains that Noah built the ark by faith. Faith is trusting that something is true even when you cannot see it. Even though Noah could not see the coming Flood, he built the ark trusting that what God said was true.

The Majority was Wrong:

According to **2 Peter 2:5**, Noah must have also been pleading with the people around him, urging them to trust what God had said. They, however, refused to believe. In the entire world, only eight people chose to follow God; Noah and his wife, and his three sons Shem, Ham and Japheth and their wives. (**Genesis 7:7**) So many times we tend to decide what we will believe about what is right and wrong based upon what the *majority* of the people around us think...but what about when the majority is wrong?

God Provided One way to be Saved:

It would have been impossible to ignore the fact that something divine was happening when God miraculously sent animals to the ark! (**Genesis 7:15-16**) Not only was God planning for the survival of each species, God was giving one last chance for the world to see the reality of the coming Flood! The end of verse 16 says, that after Noah and his family were safe inside the ark, God Himself shut the door! The time for choosing whether or not to follow God was over.

For those who had delayed their decision, it was too late. (**Genesis 7:11**) God's Word had really come to pass, and they realized they had rejected the truth! Although God had provided *one way* for them to be saved, they had turned their backs on God. (**Genesis 7:17-21**) Noah and his family were rescued from the flood not because they were not sinners, but because they had believed God. Just as God provided the ark as the only way to be saved from judgment, this event pointed to the future, and a day when God in His love, would provide *one way* for all of humanity to be saved.

The Story of Abraham:

Genesis 9-11 tell us that Noah lived for another 350 years after the Flood. It was during his son Shem's lifetime, only two years after Noah's death, that one of the most famous men in all of history was born: Abraham. **Genesis 12-25** records the history of Abraham's life. Abram, as he was first called, was a descendant of Shem. A rich man with many servants and flocks, Abram was married to Sarai, but they had no children because she was barren.

God's Promise to Abram:

In **Genesis 12:1-3**, God revealed a special plan that He had for Abram. First, God said He would be guiding Abram to a land that would be his and his descendants' future possession. Second, God would be birthing a great nation through Abram. And third and most important, God promised that all people on earth would be blessed through him. (**Genesis 12:3**)

Because of sin, all people are under a curse of judgment. God promised a blessing for all people through Abram. This was because the coming Deliverer would be a physical descendant of Abram and bring blessing to all people, for He would come to free humanity from the curse of sin and death!

Abram Believed God's Promise:

Years later, God repeated His promise to give Abram a son. (**Genesis 15:4-6**) Verse 6 says that Abram, *"...believed the LORD."* When Abram put his faith in God's promise the rest of the verse tells us God, (**Genesis 15:6**) *"...credited it to him as righteousness."* Abram was declared to be righteous. But what had Abram done to deserve this? Abram hadn't given anything to God or performed any religious ceremony. He hadn't done any good works to merit this. God said Abram was righteous simply because he *believed* God's promise.

God Fulfills His Promise to Abram:

As the years went by, however, and Abram and Sarai remained childless, their situation seemed hopeless. **Genesis 16** tells us that Sarai convinced Abram to produce a child through Hagar, her Egyptian maidservant. Hagar gave birth to Ishmael. God graciously blessed Ishmael and caused a nation to descend from him as well. But Ishmael was not the son God had promised.

Finally, in **Genesis 17**, when Abram was 99 years old, the LORD appeared to Abram and told him that just as God had promised earlier, his wife, *Sarai,* would miraculously give birth to a son. (**Genesis 17:19**) On that same day, God changed their names to Abraham and Sarah. (**Genesis 17:5,15**) How exciting that year must have been as they dreamed of the day when they would hold their son, the son through whom the Deliverer would come. (**Genesis 21:1-2**)

The Worship of God:

As little Isaac grew up, Abraham surely taught him how to worship the Lord. Scripture tells us that one of the ways God's followers would worship Him, was through sacrifices. They would build an altar, and on this altar they would place an animal, often times a lamb. God's people realized they were sinners and that the payment for sin was death. The lamb was then killed and burned in God's presence. It was a sobering illustration of an innocent one dying in the place of those who were guilty…. dying that they might live.

The Unforgettable Sacrifice:

Although they must have offered many sacrifices to the LORD, both Isaac and Abraham were about to face a sacrifice neither of them would ever forget. In a divine test, God asked Abraham to offer his son, Isaac, as a sacrifice. (**Genesis 22:1-2**) Abraham had waited 25 years for this son! Would Isaac now have to die? Abraham did not understand what God was doing, but he determined to obey the LORD. (**Genesis 22:3-5**) Abraham realized that somehow God had a higher plan. For God had promised that a nation, and eventually the Deliverer, would come through Isaac. Therefore, based on God's promise, Abraham reasoned that perhaps God was planning to raise Isaac from the dead. (**Hebrews 11:17-19**) When they arrived in the region of Moriah, Abraham confidently told his servants that after he and Isaac offered the sacrifice, they would both return.

God Will Provide a Substitute:

As Abraham and Isaac climbed Mount Moriah, Isaac carried the very wood on which he would die. (**Genesis 22:6-8**) After they built an altar, Isaac was bound and placed on top of the wood on the altar. But when Abraham took the knife to slay his son, the angel of the LORD stopped him. (**Genesis 22:9-12**) Then Abraham looked up and saw a ram caught by its horns in a thicket. (**Genesis 22:13**) Abraham took the ram and sacrificed it instead of his son, Isaac.

The wood had been for Isaac. The knife and the fire had been for Isaac's death. At the last moment, however, in the face of certain death, God had provided a *substitute*. A substitute is one who takes the place of another. That day, the ram died in Isaac's place so that Isaac would live. As a reminder forever of what God had done, Abraham named the place, (**Genesis 22:14**) *"The LORD will provide"*. You would think that Abraham would have named it, "The LORD *has* provided." A future day was coming, however, when God would once again provide a Substitute. One would die in order that others might live. He would be the ultimate *provision*.

Group discussion time: Personal & Relevant

1. Divide into groups of 3-5 people.
2. Distribute the topics listed below, giving a topic to each group to discuss. *(If you have more than 3 groups, just repeat the topics.)*
3. Allow the groups ten minutes to discuss their topic and record their answer in their Study Guide.
4. After ten minutes, have everyone come back together again.
5. Ask each group to choose a representative to read their group's answer. Encourage everyone to take notes in their Study Guide as the other groups share the answers to their topics.
6. After "Topic One's" answers are shared, read the "Summary" for Topic One before moving on to Topic Two and so on.

Topic One: The choice to believe

Question: Were Noah and his family sinners? Why did Noah and his family live while the others perished? (See **Hebrews 11:7**) What does **II Peter 3:9** say about God?

_____

_____

> **Facilitator's Summary:** Noah and his family were born sinners just like the people around them. All people are sinners. (**Romans 3:23**) The difference between Noah's family and those who perished in the Flood, is that Noah chose to follow God and accept His _forgiveness_ for his sins. (**Hebrews 11:7**)
>
> **II Peter 3:9** says that God does not want anyone to perish, but for all to come to repentance. Repeatedly in the Bible when evil people have repented, God has shown mercy and withheld His judgment.
>
> _(*For further insight: See **Jonah 3:1-10** where God has mercy on the city of Nineveh when they repent and believe what God says. Nineveh was the capital of the Assyrian Empire, an extremely violent people known to torture their captives by skinning them alive, impaling them or cutting off their arms and legs! Yet, God forgave them when they repented!_
> _In **II Peter 2:5** we see a description of Noah as a preacher of righteousness. Surely he must have been pleading with the people around him to also accept God's forgiveness and escape judgment.)_

Topic Two: One way to be saved

Question: The Flood was a divine judgment of cataclysmic nature, but it wasn't a death sentence for everyone. How did this same event also showcase God's gracious provision?

_____

_____

> **Facilitator's Summary:** It was impossible for someone to save himself through his own efforts. God did, however, provide a way to escape the Flood.
>
> There are some very important points we learn from this narrative:
>
> 1. ***God is Holy*** which means He is completely pure with nothing evil in Him.
> 2. ***God must punish sin.*** Sin is anything that goes against God's perfect character.
> 3. ***God is loving and merciful*** and provides a way to be saved from His judgment.
>
> There was only one way to be saved. All those who believed what God said entered the ark. All who rejected God were also rejecting the only way to be saved from the Flood.

Topic Three: Facing certain death

Question: When Isaac lay upon the altar with a knife above him, he faced what seemed to be certain death. How is this a picture of our condition before God?

Hint: **Romans 3:23** *describes our condition before God and* **Romans 6:23** *tells us the payment for this is death.*

_____

Why didn't Isaac die that day?

_____

> **Facilitator's Summary:** Just as Isaac faced death, the Bible says that our sins condemn us: The payment for our sins is death. In this breathtaking story, God rescues Isaac. He was painting a dramatic picture to illustrate His incredible provision of a Substitute. Just as God provided the ram to die so that Isaac could live, this pointed to God's future plan for rescuing humanity.

Watch Episode 3 -"What does this mean for you?"

1. The choice to believe... is up to you.

"As Adam and Eve's descendants populated the earth, each of them had a choice to obey God or to reject Him. Noah and his family, chose to follow God while the rest of the world turned their backs on God becoming evil, violent and corrupt. Because God is holy and sin must be punished, God told Noah that He would send a judgment of floodwaters because of their wickedness. God in His love, however, provided one way to be saved from the Flood. All those who believed in what God said entered the ark. All those who refused, perished. In the same way, God must punish your sin, but God in His love has provided one way for you to be saved as well."

2. A blessing... for you.

"After the Flood, when the world began to be repopulated, God chose a man named Abraham to be the father of a nation. It was through this nation that the Deliverer would one day come. Through Him, all people on earth would be blessed. It was the promise of a blessing for you."

3. God provided a substitute... for you.

"In a divine test, God asked Abraham to offer Isaac as a sacrifice. But before Abraham could slay his son, God provided a substitute to die in his place! A ram died so that Isaac could live. Isaac is a picture of you! This day was pointing to a future event... a day when God would provide Someone who would die as a substitute for you."

Closing Checklist:

- ❏ "Does anyone have any questions?" (Either as a group or one on one.)
- ❏ Encourage them to jot down any questions or comments during the week.
- ❏ Encourage them to read the Bible and articles contained in their Study Guide. (See list below)

Read it for yourself:

Romans 3:23	All people are sinners
Romans 6:23	The payment for sin is death.
Genesis 6:9-22 and 7:1-34; 8:13-20	The Flood
Genesis 12:1-3	God's promise to Abraham
Genesis 21:1-3	Isaac is born.
Genesis 22: 1-14	The ram dies in Isaac's place.

Dig Deeper

Evidence for a Global Flood	**Pg. 204** (Study Guide 136)
God does not want anyone to perish.	**II Peter 3:9**
What happens when wicked people repent.	**Jonah 3**

* Ask someone to read the verse out loud from their Study Guide:

Memorize this:

"...He is patient with you, not wanting anyone to perish, but everyone to come to repentance." **II Peter 3:9**

Facilitator's Comment on Verse:

This verse reminds us of God's character. God is holy and must punish sin, but He is also loving and always provides a way to be saved. It is never His desire that anyone should perish.

Facilitator's Closing Comment:

Don't miss next time. We are going to witness a clash between opposing supernatural powers. We'll also see that's God's power is always greater!

Questions your group *might* have:

Remember: *Keep your group on track! If you find a question is more disruptive than beneficial, graciously thank them for their question and tell them you look forward to talking about it one on one.*

1. Did the Flood really happen?	**Pg. 58**
2. How could God be so cruel in the Flood?	**Pg. 58**
3. Is God in favor of child sacrifice?	**Pg. 58**
4. What about Ishmael?	**Pg. 59**
5. Aren't animal sacrifices cruel?	**Pg. 59**

1. Did the Flood really happen?

The Bible clearly teaches that a global Flood took place. The earth shows everywhere the effects of this Flood. Scientists who believe in God and His Word, have carefully documented the evidence. Unfortunately, scientists who are anti-theists and take God out of the equation, will look at the same evidence and try to find an alternative solution. (For example - the Grand Canyon is an amazing testimony to what a lot of water can do in a short amount of time. Those in opposition to the Bible will look at the same Grand Canyon and claim it is a small amount of water over a long period of time.) There are fascinating articles written on this subject. Take time out to read some of them.

Recommended Resource:

Evidence for a Global Flood Pg. 204

2. How could God be so cruel in the Flood?

God is far from cruel, and is more than willing to forgive even the vilest sinner who repents. See the discussion listed in the first topic of the Group Discussion "The Choice to Believe" for an extensive reply on the love of God, His mercy, and others who have repented.

3. Is God in favor of child sacrifice?

No! God is the giver of life and abhors the killing of the innocent. The Bible speaks out extensively against this describing it as detestable and evil. (**Deuteronomy 12:31**; **Ezekiel 23:36,37**; **2 Kings 21:6**)

When God asked Abraham to sacrifice Isaac, it was a test. God always intended to stop Abraham and save Isaac. This entire event also served as a dramatic illustration of how God would rescue humanity and ultimately provide a Substitute for all of humanity.

4. What about Ishmael?

The conflict and rivalry that was caused between Hagar and Sarah and then consequently between Isaac as a toddler and adolescent Ishmael is very sad. This story shows us how tragic it is when we try to take things into our own hands instead of trusting God in His timing. Sarah's impatience in seeing God's promise fulfilled and attempt to "help things out" caused a lot of grief.

The Bible does say that despite these unfortunate circumstances God made Ishmael into a great nation (**Genesis 21:13**) and that God was with Ishmael. (**Genesis 21:21**) Ishmael did go on to have a large family. (**Genesis 25:12–18**) Moreover, it tell us that when Abraham died, Isaac and Ishmael together buried their father.(**Genesis 25:9**)

*Muslims might want to discuss this further due to Islamic teaching surrounding Ishmael. According to Islam, Ishmael was the one God asked Abraham to sacrifice. They use the phrase "only son" to justify this belief. (**Genesis 22:1,2** - God asks Abraham to sacrifice his "only son" Isaac.) They state that Ishmael was the only son for at least 13 years before Isaac was born, thus they say that Ishmael was the sacrificial son, not Isaac. However, when God referred to Isaac as the "only son" He was referring to the fact that he was the only promised son. Ishmael was not the promised son, Isaac was. Even Muslims will agree with the fact that God had not given any promise in regards to Ishmael's birth.*

*Remind your Muslim friend that we are studying the Biblical account, and gently reaffirm him or her of God's love for Ishmael, and God's love for all of us. Point out the story of God's tender care that He showed to Hagar (**Genesis 21:14-21**) and how this story encourages all of us, especially if we find ourselves in a difficult family situation. God is not a God who only interacts with people in ideal circumstances. He meets us right where we are.*

5. Aren't animal sacrifices cruel?

Sin and the consequences of sin are equally horrible. God chose this graphic act to show us, his people, how serious sin is and how the payment for sin is death. The sacrifices also pictured the price God would one day pay in order to rescue humanity.

TELELESTAI

CHAPTER 4

DELIVERANCE

Pre Bible Study Checklist:

❏ Have extra Bibles and pens on hand.

❏ Have chocolates for prizes for anyone who memorized the verse.

❏ Pray for each participant to come and be open to God's Word and His Spirit.

❏ Be familiar with the Synopsis.

❏ Be familiar with the questions and dynamics of how the Group Discussion will flow.

❏ Glance through the *"Questions Your Group Might Have"* located at the end of this lesson.

Synopsis of the Episode:

The episode Deliverance finds the descendants of Abraham, the nation of Israel, enslaved in the land of Egypt. God preserves the life of a Hebrew baby named Moses, and raises him up to deliver His people. When a showdown between Moses and Pharaoh's magicians takes place in Pharaoh's court, Deliverance reveals what the Bible teaches concerning invoking demonic powers. After Pharaoh refuses to release the slaves, God powerfully demonstrates that He alone is God through a series of ten plagues. At the last plague during the Passover, the blood of lambs is shed, the power of God's Enemy is broken, and slaves are set free, providing a stunning picture for God's future Deliverance of the world.

Greeting

❏ Note the attendance.

❏ Verse and chocolates.

❏ Brief open discussion of their Bible reading or articles.

Watch Episode 4 - *Deliverance*

Moses is Born:

As the years went by, Abraham's son, Isaac, had a son named Jacob. As an adult, God gave Jacob a new name and called him Israel. Israel had 12 sons. The families of these 12 sons grew into what became known as the 12 tribes of Israel. When a famine ravaged the land of Canaan, they went to live in Egypt. There, the children of Israel lived as strangers in a country that was not their own, and their nation grew.

Over time, a new ruling Pharaoh of Egypt feared that the Israelites might become too numerous and powerful, so Egypt enslaved them. (**Exodus 1:1-14**) In an attempt to control the Israelite population growth, Pharaoh ordered that every Israelite boy be thrown into the River Nile. (**Exodus 1:22**) At this tumultuous point in history, a baby named Moses was born to an Israelite family. (**Exodus 2:1-2**) In a series of providential events, God protected Moses' life, and he was adopted by Pharaoh's daughter. (**Exodus 2:3-10**)

Egypt Worshipped Many Gods:

Egypt had rejected the One true God and had exchanged the truth of God for a lie. They worshipped and served created things instead of the Creator. The Egyptians didn't worship God, who had created the River Nile, they worshipped the river itself, even offering a national sacrifice of a boy or a girl each year to appease Hapi, the Nile "god". They had a host of other false gods they worshipped: Heket, the frog headed goddess of life and birth, Hathor the cow goddess, Shu the god of the sky, and Amun-Re the sun god. Egypt's ruler, the Pharaoh, had gone so far as to declare himself to be a god-king.

Moses Chose to Follow the One True God:

For prince Moses, Egypt appeared to have everything: military might, influence, prestige and power. (**Acts 7:22**) Moses knew that there was only one true God, the Creator of the heavens and the earth. For Moses, following God and believing in His promise to send a Deliverer was of greater worth than all the treasures of Egypt. (**Hebrews 11:24-25**) Like Moses, you and I also have a choice to make. Following God may not be easy, but it will be of greater worth than all this world has to offer.

Moses Called to Deliver the Israelites:

Scripture tells us that one day, in an attempt to bring justice for the Israelites in his own strength, Moses killed an Egyptian, and as a result had to flee to the land of Midian where he lived as a shepherd. (**Exodus 2:11-15**)

Though years passed, God however, had not forgotten His promise to His people. One day on Mt. Sinai[15], God called Moses to deliver the Israelites from slavery. (**Exodus 3:1-10**) God assured Moses that He would be with him and that He, Himself, would rescue His people and bring them out of Egypt to worship Him on that very mountain. (**Exodus 3:11-12**) "I AM" would be the name by which his people would know Him[16]. (**Exodus 3:14**) For God is not the "I Was", nor the "I Will Be". He is the "I AM", eternal, unchanging, and all-powerful.

Moses Demands the Release of the Israelites:

However, it would not be easy for Moses to face the Pharaoh and tell him that the LORD demanded the release of the slaves. God allowed Aaron, Moses' brother, to go with Moses into Pharaoh's presence. When confronted however, Pharaoh refused to release the slaves and was insulted that the God his slaves worshipped was telling him what to do! (**Exodus 5:2**) Pharaoh mocked God by asking: "Who is the LORD[17]?" His question was about to be answered by God Himself. (**Exodus 7:10-12**) In demonstration of God's power, Aaron threw down his staff and it became a snake, through the power of God.

Two Sources of Supernatural Power:

The Egyptian sorcerers also threw down their staffs and they turned into snakes. One may wonder *how* the sorcerers were capable of turning their staffs into snakes. According to the Bible, there are only two sources from which supernatural power is available: from God or from God's enemies, Satan and the demons. The Bible tells us that Satan is a liar and a deceiver. In his offer to people of solutions or power, he can often appear harmless. Satan can even masquerade as an angel of light. However, his intentions are always to use people for his own evil purposes, and destroy them in the process. That is why the Bible strictly prohibits calling upon any force or power other than God. (**Deuteronomy 18:10-11**) God says that divination, sorcery, witchcraft, casting spells, being a medium or spiritist or other activities like these, are detestable. God urges us to put our confidence in Him alone! And in **Exodus 7:12** when God's staff swallows the sorcerers' staffs, God demonstrated that no power is greater than His power. God always has the victory!

The LORD Judged their False Gods:

Despite all of this, Pharaoh refused to listen to God. (**Exodus 7:13**) At that moment, God could have stretched out His hand with one plague, and simply wiped Egypt off the face of the earth. But He had other

---

[15] Mt. Sinai is also called Mt. Horeb or the "mountain of God"

[16] "I AM" is often translated in later passages of the in English versions of the Bible as "LORD"

[17] "The LORD" is the same name "I AM." Pharaoh was saying, "Who is this 'I AM' God telling me what to do?!"

plans. **Exodus 7-12** describe a series of ten plagues that God brought upon Egypt. Each one demonstrated the power of God over the false gods of the Egyptians. (**Numbers 33:4**) God's heart was not only for the Israelites. (**Exodus 6:6-7**) He also wanted the Egyptians to know that He alone was the one true God. (**Exodus 7:5**) Each plague exposed to the Egyptians that the false gods in whom they trusted, were completely incapable of saving them.

One Way to Escape Death:

Pharaoh's heart remained hardened through the first nine plagues. As the tenth plague approached, the LORD explained to Moses what was about to take place. At midnight, the LORD would send the death angel to strike down the firstborn son of every household. (**Exodus 11:4-5**) There was only one way to escape death. If a year old[18], perfect, male lamb's blood was shed and placed on the doorposts of the home, God promised that He would not permit the Destroyer to enter that home and strike them down. (**Exodus 12:3-23**)

You Must Believe God's Message in order to be Saved:

What if that day someone heard God's message through Moses, but did not put blood on their doorway. Would simply knowing the truth be enough to save them? No. They had to also believe and apply the blood to their doorway. What if someone else decided that instead of the blood of the lamb, they would put a sign on their doorway that stated: "We are good people. We are religious. We give to the poor. We are law-abiding citizens." Would God be so impressed with their good deeds and spare them? No! Before God, only one factor determined whether the firstborn son lived or died. If a lamb, perfect and without blemish had died in his place, God said, (**Exodus 12:13**) *"When I see the blood I will pass over you."*

Slaves Set Free:

That night, the Israelites obeyed what the LORD had commanded Moses and Aaron, and lived. It was only after the Pharaoh had lost his oldest son that he released the Israelites. (**Exodus 12:28-31**) God's people would forever remember the events that led up to their deliverance: certain death, only one way to be saved, an innocent lamb dying so that they might live, no broken bones, shed blood, the power of the enemy broken… slaves set free! That night, about six hundred thousand men set out from Egypt, along with their families and also many other people. (**Exodus 12:37-38**) Surely, some of the Egyptians must have seen the futility of their false gods and chosen to believe the one true God who is LORD of all the earth.

---

[18] A year old lamb was a young adult.

Total Deliverance:

Yet, Pharaoh's heart became hardened once more. He sent his army in pursuit of the Israelites, where they overtook them as they were camped by the Red Sea. (**Exodus 14:5-9**) Unbeknownst to the Egyptians, this was also part of the sovereign plan of God. To the terror-stricken Israelites Moses said, (**Exodus 14:13-14**) *"Do not be afraid. Stand firm and you will see the Deliverance the LORD will bring you today… The LORD will fight for you; you need only to be still."*

As Moses stretched out his hand over the sea, the LORD drove back the sea with a strong east wind. All night the Israelites crossed the sea. When Pharaoh's army rushed after them into the sea, God threw their horses into confusion. When all the Israelites had safely crossed to the other side, Moses extended his hand out over the sea, and the waters flowed back and covered the Egyptian army; not one of them survived. (**Exodus 14:19-28**) The Israelites had now been totally freed from the bondage of the Egyptians, never to be enslaved by them again. The LORD had fought for them and had given them total Deliverance!

Group discussion time: Personal & Relevant

1. Divide into groups of 3-5 people.
2. Distribute the topics listed below, giving a topic to each group to discuss. *(If you have more than 3 groups, just repeat the topics.)*
3. Allow the groups ten minutes to discuss their topic and record their answer in their Study Guide.
4. After ten minutes, have everyone come back together again.
5. Ask each group to choose a representative to read their group's answer. Encourage everyone to take notes in their Study Guide as the other groups share the answers to their topics.
6. After "Topic One's" answers are shared, read the "Summary" for Topic One before moving on to Topic Two and so on.

Topic One: Not an easy choice

Question: Moses chose to turn his back on all the power and pleasures that Egypt had to offer in order to follow God. This choice held obvious suffering and loss. Why would he would do that?

What are some possible consequences that people face today when they choose to follow God? Is it worth it?

_____

_____

> **Facilitator's Summary:** For many people like Moses, the decision to follow God is a weighty decision. Sometimes it means facing negative social pressures, hostile family reactions... and in some contexts or cultures, even threats on your life.
>
> Knowing that all of this could be at stake, why then do people make the choice to follow God? For the same reason that Moses did! When faced with the choice of believing the truth or believing a lie - he chose truth. When faced with living with temporary pleasures or eternal rewards he chose that which is eternal. I'm sure Moses has never regretted it... and neither will you.

Topic Two: Power from beyond this world

Question: What are the venues in which our culture encourages people to seek after other powers or forces? According to the Bible, if God is not the source of this power who is?

Spirit healings? Psychic readings? What examples can you think of?

> **Facilitator's Summary:** Whether it be through ouija boards, tarot cards, palm readings, spirit healings, or channeling, there are many people seeking out or invoking spirit powers or forces. Did you know that there are more people earning a living in France in this way than there are registered doctors?
>
> The Bible is very clear when it tells us that all supernatural power comes from *either* God *or* Satan and the demons. There is no such thing as neutral. There is no middle ground. If you are relying on a being or force other than *God* it is a demonic power. There are no exceptions.
>
> Why does God strictly forbid seeking after other powers in His Word? It is because Satan is our enemy. The Bible says he seeks to steal, kill and destroy.
> **(John 10:10)**

It has been rightly said: "It is not bad for you because it is forbidden, rather the reason it is forbidden is *because* it is bad for you! When God prohibits you from doing something it is always for your safety. He wants to protect you.

Just as God's staff swallowed the sorcerers' staffs, God assures us in His Word, there is no One who is more powerful than God! He loves you. Trust in Him alone.

(*__Further insight:__ *These practices may not look sinister or evil. In* **John 8:44** *Satan is called the "father of lies."* **II Corinthians 11:14** *says that Satan can masquerade as an angel of light. He seeks to entice people by wrapping his messages in harmless, beautiful or beneficial looking packages. Remember, however, it only takes a little bit of poison to kill someone!)*

Topic Three: Really bad? Really good? Did it make a difference?

Question: What if someone were an outstanding citizen, conscientious and responsible, (the type of person everyone wants for a neighbor!) but that person didn't put blood on their doorway during the last plague. What would happen?

Or, what about a reverse scenario: What if some jerk (who no one liked) put blood on his doorway, what would happen to him? What do you think God was showing His people that night?

_____

_____

Facilitator's Summary: It wasn't about being good or bad, and it wasn't about lists of good deeds to impress God. It wasn't even about participating in religious activities, ceremonies or pilgrimages. For God, the only thing that determined whether the firstborn son lived or died was whether or not they had placed the blood of the Lamb on their doorposts.

In this way, then, life instead of death was accessible to every single household… simply because the Lamb had already died for them. God said, *"When I see the blood, I will pass over you."* (**Exodus 12:13**) This event was pointing to the future as a picture of when God would provide the ultimate Substitute who would shed His blood to bring eternal deliverance.

Watch Episode 4 -"What does this mean for you?"

1. The choice to follow God will be worth it for you.

"God miraculously preserved the life of a Hebrew baby named Moses. As an adult, he made a choice to follow the one true God. For Moses, this decision held possible suffering and loss. He realized however, that Egypt's pleasures were temporary, but the reward of following God would be eternal. Perhaps you also face a similar decision. The choice to follow God will be just as worth it for you, as it was for Moses."

2. God wants you to rely on Him alone.

"When Pharaoh refused to free the Israelite slaves, God demonstrated his power over the Egyptian gods in a series of supernatural events. When God turned Aaron's staff into a snake, Pharaoh's sorcerers also transformed their staffs into snakes. They did this by relying on the power of demons, or false gods. God then sent ten plagues on Egypt, each one showing that the false gods the Egyptians worshiped were completely incapable of saving them. Satan and the demons have always sought to entice people into invoking their power through sorcery, witchcraft, and divination, but God strictly prohibits this in his Word. When you need to turn to someone for help, remember that there is no power greater than the power of God. He loves you, and wants you to rely on Him alone."

3. The Lamb was a picture of a future Substitute for you.

"During the tenth plague, God sent the death angel to strike down the firstborn son of every household, but He also provided a way for the son to be saved. God said that if they took a perfect lamb, killed it and placed it's blood on their doors, the firstborn son would not die during the plague. The lamb became a substitute for those who believed God, and did as He instructed. These dramatic events were pointing to the future when God would provide a Substitute who would shed His blood for you, in order to give you eternal Deliverance."

Closing Checklist:

- ❏ "Does anyone have any questions?" (Either as a group or one on one.)
- ❏ Encourage them to jot down any questions or comments during the week.
- ❏ Encourage them to read the Bible and articles contained in their Study Guide. (See list below)

Read it for yourself:	
Exodus 1	The Israelites are slaves in Egypt.
Exodus 2	Moses is born and adopted by the princess.
Hebrews 11:24,25	Moses' choice to follow God
Exodus 7-11	Plagues on Egypt
Exodus 12	The Passover Lamb
Exodus 14	Crossing the Red Sea
Deuteronomy 18:10,11	God forbids seeking after other powers

Dig Deeper	
Is there Demonic Activity in the World Today?	**Pg. 206** (Study Guide 138)
What is the Christian View of Psychics or Fortune Tellers?	**Pg. 209** (Study Guide 141)
Satan comes to steal, kill and destroy.	**John 10:10**
We are told to trust in God with all our hearts.	**Proverbs 3:5,6**

* Ask someone to read the verse out loud from their Study Guide:

Memorize this:

"In Him we have redemption through His blood, the forgiveness of sins, in accordance with the riches of God's grace." *Ephesians 1:7*

Facilitator's Comment on the Verse:

We saw the dramatic events that happened during the tenth plague were pointing to the future when God would provide a Substitute who would shed His blood for the world. The verse we're memorizing this time is about that. We're not going to talk very much about the verse because it will make more sense as we watch more episodes together and see God's Story unfold.

Facilitator's Closing Comment:

Don't miss next week! We're going to see God's perspective of an entire nation that claims they can live good enough lives to be accepted by God. We'll see how they match up to God's standards.

Questions your group *might* have:

Remember: *Keep your group on track! If you find a question is more disruptive than beneficial, graciously thank them for their question and tell them you look forward to talking about it one on one.*

1. **More on those who seek after demonic powers**	**Pg. 71**
2. **Does God love Egypt? Was He being cruel to Egypt?**	**Pg. 72**
3. **Why did the Lamb have to be perfect?**	**Pg. 72**
4. **Did God really open the Red Sea?**	**Pg. 73**

1. More on those who seek after demonic powers.

Towards the end of the ten plagues in Egypt, the sorcerers as well as Pharaoh's counselors, realized the demonic powers they were trusting in were incapable of helping them or reversing what God was doing. They realized that God, the "I Am" who had come and demanded the release of the slaves, really was more powerful than the false gods they served.

- **Exodus 8:19** When the sorcerers are incapable of imitating what God is doing by use of their "secret arts" they must finally admit that God is stronger. They tell Pharaoh, "This is the finger of God," but Pharaoh won't listen to them.
- **Exodus 9:20-** Some of Pharaoh's own officials begin to fear the Lord, and when Moses tells them God is going to send a devastating plague of hail, they rush to bring their slaves and livestock into a shelter.
- **Exodus 10:7** some of the the officials beg Pharaoh to listen to Moses, and realize their country is being destroyed.

If you have dabbled in these areas or sought after spirits or powers other than God you must repent - which means to change your mind. You need to come to grips with the fact that you are seeking power from God's Enemies: Satan and the Demons. Then you need to stop participating in these activities and get rid of everything that is connected to this.

- **Acts 17:17-19 -** *"Many of those who believed now came and openly confessed their evil deeds. A number who had practiced sorcery brought their scrolls together and burned them publicly. When they calculated the value of the scrolls, the total came to fifty thousand drachmas. [a huge sum of money.]"*

TETELESTAI FACILITATOR GUIDE

Recommended Resources:

Is there Demonic Activity in the World Today? Pg. 206

What is spiritualism? Pg. 278

What is spiritism? Pg. 280

What is the Christian View of Psychics or Fortune Tellers? Pg. 209

2. Does God love Egypt? Was He being cruel to Egypt?

In **Exodus 9:15,16** God says,"*For by now I could have stretched out my hand and struck you and your people with a plague that would have wiped you off the earth. But I have raised you up for this very purpose, that I might show you my power and that my name might be proclaimed in all the earth.*"

Each one of God's plagues revealed the futility of Egypt's false gods and unmasked their false religion. During these plagues, God was also very merciful in giving them ample warnings (See **Exodus 9:20** when the Egyptians heed God's warning of the impending hail judgment and seek shelter.)

God's heart has always been for the world. He desires that all people come to know Him. The more we study the Bible, the more you will see God's global plan unfolding.

Check out the following interesting verses concerning Egypt:

- **Deuteronomy 23:7 -** *In instructions to the Israelites about how to live once they entered the land God has promised them, God said, "Do not abhor an Egyptian, because you lived as an alien in his country."*

- **II Peter 3:9 -** *"The Lord is... not wanting anyone to perish, but everyone to come to repentance."*

- **Isaiah 19:19-25 -** *God said that someday as a nation the Egyptians would follow Him and He would declare, "Blessed be Egypt my people."*

3. Why did the Lamb have to be perfect?

The "perfect lamb" (i.e. a lamb with no defects) was to symbolize the moral perfection that God requires. We'll see more about this in Episode 6 - *Atonement.* All of it was deeply symbolic of the future Deliverer, and the fact that He would be sinless and perfect.

4. Did God really open the Red Sea?

The Bible says He did. Some people have suggested that the "Red Sea" in the Bible should be translated to say "Sea of Reeds" claiming that it was more probable that the Israelites crossed over in a marsh that was temporarily drier because of wind. This is not what the Bible says happened. Check out the following verses:

- **Exodus 15:8 -** *"[T]he waters piled up. The surging waters stood firm like a wall…congealed in the heart of the sea."*

- **Psalm 78:13 -** *"He divided the sea and led them through; He made the water stand firm like a wall."*

(How could Pharaoh's army drown in a knee high marsh, anyway?!)

TE✝ELESTAI

CHAPTER 5

THE LAW

Pre Bible Study Checklist:

❑ Have extra Bibles and pens on hand.

❑ Have chocolates for prizes for anyone who memorized the verse.

❑ Pray for each participant to come and be open to God's Word and His Spirit.

❑ Be familiar with the Synopsis.

❑ Be familiar with the questions and dynamics of how the Group Discussion will flow.

❑ Glance through the *"Questions Your Group Might Have"* located at the end of this lesson.

Synopsis of the Episode:

In The Law, the nation of Israel begins their journey to God's Promised Land. At the base of Mt. Sinai, God gives His people the Ten Commandments. They confidently assure God of their perfect obedience. In The Law, each commandment is examined to show how the people are incapable of perfect obedience. God's Law serves as a mirror to show His people how sinful they are so they will realize their only hope is in the coming Deliverer.

Greeting

❑ Note the attendance.

❑ Verse and chocolates.

❑ Brief open discussion of their Bible reading or articles.

Watch Episode 5 - *The Law*

The Ten Commandments and God's Covenant:

God began to lead the Israelites to the land He had promised to Abraham. As they journeyed through the desert, God miraculously led the Israelites and provided food and water for them. After three months of traveling, they finally arrived at Mt. Sinai[19]; the mountain to which God had promised to bring Moses and the Israelites. There at Mt. Sinai, God made a covenant with the Israelites. The core terms of this covenant are known as the Ten Commandments. The terms of the covenant, or the Law, revealed more of God's character and His perfect standard of right and wrong. The Ten Commandments were inscribed on two tablets of stone by the very finger of God. The Israelites were required to perfectly obey all of God's laws. In response, they confidently told Moses, (**Exodus 19:8**) *"We will do everything the LORD has said."* But would they be able to keep the terms of the covenant and obey God's laws? As we look at these commands, ask yourself the same question. How many of these laws do you obey?

1: You shall have no other gods before me: Exodus 20:3

Exodus 20:1-2 reminds us that Israel had just left a country that believed there were a multitude of gods and goddesses to be served and appeased. But God's first commandment to His people was: (**Exodus 20:3**) *"You shall have no other gods before me."* God commanded His people to worship, trust, and serve Him alone. God explains that, (**Isaiah 45:5**) *"...[A]part from Me there is no [other] god."* Do you daily put your trust in God alone? What about when you are faced with a serious problem such as a sickness or a financial crisis; where do you go for help? Who or what do you seek after in order to gain guidance, protection, or prosperity? Or perhaps you have lived your whole life completely trusting in yourself? (**Jeremiah 17:5**) If you placed your trust in yourself or in any other being, spirit or source of power other than God, then you have broken this commandment.

2: You shall not make for yourself an idol: Exodus 20:4-6

God forbade His people from making an idol made to look like any heavenly being, angel or even God Himself. God also commanded them not to make idols in the form of animals, vegetation, or people; either living or dead. God also prohibited worshipping idols, bowing down to them or venerating them. (**Isaiah 42:8**) Have you ever given your praise to an idol or bowed down to it? Have you ever worshipped or prayed to an image? If so, you've broken this commandment. There are over 200 verses in the Bible against idolatry. Isaiah explains that

---

[19] Also known as Mt. Horeb, or the "Mountain of God"

those who are worshipping idols have had their hearts deceived without ever questioning, (**Isaiah 44:20**) *"Is not this thing in my right hand a lie?"* Over and over again, God commands His people to not trust in idols, (**Isaiah 46:5-10**) urging them, "I am God! I am your Creator! Worship, serve and trust Me alone!."

3: You shall not misuse the name of the Lord your God: Exodus 20:7

God's name is to be used with utmost honor. God prohibited His people from using His name in a curse or simply in an empty expression. Think about it. When someone says, "Oh my God, it is so hot today!" or " Oh my God, that is so awesome!", were they thinking about God or praying to Him? No! Have you ever used God's name as an expression? Have you ever blurted out God's name without even thinking about what you were saying? If you have, then you have broken this commandment.

4: Remember the Sabbath day by keeping it holy: Exodus 20:8-11

God commanded His people to not work on the seventh day of each week, but instead, dedicate that day to Him. Observance of this day not only gave His people a day of rest in which they could worship Him, but also uniquely set the nation of Israel apart from the other nations around them. Have you obeyed this law? If you are basing your acceptance by God on the fact that you keep the Sabbath, you need to realize failing to dedicate even one Sabbath to God means you have broken this commandment.

5: Honor your father and your mother: Exodus 20:12

God not only commanded us to obey our parents, but also to honor them. Honoring goes beyond outward conformity and deals with the heart. The opposite of honoring would include disobedience, talking back, arguing or being disrespectful. Have you ever done any of these things to your parents? If so, then you've broken this commandment.

6: You shall not murder: Exodus 20:13

God, as the Author and Giver of life, views every human being as precious. Many of us read the command to not murder and think, "Well, at least, this is one commandment that I've never broken! I've never killed anyone." Are you sure? Listen to these verses from **Matthew 5:21-22**: *"You have heard that it was said to the people long ago, 'Do not murder, and anyone who murders will be subject to judgment.' But I tell you that anyone who is angry with his brother will be subject to judgment."* All our actions flow from our hearts. God will judge not only the act of murder, but a heart with murderous thoughts. **I John 3:15** says: *"Anyone who hates his brother is a murderer..."* Have you ever hated anyone, or been angry with them? If so, you've also broken this commandment.

7: You shall not commit adultery: Exodus 20:14

God is also the Author and Designer of marriage. From the very beginning, God intended marriage to be one woman for one man for a lifetime. In **Proverbs 5:18**, God tells the husband: *"...[R]ejoice in the wife of your youth."* In **Proverbs 5:19** He says: *"...[M]ay you ever be captivated by her love."* The physical intimacy that a husband and wife share is a precious gift to their marriage.

Adultery, is being sexually intimate with someone to whom you are not married. God says: "Don't do that! If you do, you'll destroy yourself, and your marriage!" Some people read this commandment and think, "I'm not even married, so I haven't broken this commandment." God demands all people to be pure, not only in their actions, but with their eyes and heart as well. **Matthew 5:28** says, *"...[A]nyone who looks at a woman lustfully has already committed adultery with her in his heart."* If you have looked in lust at the body of a person you are not married to, then you are guilty of breaking this commandment.

8: You shall not steal: Exodus 20:15

Stealing is taking anything that doesn't belong to you, but belongs to someone else. Have you ever cheated, taking answers that weren't rightfully yours? Have you ever taken music, movies, or information that you didn't pay for? Have you ever cheated on your taxes, or at your job, saying that you worked eight hours when you only worked seven? If under any circumstance you have taken something that does not belong to you, then you have broken this commandment.

9: You shall not give false testimony against your neighbor: Exodus 20:16

God only speaks the truth, and He requires that we also speak the truth in everything that we say. We have a tendency, however, to think, "Oh, it's just a little white lie; it's ok, nobody's going to get hurt." But **Matthew 12:36** says that all people, *"...[W]ill have to give account on the Day of Judgment for every careless word they have spoken."* Have you ever told a lie? If so, then you've broken this commandment.

10: You shall not covet: Exodus 20:17

Not only is coveting a sin, but it often leads a person to break other commands of God in order to get whatever it is they are coveting. What about you? Have you ever become dissatisfied with what you already have, and been consumed with the desire to have something that is not yours? If so, you've coveted and are guilty of breaking this commandment.

God will judge every single action:

The truth is, every single person who honestly evaluates their life will have to admit they have broken God's commandments. And like the Israelites, we have done it over and over again. We have a problem then because God is holy. He is completely pure with nothing evil in Him. He requires absolute obedience to these laws. God says, (**Galatians 3:10**) *"Cursed is everyone who does not continue to do everything written in the Book of the Law."*

What gives eternal magnitude to these commandments is the fact that God also says, (**Hebrews 9:27**) *"...[M]an is destined to die once and after that to face judgment."* Rich or poor, educated or not, good or bad, no one escapes death. After death, God will judge every single person. He knows all the careless words that you have spoken. He has taken note of of everything that your hands have done, and each place that your feet have gone. All the hidden secrets you thought no one knew were recorded by God. (**Revelation 20:12**) He will judge every single one of these actions.

The Law functions like a mirror:

In light of these sobering facts, the question begs to be asked: If God already knew that we wouldn't be able to obey His laws, *why* then did He give them to us? **Romans 3:20** explains, *"...[T]hrough the law we become conscious of sin."* The reason God gave us the Ten Commandments was so that we would realize we are sinners! God's holy laws functioned like a mirror showing the people their own sinfulness. When we look at the Law, we realize our own lives are full of evil.

The Law leads us to the Deliverer:

Galatians 3:24 says that God also gave the Law in order to lead people to the coming Deliverer! God knew if the people could recognize the fact they were sinners, they would realize they needed Someone to rescue them from their sins. The Deliverer would be the only One who would be able to perfectly obey God's laws. His life would be completely pure with nothing evil in Him. He would be the only One who would be able to resolve the problem of their sins. God knew, in order for the people to realize their only hope was in the coming Deliverer, they needed *the Law*.

Group discussion time: Personal & Relevant

1. Divide into groups of 3-5 people.
2. Distribute the topics listed below, giving a topic to each group to discuss. *(If you have more than 3 groups, just repeat the topics.)*
3. Allow the groups ten minutes to discuss their topic and record their answer in their Study Guide.
4. After ten minutes, have everyone come back together again.
5. Ask each group to choose a representative to read their group's answer. Encourage everyone to take notes in their Study Guide as the other groups share the answers to their topics.
6. After "Topic One's" answers are shared, read the "Summary" for Topic One before moving on to Topic Two and so on.

Topic One: Measuring up?

Question: What are some New Year's resolutions you have made in the past? Have you always been able to measure up to the standards *you* set for yourself? After watching this episode, *The Law,* do you feel like you've been able to measure up to *God's* standards?

Facilitator's Summary: Whether it's the decision to exercise, lose weight or read more books, most of us have resolved to do better. Usually it works out for a little while, but sooner or later we fail. We can't even measure up to our *own* standards, let alone God's standards!

God's standards go far beyond even outward actions and deal with our motives, intentions and the deepest feelings of our heart:.... Feelings like lust or hate. **I John 1:8** puts it this way: *"If we claim to be without sin, we deceive ourselves and the truth is not in us."* Because of our sin, it is impossible to perfectly obey God's laws.

Topic Two: Can the bad be balanced out by good?

Question: Is it possible to do enough good deeds to outweigh your bad ones?

If you cheated on a test but then walked out and bought a beggar some food, would that help settle the account with God?

*See **James 2:10**

Facilitator's Summary: Most people are under the impression that God has a giant scale where He is measuring all of the bad things they've done. Secretly they hope that at the end of their life somehow their good deeds will have outweighed their bad ones.

The problem is, according to God, that's impossible! In **James 2:10**, God tells us that it only takes *one* little sin to "tip the scale" to condemnation! **James 2:10** says, "Whoever keeps the whole law and yet stumbles at just one point is guilty of breaking all of it."

God is perfectly holy. He doesn't demand a good try. He demands perfection.

Topic Three: Do you *really* think of yourself as that good?

Question: How would you feel about a movie that portrayed one week of your life, and in this movie it revealed every single action, word and thought you had during that week? What does **Hebrews 4:13** say?

Facilitator's Summary: Hebrews 4:13 says, *"Nothing in all creation is hidden from God's sight. Everything is uncovered and laid bare before the eyes of Him to whom we must give account."* **Revelation 20:12** says God is keeping a record of your every word, thought and action. Someday you will stand before God and be judged according to this record of your life.

God's Law functions like a mirror for our hearts, showing us how sinful we really are. When we truly examine our lives in light of the Ten Commandments, we realize how we are unable to measure up to God's Holy Standards. These Laws helped the people realize how much they needed the coming Deliverer. This Promised Deliverer would be the Only One who would be able to measure up to God's perfect standard. He would be the One to rescue humanity from their sins.

Watch Episode 5 -"What does this mean for you?"

1.You have broken God's laws.

"God required perfect obedience to His laws. Although the Israelites were confident they would be able to keep them, because of their sinfulness, they could not. They broke His Laws over and over again. An honest evaluation of your life will reveal that you also have broken God's commandments. Because of your sin, perfect obedience is also impossible for you."

2. You will have to give account to God.

"In Hebrews 9:27 it is written that "...[M]an is destined to die once and after that to face judgment. "After death, God will judge every single person according to what they have done. Even if you have kept the whole law, and only broken one command, James 2:10 says that you are guilty of breaking all of it. The day will come when you will have to give account to God for every action, every word and every thought."

3. Someone to rescue you

"When God gave the people the Law, He already knew that they would not be able to keep His commandments. Like a mirror that reveals to us an imperfection, the Ten Commandments reveal to people the sin in their lives and hearts. The Law pointed people to the coming Deliverer. Their only hope would be in Someone who could rescue them from their sins.... this is the only hope for me and for you."

Closing Checklist:

- ❏ "Does anyone have any questions?" (Either as a group or one on one.)
- ❏ Encourage them to jot any questions or comments during the week.
- ❏ Encourage them to read the Bible and articles contained in their Study Guide. (See list below)

Read it for yourself:

Exodus 20:1-17	The Ten Commandments
James 2:10	Breaking one commandment condemns you
Isaiah 42:8	God will not share His glory with idols
Matthew 5:21-22	God judges hate like murder
Matthew 5:28	God judges lust like adultery
Revelation 20:12	Everyone will be judged by God.
Romans 3:20	The Laws makes us conscious of our sin.

Dig Deeper

God knows everything about us and we will give account to Him.	**Hebrews 4:13**
All of us have sinned.	**Romans 3:23**
If we say we have never sinned, we're lying!	**1 John 1:8**

*Ask Someone to read the verse out loud in the Study Guide

Memorize this:

"...[N]o one will be declared righteous in God's sight by the works of the law; rather, through the law we become conscious of our sin." **Romans 3:20**

Facilitator's Comment on the Verse:

According to this verse there is not one single person on the planet to whom God will say, "That person is righteous because they follow my laws." Today we've seen that no matter how hard we try, we break God's commandments! This verse tells us that, "through the law we become conscious of our sin."

Facilitator's Closing Comment:

God wanted His people to realize their only hope was in the coming Deliverer who would rescue them and resolve the problem of their sin. Don't miss next time, we're going to see how God gave His people a way for their sins could be covered while they waited for the Deliverer to come and restore their broken relationship.

Questions your group *might* have:

Remember: *Keep your group on track! If you find a question is more disruptive than beneficial, graciously thank them for their question and tell them you look forward to talking about it one on one.*

1. What about the Sabbath?	**Pg. 84**
2. The Ten Commandments List I learned was different.	**Pg. 85**
3. Does God encourage the use of images?	**Pg. 90**
4. Why does God prohibit sex outside of marriage?	**Pg. 90**
5. LGBTQ?	**Pg. 91**
6. What about reincarnation?	**Pg. 92**

1. What about the Sabbath?

** If you have a listener in your group who you perceive is putting their confidence for salvation in the fact that they religiously keep the Sabbath, gently remind them of everything we just saw in the episode **about the reason for the Law.** Try to keep the discussion off of the whole "Saturday or Sunday" issue. The real issue is the fact that we are incapable of earning salvation in our own efforts and through our own good works. Keep emphasizing that if their confidence in going to Heaven is based on their own effort (i.e. keeping the Sabbath) then they are lost! Look at the following verses with them:*

- **Galatians 3:20 -** We are cursed if we cannot keep the whole law

- **James 2:10 -** Even if we break one commandment we are guilty of breaking all of them (i.e. if you told a lie then you're condemned even if you faithfully kept the Sabbath. What about lust? Anger? All of us have sinned more than once.)

- **Romans 3:20 -** Not one single person will be declared righteous by following the Law, the Law was given to show us we are sinners, and to lead us to the Deliverer.

If they want to continue talking about whether or not keeping the Sabbath is important just say, "It's fine if you want to worship God on the Sabbath. The important thing that you need to realize from this episode is that we are sinners and we break God's Laws."

For now, I want you to remember the main point of this episode is not about whether we should worship God on Saturday or Sunday... the main point of this

episode is that we've all messed up, and that we're all sinners in need of Someone to rescue us.

The following article might be helpful for <u>you</u> to read on your own for more information. Although perhaps it is not something you want to share with them just now, as it is not worth making an issue over. Always keep the main point, the main point.

Recommended Resource for your own reading:

What about the Sabbath? Pg. 282

2. I'm confused, the list I was taught for the Ten Commandments was different.

Sometimes we shorten the wording of the Ten Commandments in order to make it easier for people to memorize. For example, we could say: "You shall not misuse the name of the Lord your God," to remind us of the entire commandment: "You shall not misuse the name of the Lord your God, for the Lord will not hold anyone guiltless who misuses his name. "

In creating these "Short Lists", various people have divided up the verses in **Exodus 20:1-17** in different places coming up with slightly varying "Short Lists" because of how they numbered their lists. This might be why you're confused.

Read on to examine **Exodus 20:1-17**. You will notice how these verses have been historically numbered three different ways:

Exodus 20:1-17: Ten Commandments: (Numbering Version 1)

1 And God spoke all these words:

1st Commandment:

2 "I am the Lord your God, who brought you out of Egypt, out of the land of slavery."

2nd Commandment:

3 "You shall have no other gods before Me."

4 "You shall not make for yourself an image in the form of anything in heaven above or on the earth beneath or in the waters below. **5** You shall not bow down to them or worship them; for I, the Lord your God, am a jealous God, punishing the children for the sin of the parents to the third and fourth generation of those who hate Me, **6** but showing love to a thousand generations of those who love me and keep my commandments."

3rd Commandment:

7 "You shall not misuse the name of the Lord your God, for the Lord will not hold anyone guiltless who misuses His name."

4th Commandment:

8 "Remember the Sabbath day by keeping it holy. **9** Six days you shall labor and do all your work, **10** but the seventh day is a Sabbath to the Lord your God. On it you shall not do any work, neither you, nor your son or daughter, nor your male or female servant, nor your animals, nor any foreigner residing in your towns. **11** For in six days the Lord made the heavens and the earth, the sea, and all that is in them, but He rested on the seventh day. Therefore the Lord blessed the Sabbath day and made it holy."

5th Commandment:

12 "Honor your father and your mother, so that you may live long in the land the Lord your God is giving you."

6th Commandment:

13 "You shall not murder."

7th Commandment:

14 "You shall not commit adultery. "

8th Commandment:

15 "You shall not steal."

9th Commandment:

16 "You shall not give false testimony against your neighbor."

10th Commandment:

17 "You shall not covet your neighbor's house. You shall not covet your neighbor's wife, or his male or female servant, his ox or donkey, or anything that belongs to your neighbor."

Exodus 20:1-17: Ten Commandments: (Numbering Version 2)

1 And God spoke all these words:

2 "I am the Lord your God, who brought you out of Egypt, out of the land of slavery."

1st Commandment:

3 "You shall have no other gods before[a] Me."

2nd Commandment:

4 "You shall not make for yourself an image in the form of anything in heaven above or on the earth beneath or in the waters below. 5 You shall not bow down to them or worship them; for I, the Lord your God, am a jealous God, punishing the children for the sin of the parents to the third and fourth generation of those who hate Me, 6 but showing love to a thousand generations of those who love Me and keep My commandments."

3rd Commandment:

7 "You shall not misuse the name of the Lord your God, for the Lord will not hold anyone guiltless who misuses His name."

4th Commandment:

8 "Remember the Sabbath day by keeping it holy. 9 Six days you shall labor and do all your work, 10 but the seventh day is a Sabbath to the Lord your God. On it you shall not do any work, neither you, nor your son or daughter, nor your male or female servant, nor your animals, nor any foreigner residing in your towns. 11 For in six days the Lord made the heavens and the earth, the sea, and all that is in them, but He rested on the seventh day. Therefore the Lord blessed the Sabbath day and made it holy.

5th Commandment:

12 "Honor your father and your mother, so that you may live long in the land the Lord your God is giving you."

6th Commandment:

13 "You shall not murder."

7th Commandment:

14 "You shall not commit adultery."

8th Commandment:

15 "You shall not steal."

9th Commandment:

16 "You shall not give false testimony against your neighbor."

10th Commandment:

17 "You shall not covet your neighbor's house. You shall not covet your neighbor's wife, or his male or female servant, his ox or donkey, or anything that belongs to your neighbor."

Exodus 20:1-17: Ten Commandments: (Numbering Version 3)

1 And God spoke all these words:

2 "I am the Lord your God, who brought you out of Egypt, out of the land of slavery."

1st Commandment:

3 "You shall have no other gods before[a] Me."

4 "You shall not make for yourself an image in the form of anything in heaven above or on the earth beneath or in the waters below. **5** You shall not bow down to them or worship them; for I, the Lord your God, am a jealous God, punishing the children for the sin of the parents to the third and fourth generation of those who hate Me, **6** but showing love to a thousand generations of those who love Me and keep My commandments."

2nd Commandment:

7 "You shall not misuse the name of the Lord your God, for the Lord will not hold anyone guiltless who misuses His name."

3rd Commandment:

8 "Remember the Sabbath day by keeping it holy. **9** Six days you shall labor and do all your work, **10** but the seventh day is a Sabbath to the Lord your God. On it you shall not do any work, neither you, nor your son or daughter, nor your male or female servant, nor your animals, nor any foreigner residing in your towns. **11** For in six days the Lord made the heavens and the earth, the sea, and all that is in them, but he rested on the seventh day. Therefore the Lord blessed the Sabbath day and made it holy."

4th Commandment:

12 "Honor your father and your mother, so that you may live long in the land the Lord your God is giving you."

5th Commandment:

13 "You shall not murder."

6th Commandment:

14 "You shall not commit adultery."

7th Commandment:

15 "You shall not steal."

8th Commandment:

16 "You shall not give false testimony against your neighbor."

9th and 10th Commandments:

17 "You shall not covet your neighbor's house. You shall not covet your neighbor's wife, or his male or female servant, his ox or donkey, or anything that belongs to your neighbor."

In this version's "Short List" verse 17 is summarized like this:

#9:"You shall not covet your neighbor's wife."

#10 "You shall not covet your neighbor's goods."

Note, however, that regardless of how the commandments are numbered, the content of the verses *does not change!* Keep in mind at all times that a "Short List" is only valuable if we are aware of the full content that the list represents. **Always compare every "Short List" of the Ten Commandments with the Word of God.**

3. Does God encourage the use of images?

Someone might say, "God is not against images, He even commanded the Israelites to make the cherubim above the Ark of the Covenant."

God did command the Israelites to make the lid of the Ark of the Covenant with cherubim. However, God never commanded the Israelites to pray to the cherubim! The Ark of the Covenant was in the Most Holy Place, a place that only the High Priest could access once a year on the Day of Atonement. Furthermore, when the Ark of the Covenant was transported, it was always covered. With the exception of the High Priest, no one ever saw the cherubim and they most certainly did <u>not</u> worship them.

The Bible does not contradict itself. Idolatry is always, always prohibited. God compares it to prostitution! He says, "I love you! I made you for Me! Why are you giving your love to this idol?!"

Recommended Resources:

Does God encourage the use of images/icons in worship? Are icons wrong? Pg. 287

Idolatry - What the Bible says. Pg 284

Does the Bible promote or prohibit praying to angels? Pg. 289

Is worship of saints wrong? Pg. 291

4. Why does God say you can't have sex outside of marriage?

(See Pg. 46 for "I thought the first sin was sex?" for more on how God is the designer of sex and made it to be beautiful and pleasurable.)

Sex is not just the uniting of two bodies, but the uniting of two souls. God intended this mystical union to take place in the protection of marriage - a forever commitment. This shields both your heart and your body, allowing you to give yourself to your spouse in complete trust and security, knowing that not only has your spouse guarded his or her body and waited just for you - but he or she will continue to love you, protect you, and cherish you till the end. God's commands are always for our best. They set us free to live in freedom from the fear, bondage and suffering that corruption of His perfect plan brings.

I had a professor who put it this way: What if someone used a Stradivarius violin to pound a nail into the wall? (It makes me cringe just picturing it!) Would they get the nail pounded in? Probably. Is it what the Stradivarius was intended for? Absolutely not! The maker of that Stradivarius would be devastated and furious to see the wreckage and damage you had brought about to his creation! In the same way, we humans do a lot of damage to our bodies in activities that God never intended for us to participate in. He is heartbroken when He looks at His creation and sees the pain, heartache and suffering that we are causing to ourselves and others. He says, "I made you for so much more! This is not my perfect plan!"

However, if you are thinking, "Well, too late for me", know that with God there is complete forgiveness, restoration and healing. He has a better way for you and He wants you to continue getting to know Him!

Recommended Resource:

What does the Bible say about sex before marriage? Pg. 293

5. One man for one woman?! What if someone is LGBTQ?[20]

If you are asked this question regarding those who identify themselves as lesbian, gay, bisexual, transexual or queer, tread very lightly, remembering that if the person asking the question has not yet come to a complete understanding of the gospel, then **the most important issue at hand is not this question. True transformation is only possible in Christ.** *Helping someone come to a complete understanding of freedom through Christ, and how to live a biblical lifestyle instead of living in bondage to lies and sin, will be a necessary and important part of discipleship* <u>after</u> *someone has come to Christ. Since you are still introducing him or her to Christ, be very careful to answer in love and patience. Since people are being bombarded with lies in regard to this issue, the questioner is understandably confused over this topic. It may be best to respond in the following way:*

When God created the first couple in the Garden, whom did He create? Adam and Eve. One man for one woman. This is God's design. **Psalm 139** says that God created us in our mother's womb. Scientists have told us that the sex of the baby is determined at the very moment of conception. Isn't that amazing? God makes either a boy or a girl. That doesn't mean that later on people won't be

---

[20] Once again, we want to see all people walking in newness of life and Biblical freedom from sin. This life transformation is only possible, however, with new birth in Christ and the indwelling of the Holy Spirit. Only God can give someone the love and acceptance they long for and the power to say "no" to sin and thus "no" to every harmful desire. The reason we recommend constantly pointing people towards salvation is that ultimately new life in Christ will lead to transformation in <u>every</u> area of a person's life and that includes how they view themselves and the choices they make. A wise man once said: "The gospel is not about making bad men *good*; it is about making dead men *alive!*"
Once someone is "alive in Christ" God can begin to transform them, and you will be able to step into the vital role of a mentor and discipler helping someone learn to walk with God, moving from "bad" to "good."

confused or make harmful choices, but God's purpose and plan for them is to be what He created them to be.

I'm sure you still have a lot of questions about this. I'll tell you what, though, we're not even halfway through this Bible Study series. As we progress, we're going to find out a whole lot more about God's character, His incredible plan for humanity, and His love for *you*. So, hang in there and keep listening, ok?

I *do* want you to understand what the Bible says. I'm not trying to avoid your question. I think a lot will fall into place as we keep studying the Bible. If you still have questions at the end of the series, let's make a point to go out for coffee and talk about this more, ok?

For now, I want you to remember the main point of this episode is not about sexuality... the main point of this episode is that we've all messed up, and that we're all sinners in need of Someone to rescue us.

Recommended Resources for a Believer:

Can you be born gay? Pg. 295

If God is Love, how can He condemn homosexuality? Pg. 298

Recommended Resource for a Seeker: * Be aware that the purpose of the following article is not to discuss what the Bible says about homosexuality, but rather to focus only on salvation and the fact that all are in need of a Savior, and that He extends His offer of salvation to all.

God loves you even if you're LGBTQ. Pg. 300

6. What about reincarnation?

God makes it clear in His Word that each person He creates is uniquely and fearfully made. You are not a "recycled soul" that has lived in another body. You are completely and uniquely *you*, with your DNA, your body and your personality. He loves you and desires to have a relationship with you.

God gives us one life to live on this earth and after that we will stand before Him and give account to Him. We do <u>not</u> return to this world to live again as a different human being.

- *Hebrews 9:27* - "... [P]eople are destined to die once, and after that the judgment."

Recommended Resource:

What does the Bible say about reincarnation? Pg. 306

TETELESTAI

CHAPTER 6

ATONEMENT

Pre Bible Study Checklist:

❏ Have extra Bibles and pens on hand.

❏ Have chocolates for prizes for anyone who memorized the verse.

❏ Pray for each participant to come and be open to God's Word and His Spirit.

❏ Be familiar with the Synopsis.

❏ Be familiar with the questions and dynamics of how the Group Discussion will flow.

❏ Glance through the *"Questions Your Group Might Have"* located at the end of this lesson.

Synopsis of the Episode:

The episode Atonement shows how God provides a way for the turning aside of His punishment through the sacrificial system that centers around the Tabernacle. This is God's way of providing the means by which the people's sins are dealt with until the Deliverer arrives. When a rebellion against God takes place in the desert, venomous snakes are sent to punish the people. Full healing from this snakebite is offered to all who will simply look upon the bronze snake lifted up on a pole. The innocent substitute shedding its blood in the sacrificial system to turn aside God's punishment, and the life being offered to all who look at the bronze snake, are two more breathtaking pictures set in place that point to the work of the coming Deliverer.

Greeting

❏ Note the attendance.

❏ Verse and chocolates.

❏ Brief open discussion of their Bible reading or articles.

Watch Episode 6 - *Atonement*

God's Plan of Atonement:

Until the Deliverer came, God continued to reveal a way in which His people could be forgiven, and not receive the punishment they deserved for their sins. There, at Mt. Sinai, God not only gave His people the Law, but God also revealed to Moses His plan of Atonement. Atonement is the turning aside of God's punishment. Instead of pouring out His punishment upon the sinful people, God would provide a way in which His punishment would be turned aside.

Atonement was made at the Tabernacle:

All the requirements for atonement were to be performed at a magnificent, portable structure called the Tabernacle. At the Tabernacle, God manifested His presence by a cloud that came to rest above the Tabernacle. Later on, the Tabernacle would be replaced by a permanent structure called the temple. But until that day came, the Tabernacle would be the center of all activity concerning atonement. God also chose men called priests to represent the nation in fulfilling the requirements that God had instituted. The priests were the ones who were to now bring the offerings and sacrifices to God at the Tabernacle, and the leader of the priests was called the high priest.

A Perfect Substitute:

When the Israelites came to the Tabernacle to make atonement for their sins, they weren't to offer just any animal. God gave them very specific instructions. (**Leviticus 1:2-3**) All animals offered to the Lord were to be perfect, they with no defects. This was to symbolize the moral perfection that God required. Notice that when a man offered a sacrifice, the man was not inspected for perfection. (**Leviticus 1:3**) No one asked him, "Have you been saying prayers? Have you been helping the poor? Have you been a good citizen?" No! The man was not examined; the man was a sinner! Rather, the animal was examined, and had to be found perfect. The *animal* was examined in the man's place as his substitute.

God's Punishment Turned Away from the Sinner:

The man would then place his hand on the head of the animal. (**Leviticus 1:4**) By this action he was admitting, "I am a sinner, but I am bringing this animal as my substitute to die in my place." Then **Leviticus 1:4** continues: *"...[I]t will be accepted on his behalf to make atonement for him."* To the man, God was saying: "Because this animal is taking your punishment in your place, I will turn my punishment away from you." Since the payment for sin is death, that animal was then killed, instead of the man. Its blood was shed. In **Hebrews 9:22** God says that, "...

without the shedding of blood there is no forgiveness." And in **Leviticus 17:11** God also explains, *"For the life of a creature is in the blood, and I have given it to you to make atonement for yourselves on the altar..."* A life had been given in the place of another. And when God saw the blood of the sacrifice, His punishment was turned away from the man because a substitute had taken his place. This is how atonement, the turning aside of God's punishment, was made for an individual.

Atonement for the Entire Nation:

There was a special day every year in which Atonement was to be made for the sins of the entire nation. This day was called the Day of Atonement. (**Leviticus 16:34**) This was to take place in the Tabernacle. The Tabernacle was divided into two rooms: the Holy Place and the Most Holy Place. Within the Most Holy Place was a golden box containing the Ten Commandments, called the Ark of the Covenant. Inside this box were God's holy laws, the covenant that he had made with them. The Ark of the Covenant had a lid called the Atonement Cover. It was here that God promised His people that His presence would fill the Most Holy Place.

(**Leviticus 16:2**) A thick, multi-layered, richly embroidered Curtain hung between the Holy Place and the Most Holy Place, blocking access to the Most Holy Place. With this curtain, God was showing the people that sinful man is separated from Holy God. No one was allowed behind the curtain into the Most Holy Place. God had warned them that if anyone went behind the Curtain into God's presence, they would surely die.

The Blood of the Substitute over the Law that Condemns

On the Day of Atonement, however, someone did go behind the curtain, into the Most Holy Place. (**Hebrews 9:7**) Every person in the nation had sinned and because the payment for sin is death, they all deserved to die.

On that day, the High Priest represented the entire nation. Once behind the curtain, the High Priest faced the Ark of the Covenant. Inside of the Ark of the Covenant were the Ten Commandments, God's holy laws, the laws the people were unable to keep, the laws that showed their complete sinfulness. In **Leviticus 16:15**, God commanded the High Priest to take the blood of the sacrifice, and sprinkle it on the Atonement Cover, and in front of it. There, above the Atonement Cover, was the presence of God, and beneath Him, were the laws that condemned them. But now, in between Holy God and sinful man, was the blood of the sacrifice; the innocent one that had died in the place of those who were guilty. When God looked down, instead of seeing the Law that condemned them, He chose to see the blood of the one who had died for them, as their substitute. And in this way, God's punishment was turned away from the people, and atonement was made.

Illustrations of a Future Atonement:

Through the sacrifices, God turned His punishment away from the people. These sacrifices, however, did not take away their sins. Rather, day after day, and year after year, they were a constant reminder of how sinful the people were! **Hebrews 10:1** explains that these sacrifices were only a shadow of the good things that were coming, and not the realities themselves. You see, although the people may not have understood it at the time, every sacrifice was a picture in God's eternal Plan of Salvation. Each time an animal's blood was shed, it pointed to a day in the future when blood would be shed to turn away God's punishment *once and for all*. Every time an animal was offered as a sacrifice, it pointed to a future day when One who was Innocent would come and die in the place of all those who were guilty, a day when atonement would be made not only for the sins of the nation, but for the sins of the whole world.

Rebellion in the Desert:

When the Israelites reached the border to the Promised Land, there was an uprising against God. Because of their lack of trust in God's power, the Israelites refused to enter the land, and instead demanded to go back to Egypt. God declared that, as a result of their disobedience, only their children would be allowed to enter the Land. God then led them back into the desert, where they were to wander for forty years until their children were old enough to enter the Promised Land, and the older generation that had refused to enter the land, had passed away.

Numbers 21 describes an important event which took place during these forty years in the desert. God had carefully led his people through the desert, protected them from all harm, and daily provided the food and water they needed. Yet, **Numbers 21:5** says that the people, ungrateful for all of God's provision, spoke against God and against Moses. In the face of this rebellion against God, God caused a series of dramatic events that would not only be recorded in Israel's history, but would be used by God to paint another striking picture of His eternal Plan of Salvation.

God Offered Life to the Entire Rebellious Nation:

Because of the people's rebellion against Him, **Numbers 21:6** says, *"Then the LORD sent venomous snakes among them; they bit the people and many Israelites died."* There was no cure for the snakebite, no hospitals, no medicine that would reverse the effects of the venom. All who were bitten would surely die. When the Israelites realized the peril they were in, they confessed their rebellion and cried out for help. (**Numbers 21:7**) In response to the people's cry for deliverance, God was about to provide complete healing. Not only would this healing reverse the effects of the poison, it would be offered freely by God. Life instead of death would be offered by God to every single person in the nation, regardless of age, gender, social status or even past rebellion against Him.

An Opportunity to Trust God:

In **Numbers 21:8-9**, we read that in obedience to God's instructions, Moses fashioned a snake out of bronze and hung it up on a pole. This snake was not to be an idol to be worshiped. Throughout the Bible, God strictly prohibits the worshiping of idols. Nor did this bronze snake have any magical powers. The reason God told Moses to place this snake on a pole was to give the people an opportunity to trust Him. The healing that God would provide would not be forced upon anyone. Every single person would have to *choose* whether they would accept or reject the healing God offered.

Trust, Look, Live:

God told Moses to announce to the people, (**Numbers 21:8**) *"...[A]nyone who is bitten can look at it and live."* When someone believed what God said, and looked at that snake on the pole, that person would instantly be healed and given life.

What if that day someone in the crowd said, "What?! That's all I have to do...just look?! No, that's too easy. That just seems too simple. I can't believe that. I'm not going to look." What would you say to that person? I would say, "Stop being prideful! Just look! Believe what God says; trust Him!"

What if someone else said, "I don't think it's necessary for me to look. I'm a very good person. I really think that God will see my heart and all of my good works, and heal me!" Do you think that's true? Would God heal them simply because they were a good person? No! It did not matter how good a person was! If they refused to look, then that person would die!

Lastly, what if someone else said, "I would like to look, I really would, but the problem is I'm not sure how my family and friends will react. They have already decided they are not going to look, so what will they think of me if I do? Because of this, I've decided not look either." What would you say? I would say, "Friend, I am so sorry that the others around you are choosing to reject life! You, though, can still choose life! You do not have to reject life because of them! This is your only hope!"

God will Always Do what He Says:

That day in the desert, thousands stood between life and death. They all had the same choice to make: Do I trust what God said and look, or do I refuse to listen to Him and die? **Numbers 21:9** says, *"When anyone was* *bitten by a snake and looked at the bronze snake, he lived."* God will always do what He says. You can trust His Word. Unbeknownst to the people that day, was the fact that in the same way that Moses had lifted up the snake in the desert, a day was coming when, like the bronze snake, the coming Deliverer would also be lifted up. This event in the desert pointed to a future day when those who faced eternal death would be given the choice to not receive the punishment for their sins, but instead accept eternal life.

Group discussion time: Personal & Relevant

1. Divide into groups of 3-5 people.
2. Distribute the topics listed below, giving a topic to each group to discuss. *(If you have more than 3 groups, just repeat the topics.)*
3. Allow the groups ten minutes to discuss their topic and record their answer in their Study Guide.
4. After ten minutes, have everyone come back together again.
5. Ask each group to choose a representative to read their group's answer. Encourage everyone to take notes in their Study Guide as the other groups share the answers to their topics.
6. After "Topic One's" answers are shared, read the "Summary" for Topic One before moving on to Topic Two and so on.

Topic One: Examination

Question: At the time a sacrifice was offered, the priest had to make sure that there was perfection. Who or what was the priest examining? Why do you think this is significant?

_____

_____

> **Facilitator's Summary:** When a sacrifice was being offered, the priest examined the *lamb*, not the man or woman bringing the sacrifice! The lamb had to be perfect because it represented the *moral* perfection that God requires. God is absolutely perfect. He is Holy; which means He is completely pure with no evil in Him.

What if the man or woman themselves were examined? Would they pass the examination and be found perfect? No! Of course not! Remember the Ten Commandments? No matter how hard someone tries, we have all broken God's commandments, we fail to meet God's standard. (**Romans 3:23**)

God allowed the people to bring a substitute to be examined in their place, and found *perfect* and acceptable on their behalf.

This was an amazing picture pointing ahead to the Deliverer, Someone would come who would perfectly obey God's Laws and meet God's standard. This Deliverer would come to "take the test for you," so to speak. God required perfection. We can't be perfect. God says, "I will provide Someone to be perfect in your place."

Topic Two: Death on behalf of someone else

Question: Why the bloodshed? Why did God instruct them to sacrifice an animal on their behalf?

Wouldn't it have been shocking to participate in something like this and see a living thing killed?

*See **Leviticus 17:11***

Facilitator's Summary: Do you think these sacrifices were horrible? I do. I hate death! God hates death even more than we do. God wanted His people to realize how terrible and how serious sin is. I can't imagine what it must of been like for these people to see that animal alive one minute and then watch its blood poured out as it was killed… because of them!

Leviticus 17:11 says that the "life is in the blood." **Romans 6:23** states that payment for sin is death. The man or woman offering the sacrifice was the sinner who deserved to die. God in His love, however, allowed a *substitute* to die for them. An innocent one was dying so that the guilty person could live. Each sacrifice was pointing to the ultimate sacrifice that would one day be paid for your sins and mine.

Topic Three: The Most Holy Place

Answer the following questions:

Where did God manifest His presence in the Most Holy Place? (**Exodus 25:21,22**)

_____

What was the most important item placed inside the Ark of the Covenant? (**Deuteronomy 10:4,5**)

_____

On the Day of Atonement, what was sprinkled on the lid of the Ark of the Covenant? (**Leviticus 16:14**)

_____

Why is this significant?

_____

> **Facilitator's Summary:** On the Day of Atonement, God manifested His presence above the Ark of the Covenant. God's Holy Laws were placed inside the Ark of the Covenant. On the Day of Atonement the blood of the sacrifice was placed on the Ark of the Covenant. At that moment, *in between* God's presence and the Ten Commandments was the blood.
>
> In a sense, it was as if God was saying, "Yes, you have broken My Laws. Yes, they condemn you, but because an innocent one died for you, My punishment will be turned away from you! You will not be condemned for the wrong you've done. I have provided atonement for you!"

Topic Four: Reasons to not believe?

Question: When God offered healing in the desert to all those bitten by the venomous snakes, we saw three hypothetical scenarios of people rejecting His offer of life.

Think through each one of the following excuses someone might have for not looking at the bronze serpent. How do they reveal a faulty perspective?

1.   "It's too easy, so I'm not going to do it."
2.   "I'm such a good person, surely God will accept me because of that."
3.   "My friends and family are not going to look so I'm not either."

Facilitator's Summary:

We also have a fatal condition called sin, and God offers us Life. Not everyone is willing to accept His offer, though. Let's look at each one: At that moment, *in between* God's presence and the Ten Commandments was the blood.

1. **"Sounds too easy; surely I have to do something."**

    It seems counterintuitive for someone to say they can't accept an offer of life because it's too easy. Unfortunately though, we have a tendency to look for a list of things to <u>do,</u> a checklist we have to fulfill:

    "If I go to this meeting, say these prayers, perform this ceremony, then I will earn eternal life."

    The event that took place that day is a wonderful picture of how God provides salvation. You see, that day in the desert, God didn't tell them to *do anything*. The life He promised to give them would not be based on anything they could *do*. God wanted His people to simply *believe* what He said and accept the life He offered.

2. **"I'm such a good person, surely God will accept me because of that."**

Whether people were good or bad didn't make a difference. They were *dying*. The need of each person was the same! They needed life!

3. **"My friends and family are not going to look so I'm not either."**

We all care deeply about what our family and friends think of us. It seems crazy, however, to think that someone who is dying would reject the opportunity to have life based on peer pressure or family expectations.

As you study God's Word and consider the life He is offering you, ask yourself if any of these reasons are keeping you or someone you know away from Him.

Watch Episode 6 -"What does this mean for you?"

1. Examined in your place.

"When a man brought a sacrifice, instead of examining the man, the priest examined the lamb. The man who brought the lamb was a sinner who had broken God's laws and could not please Him. It was the lamb who had to be found perfect, with no defects. In the same way, God knew that you would break His laws. That's why He already planned to send the Deliverer: He would live the perfect life and be examined by God in your place."

2. An Innocent One for you.

"After being examined, the lamb was then killed. The man was guilty, yet it was the lamb who died. In this way, God allowed His punishment to be turned away from the man. Each time a sacrifice was offered, an innocent one died in the place of the guilty. Every death pointed to the ultimate sacrifice that would be made in order to resolve the problem of your sin."

3. Atonement for you.

"Once a year, on the Day of Atonement, when the High Priest entered God's presence, the blood of the sacrifice was sprinkled on the Atonement Cover. Instead of condemning the nation, God chose to see the blood of the one who had died for them, and turned away His punishment

This too was pointing to a future day when blood would be shed for the forgiveness of the entire world. A day when God would provide atonement for you."

4. A life for you.

"During a rebellion against God in the desert, poisonous snakes were sent to bite the people. God provided a way that all those who were bitten could live. They had only to look at the bronze snake and they would be healed. Just as the snake bite was fatal, you too have a fatal condition called sin. When God provided a way for the people to live, this was a picture of the salvation God would offer the world, life He would offer to you."

Closing Checklist:

- ❏ "Does anyone have any questions?" (Either as a group or one on one.)
- ❏ Encourage them to jot down any questions or comments during the week.
- ❏ Encourage them to read the Bible and articles contained in their Study Guide. (See list below)

Read it for yourself:

Leviticus 16:2	God's presence in the Tabernacle.
Leviticus 1:1-4	How sacrifices were brought.
Hebrews 9:7	Only the high priest could enter the Holy Place on the Day of Atonement.
Hebrews 10:1-3	These sacrifices could not take away their sins but only reminded them of how sinful they were. (Only the Deliverer would be able to fully pay for their sins.)
Numbers 21:1-9	The bronze snake.

Dig Deeper

Forgiveness could only take place because of the shedding of blood	**Hebrews 9:22**

*Ask someone to read the verse out loud from their Study Guide:

Memorize this:

"...He was pierced for our transgressions, He was crushed for our iniquities; the punishment that brought us peace was on Him..." **Isaiah 53:5**

Facilitator's Comment on Verse:

This verse reminds us of God's character. God is holy and must punish sin, but He is also loving and always provides a way to be saved. It is never His desire that anyone should perish.

Facilitator's Closing Comment:

Don't miss next time. We are going to witness a clash between opposing supernatural powers. We'll also see that God's power is always greater!

Questions your group *might* have:

Remember: *Keep your group on track! If you find a question is more disruptive than beneficial, graciously thank them for their question and tell them you look forward to talking about it one on one.*

I. Was the Ark of the Covenant an idol?	**Pg. 105**
2. Did the sacrifices pay for their sins?	**Pg. 105**
3. Do we have to offer sacrifices today?	**Pg. 106**
4. Aren't animal sacrifices cruel?	**Pg. 106**
5. Do we have to worship God at a tabernacle or temple today?	**Pg. 106**
6. Was the bronze snake an idol?	**Pg. 106**

I. Was the ark of the covenant an idol?

(This answer is copied from an answer given in the "The Law.")

God never commanded the Israelites to pray to the cherubim and no one even saw them for that matter! The Ark of the Covenant was in the Most Holy Place, a place that only the High Priest could go once a year on the Day of Atonement. They never worshipped the cherubim. Not only that, when the Ark of the Covenant was transported it was always covered.

The Bible does not contradict itself. Idolatry is always, always prohibited. God compares it to prostitution! He says, "I love you! I made you for me! Why are you giving your love to this idol?!"

See the list in the article: Idolatry - What the Bible says. Pg 284

2. Did the sacrifices pay for their sins?

No. The sacrifices temporarily turned aways God's punishment until the day came when God's promised Deliverer would completely pay for their sins once and for all. Each sacrifice offered reminded them of their sins. Although they did not understand it at the time, each sacrifice also pointed ahead to the ultimate price the Deliverer would one day pay to rescue them.

3. Do we have to offer sacrifices today?

We do not. Keep coming to Bible Study and watching, and you'll find out why we do not have to offer sacrifices.

4. Aren't animal sacrifices cruel?

Sin and the consequences of sin are equally horrible. God chose this graphic act to show His people how serious sin is and how the payment for sin is death. The sacrifices also pictured the price God would one day pay in order to rescue humanity.

5. Do we have to worship God at a tabernacle or temple today?

No. Keep listening and studying! Soon we'll see the culmination of God's Redemption Story and why we do not have to go to a physical structure to worship God.

6. Was the bronze snake an idol?

It was most certainly not an idol! God strictly forbids the worship of any object. In **Isaiah 42:8** He says, "I am the Lord; that is my name! I will not yield my glory to another or my praise to idols." The people were not to pray to the bronze snake or worship it. They were simply asked to "look at it" and that is how God chose to see who listened to Him and believed what He said, and who did not. Later on in Israel's history, the people of Israel wrongly began to worship the bronze snake and a godly king had to destroy it! (**II King 18:4**)

TETELESTAI

CHAPTER 7

LAMB OF GOD

Pre Bible Study Checklist:

- ❏ Have extra Bibles and pens on hand.
- ❏ Have chocolates for prizes for anyone who memorized the verse.
- ❏ Pray for each participant to come and be open to God's Word and His Spirit.
- ❏ Be familiar with the Synopsis.
- ❏ Be familiar with the questions and dynamics of how the Group Discussion will flow.
- ❏ Glance through the *"Questions Your Group Might Have"* located at the end of this lesson.

Synopsis of the Episode:

In Lamb of God, the promised Deliverer, the Messiah Jesus arrives! Although He is the Savior they have been waiting for and the fulfillment of the prophecies, He appears in an unexpected manner. God Himself takes on human form; the Creator becomes a part of His creation. As He grows up and lives among the people, Jesus is the only One who can fully obey God's Laws without sinning. He is victorious over Satan's temptations and declared to be the Lamb of God who takes away the sins of the world. The pictures are starting to come together in God's Story of Redemption.

Greeting

- ❏ Note the attendance.
- ❏ Verse and chocolates.
- ❏ Brief open discussion of their Bible reading or articles.

Watch Episode 7 - *Lamb of God*

The Eyewitness Accounts Spread like Wildfire:

The Roman Empire chose Greek to be the common language of communication for the entire empire. In 150 B.C., when God's Word was translated into the Greek language, everyone who could read Greek was able to read the prophecies about the Messiah, the Deliverer. With myriads of people now connected and speaking a common language, news never traveled so quickly. What took place next spread like wildfire across the empire, and changed the world forever. These events were carefully documented by eyewitnesses in four different books. These four books became known as the *euangelion*, which in Greek means Gospels, or "good news", and this is the message they carried.

Mary and Joseph were Waiting for the Promised Deliverer:

Within the Roman Empire, in the nation of Israel, in a small town called Nazareth lived a young lady named Mary. **Matthew 1:18** says that, "*Mary was pledged to be married to Joseph.*" Both she and her fiancé Joseph were devoted followers of God. **Matthew 1:19** says that Joseph was a righteous man, which is the word used to describe someone who has had their sins forgiven by God. **Luke 2:24** records Mary herself bringing an offering for her sins, and in **Luke 1:47**, Mary says, "*...[M]y spirit rejoices in God my Savior...*" Mary knew that she needed a Savior, and both she and Joseph, along with all those in Israel who loved God, surely must have longed for the coming of the Deliverer, their Messiah.

Jesus was Born of a Virgin:

Luke 1:26 says that God sent the angel Gabriel to deliver an important message to Mary. (**Luke 1:30-32**) The angel told Mary, who was a descendant of David, that she would give birth to a Son, named Jesus. He would reign forever and His kingdom would never end. This was the fulfillment of the prophecies given over a thousand years earlier when God promised that a descendant of King David would be the Messiah! (**2 Samuel 7:16**) This was the moment Israel had been waiting for!

When God chose a virgin, (**Luke 1:34-38**) a woman who had never had sexual relations with a man, to be the mother of the Messiah, God was also fulfilling the first promise He had given to Adam and Eve concerning the Deliverer who would be born without a human father! (**Genesis 3:15**) Matthew records that, (**Matthew 1:22**) "*All this took place to fulfill what the Lord had said through the prophet: 'The virgin will be with child and will give birth to a son, and they will call him Immanuel' - which means, 'God with us.' *"

Jesus' Divine Origin is Confirmed to Joseph:

Mary must have felt so honored to be the one who would carry the Messiah, but it wasn't going to be easy. In Israel at that time, if an unmarried woman became pregnant she faced public shame, rejection, and even possible death. Surely everyone in the small town of Nazareth talked about pregnant Mary. Joseph must have felt so betrayed and confused. Joseph had never had relations with Mary; he knew the child was not his. Joseph was considering quietly cutting off their engagement when God intervened by sending the angel, Gabriel, to explain to Joseph in a dream who the baby within Mary was! (**Matthew 1:20-21**) Imagine how Joseph felt when he realized that the baby inside Mary was to grow up to be their Messiah, the One who would save them from their sins! **Matthew 1:24** says that Joseph obeyed God, and immediately, *"…took Mary home as his wife."*

After Jesus was born, Joseph and Mary would enjoy the normal physical intimacy that a husband and wife share. Together they would have other children, whose names are listed for us in **Matthew 13:55** and mentioned in various other places in the Bible. Until Mary gave birth to Jesus, however, **Matthew 1:25** says of Joseph that, *"He had no union with her until she gave birth to a son."*

Jesus Born in Bethlehem:

After Mary and Joseph got married, they received more unexpected news. A Roman census was taken, ordering each citizen to return to their hometown to register. (**Luke 2:1-4**) It seemed so untimely for a pregnant woman to leave her home in Nazareth and travel roughly 80 miles[21] to Bethlehem, the town of their ancestors. This too, however, was part of God's perfect plan. 600 years earlier, God had given a prophecy found in **Micah 5:2** stating that the Messiah would be born in the town of Bethlehem.

There in Bethlehem, the promised Messiah was finally born, and yet the world was too busy or too preoccupied to even notice. (**Luke 2:6-7**) Instead of a palace, the King who was to reign forever was laid to sleep in a feeding trough. He came in a way that no one expected, in the silence of the night, in the care of peasants, in the humblest of settings.

Jesus is the Savior for All People:

(**Luke 2:8**) *"And there were shepherds living out in the fields nearby, keeping watch over their flocks at night."* The shepherds outside of Bethlehem were most likely tending the very sheep that were used for the sacrifices. Little did they realize that on that very night, the One who would save them from their sins had been born so that they would no longer need any sacrifices! God in His sovereignty chose to allow these shepherds to be the first

---

[21] 80 miles is 130 kilometers

ones to hear the announcement of the angels that the Savior, the Messiah, had been born! **(Luke 2:9-11)** The angels declared that this good news was to be for all people. Jesus had come to be the Savior for all of humanity. When the angels left them, the shepherds hurried off to Bethlehem and found the baby lying in a manger. **(Luke 2:15-16)**

Jesus is God:

He was, however, no ordinary baby. The One who had spoken the stars into existence had come to the earth as a human, and lay sleeping in a manger. The Bible clearly teaches that Jesus is God **(Philippians 2:6-7)** In order to be the Messiah, He became a servant; He came down to earth as a human. **Hebrews 2:14** and **John 1:14,18** affirm that the One who made the world, entered the world as a human. The Creator became a part of His creation.

Jesus Can Sympathize with Us:

Eventually Mary and Joseph did move back to Nazareth. Other than one story that took place when Jesus was twelve, **(Luke 2:41-50)** the Bible is silent about Jesus' childhood and growing up years. The Bible clearly states that although Jesus is God, during the first 30 years of his life here on earth, He did not perform any miracle, or display His power as God. Why did He do it? Why did He live such a simple life?

According to **Hebrews 4:15-16**, one of the reasons Jesus did this was so that we would be able to come to Him for help in our time of need, knowing that Jesus can sympathize with us. Whether it was going to school, growing up in a family, having parents misunderstand Him, or working hard to survive, He experienced all of the things that you and I go through. He wore our sandals and walked the dusty streets of our earth... for you and me.

John the Baptist Prepared the People for the Messiah:

(Matthew 3:1) John the Baptist was a messenger sent by God, to prepare the people for the Messiah. **Matthew 3:2** says he urged the people saying, "R*epent, for the kingdom of heaven is near.*" Repent: this word in the Greek literally means to change your mind. You see, many people mistakenly thought that God would automatically accept them into Heaven because of their nationality, their good works, or their religious ceremonies. This perspective was wrong.

The Bible shows us in the Ten commandments that we have broken God's holy laws and are all guilty as sinners. John told the people that they needed to repent, in other words, to change their minds, and realize they were *not* good enough to get to Heaven. They needed to admit they were sinners, and needed a Savior.

(**Matthew 3:6**) Those who agreed with John's message demonstrated this by being baptized in the Jordan River. This baptism did not save them, nor did it wash away their sins. Rather, this baptism was an outward act that showed they agreed with John's message, believed they were sinners, and were looking forward to the coming Messiah.

John the Baptist Revealed that Jesus was the Messiah:

When Jesus was about thirty years old, the time came for the rest of the world to know that He was the Messiah. John the Baptist had been sent to prepare people's hearts for the Messiah, and also to reveal the Messiah to the nation. According to **John 1:33**, God told John that the man on whom he saw the Holy Spirit visibly descend, would be the Messiah. (**Mark 1:9**) When Jesus came to be baptized by John, it was not because He was sinful, but so that John could recognize Him as the Messiah. (**Mark 1:10-11**)

Jesus is Sinless:

As the Spirit descended upon Jesus, the Father audibly proclaimed that He was well pleased with Jesus. You see, all the other people who stood there that day were sinners; they could not please God. Amongst them, however, stood Jesus. He was the only one who could perfectly obey all of God's commands and fully please Him.

If Jesus was not sinless He would not be able to the Savior, the Messiah. The fact that Jesus was sinless was proven when He was led to the desert to be tempted by Satan. (**Mark 1:12-13**) Just as Satan had tempted Adam and Eve to sin, Satan tempted Jesus. Unlike Adam and Eve, however, Jesus was victorious and did not give in to Satan's temptations and sin.

Throughout Jesus' life, Jesus was faced with all of the same temptations that you and I also face. **Hebrews 4:15** says that He was, "...*tempted in every way, just as we are - yet was without sin.*" **Luke 1:35** says that He is the "Holy One"; which means He is completely pure with nothing evil in Him. Only Jesus could fully please God. Only Jesus could live a perfect life, and not sin.

Jesus is the Lamb of God:

In the Old Testament, God instructed His people on how to bring animals as sacrifices for their sins. The man who brought the lamb was not examined. He was a sinner, not acceptable to God. As the man's substitute, however, the *lamb* had to be perfect; it could have no defects. The lamb was examined in the man's place.

In the same way that God allowed the lamb to be examined, Jesus came to be examined in our place, to be our Substitute. As Jesus was returning from the desert, victorious over sin and Satan, **John 1:29** says, "*[J]ohn saw Jesus coming toward him and said, "Look, the Lamb of God, who takes away the sin of the world!"* Jesus came to be the Lamb of God, to take our place, to be our Substitute.

God knew that you and I would fail, that we would sin. He knew that we could not perfectly obey His laws. He knew that we would need a substitute. Jesus came to be that substitute. Jesus came to live the life that you and I could not live. Jesus came to be the *Lamb of God.*

Group discussion time: Personal & Relevant

1. Divide into groups of 3-5 people.
2. Distribute the topics listed below, giving a topic to each group to discuss. *(If you have more than 3 groups, just repeat the topics.)*
3. Allow the groups ten minutes to discuss their topic and record their answer in their Study Guide.
4. After ten minutes, have everyone come back together again.
5. Ask each group to choose a representative to read their group's answer. Encourage everyone to take notes in their Study Guide as the other groups share the answers to their topics.
6. After "Topic One's" answers are shared, read the "Summary" for Topic One before moving on to Topic Two and so on.

IMPORTANT NOTE:

Today, give out only the first two topics for group discussion. Discuss Topic Three together as a group. There will be an article to read together and discuss.

Topic One: Relatability

Question: Why do people who have been through similar experiences seem to share a connection? How would Jesus coming to earth to become human help us be able to relate to Him?

Have you ever heard women exchanging pregnancy stories, or war veterans talking? Why do they feel they can relate to each other? **Philippians 2:6,7*

Facilitator's Summary: Whether they be war veterans, pregnant women, or survivors of a natural disaster, people who have been through similar circumstances connect with each other because they can relate. They feel the other person has walked in their shoes and knows what they themselves have experienced.

In light of that, it is astounding to think that God would come to earth and live a normal life for *thirty years!* He came down and ate our food, wore simple clothes, went to school, walked our dusty roads, worked a job… everything! **Hebrews 2:14** tells us that He shared in our humanity. One of the reasons He did this was so that you and I could always relate to Him.

Topic Two: Examined in your place

Question: We are incapable of perfectly keeping God's laws. What about Jesus, though? What are the implications of Jesus being called the "Lamb of God"?

If you had to take an extensive written exam, then found out an expert on the subject would be allowed to take the exam in your place, would you feel relieved? What if you had to run a race, then had the Olympic Gold medalist offer to run in your place for you?

———————————————————————————————

———————————————————————————————

Facilitator's Summary: When someone brought a Lamb to be sacrificed the priest examined the *lamb;* he did not examine the man. The lamb had to be perfect. If God were to examine our lives He would find all of our faults. We cannot fully obey God's laws. We cannot measure up to His standard. But Jesus can! As the Lamb of God, Jesus came to live the perfect life that God requires; He came to be examined in our place.

Having *Jesus'* life instead of *your* life examined by God is like having an Olympic Gold medalist tap you on the shoulder and ask, "Do you want me to run this race for you?" It's as if Jesus "ran the race" of life in your place. God knows you are a sinner; He did not come to examine you. In **John 3:17** it says, "For God did not send His Son into the world to condemn the world, but to save the world through Him."

Topic Three: Coincidence?

Question: Could the fulfillment of prophecies have been coincidence or manipulation instead of being legitimate fulfillments?

> **Facilitator's Summary:** Over the years, God had given countless prophecies about the promised Messiah, the Deliverer. Some may wonder, "Could the fulfillment of these prophecies be mere coincidence? In other words, could an alleged 'fulfillment' have just happened by chance or perhaps manipulation?"
>
> Let's read the article **"Messianic Prophecies & Fulfillments"** which addresses this question.
>
> **Choose one or two volunteers to read the Article aloud.**
>
> *The Article is provided on the Next Page in this Facilitator Guide.*

Messianic

Prophecies & Fulfillments:

Messiah Would:	Prophecy Given:	Fulfillment:
Be born in Bethlehem	Mic. 5:2	Matt. 2:1-6; Lk. 2:1-20
Be born of a virgin	Is. 7:14	Matt. 1:18-25; Lk. 1:26-38
Be a descendant of David	Is. 9:7	Matt. 1:1
Flee to Egypt	Hos. 11:1	Matt. 2:13
Have a forerunner	Is. 40:3	Matt. 1:17; Lk 1: 16-17; Jn. 1:19-28
Be a prophet like Moses	Deut. 18:15, 18-19	Jn. 7:40
Enter Jerusalem on a donkey	Zech. 9:9	Matt. 21:1-9; Jn. 12:12-16
Be rejected by His own people	Is. 53:1, 3; Ps. 118:22	Matt. 26:3, 4; Jn. 12:37-43; Acts 4:1-12
Be betrayed by a friend	Ps. 41:9	Matt. 26:14-16, 47-50; Lk. 22:19-23
Be sold for 30 pieces of silver and the silver would be used to buy a field	Zech. 11:12-13	Matt. 26:14-15
Be tried and condemned	Is. 53:8	Lk. 23:1-25; Matt. 27:1,2
Be silent before His accusers	Is. 53:7	Matt. 27:12-14; Mk. 15:3-4; Lk. 23:8-10
Be struck and spat on by His enemies	Is. 50:6	Matt. 26:67; Matt. 27:30; Mk. 14:65

Messiah Would:	Prophecy Given:	Fulfillment:
Be mocked and insulted	Ps. 22:7-8	Matt. 27:39-44; Lk. 23:11, 35
Suffer with criminals	Is. 53:12	Matt. 27:38; Mk. 15:27-28; Lk. 23:32-34
Pray for His enemies	Is. 53:12	Matt. 27:38; Mk. 15:27-28; Lk. 23:32-34
Be given vinegar and gall	Ps. 69:21	Matt. 27:34; Jn. 19:28-30
Have people gamble for his garments	Ps. 22:18	Matt. 27:35; Jn. 19:23-24
Not have any bones broken	Ex. 12:46	Jn. 19:31-36
Die as a sacrifice for sin	Is. 53:5-6, 8, 10-12	Jn. 1:29; 11:49-52; Acts 10:43; 13:38-39
Have his hands and feet pierced	Ps. 22:14, 16-17	Matt. 27:31; Mk. 15:20, 25
Be buried with the rich	Is. 53:9	Mk. 15:43-46
Be raised from the dead	Ps. 16:10	Acts 2:22-32; Matt. 28:1-10
Sit at God's right hand	Ps. 110:1	Mk. 16:19; Lk. 24:50-51

All of these prophecies and more were fulfilled by one man: Jesus Christ. Could this have happened by chance? Let's look at the mathematical probability of one man fulfilling just eight of these prophecies:

1. **He would be born in Bethlehem.**
2. **He would have a forerunner.**
3. **He would enter Jerusalem on a donkey.**
4. **He would be betrayed by a friend.**
5. **He would be sold for silver.**
6. **The silver would be used to buy a field.**
7. **He would be silent before His accusers.**
8. **He would be pierced before death.**

In their book *Science Speaks*[22], Peter W. Stoner and Robert C. Newman, S.T.M., Ph.D[23] write that the probability of these eight prophecies being fulfilled by one man is 1 in 10^{17}. In order to help us visualize this statistic, they write:

"Suppose that we take 10^{17} silver dollars and lay them on the face of Texas. They will cover all of the state two feet deep. Now mark one of these silver dollars and stir the whole mass thoroughly, all over the state. Blindfold a man and tell him that he can travel as far as he wishes, but he must pick up one silver dollar and say that this is the right one.

What chance would he have of getting the right one? Just the same chance that the prophets would have had of writing these eight prophecies and having them all come true in any one man, from their day to the present time, providing they wrote using their own wisdom. Now these prophecies were either given by inspiration of God or the prophets just wrote them as they thought they should be. In such a case the prophets had just one chance in 10^{17} of having them come true in any man, but they all came true in Christ.[24]"

Author's Note:

The preceding statistics were carefully reviewed by a committee of American Scientific Affiliation members and by the Executive Council of the same group. In his foreword to the book *Science Speaks*, H. Harold Hartzler, Ph.D wrote on behalf of the committee:

"The mathematical analysis included is based upon principles
of probability which are thoroughly sound and Professor Stoner
has applied these principles in a proper and convincing way."

---

[22] Stoner, Peter W., M.S. and Newman, Robert C.S.T.M., Ph.D.; *Science Speak*, Moody Press, Chicago, 1976, Chapter 3

[23] Peter Stoner, June 16, 1888 - March 21, 1980
PETER W. STONER, M.S.:
Chairman of the Departments of Mathematics and Astronomy at Pasadena City College until 1953; Chairman of the science division, Westmont College, 1953-57; Professor Emeritus of Science, Westmont College; Professor Emeritus of Mathematics and Astronomy, Pasadena City College.
ROBERT C. NEWMAN, S.T.M., Ph.D.:
Ph.D. in Astrophysics, Cornell University, 1967; S.T.M., Biblical School of Theology, 1972; Associate Professor of Physics and Mathematics, Shelton College, 1968-71; Associate professor of New Testament, Biblical School of Theology, 1971-

[24] http://sciencespeaks.dstoner.net/ Online edition to the book *Science Speaks*, prepared by Don W. Stoner, grandson of Peter W. Stoner

Watch Episode 7 -"What does this mean for you?"

1. A Savior for you.

"When God sent an angel to proclaim to a virgin that she would give birth to the Messiah, this was the fulfillment of the first promise that had been given to Adam and Eve. God had told them a Savior would be born without a human father who would grow up and crush Satan's head. Jesus is this Promised Savior that all of the prophets had written about and that the people had awaited, for so many years. He is a Savior for you."

2. Out of love for you.

"The Messiah came in a way no one expected. For God Himself had come down to earth in human form. As Jesus grew up, He experienced all the joys and sorrows of the people he lived among. The Creator became a part of His creation... out of love for you."

3. A Lamb for you.

"God the Father, announced that Jesus was His beloved Son; the only One who could fully please God. Only Jesus could face Satan's temptations and live a perfect life and not sin. Jesus had come to be the perfect Lamb of God who takes away the sin of the world. Jesus came to be examined by God in your place; to be a substitute for you."

Closing Checklist:

- ❏ "Does anyone have any questions?" (Either as a group or one on one.)
- ❏ Encourage them to jot any questions or comments during the week.
- ❏ Encourage them to read the Bible and articles contained in their Study Guide. (See list below)

Read it for yourself:

Matthew 1:18-25; **Luke 1: 26-37; 2:1-21**	Jesus' birth
Philippians 2:6,7	Jesus took on human form to be born.
Matthew 3:1-6	John the Baptist tells people to repent.
Mark 1:9-11	Jesus is baptized. God declares Jesus to be the One who fully pleases Him.
Hebrews 4:15	Jesus was tempted in every way but did not sin.
John 1:29	Jesus is declared to be the Lamb of God.

Dig Deeper

Messianic Prophecies and Fulfillments	**Pg. 211** (Study Guide 143)
Did the writers of the New Testament just copy from mythology?	**Pg. 214** (Study Guide 146)
The Gospels are eyewitness accounts	**Luke 1:1-4**
Jesus became flesh to share in our humanity.	**Hebrews 2:14**

* Ask someone to read the verse out loud from their Study Guide:

Memorize this:

"...John saw Jesus coming toward him and said, "Look, the Lamb of God, who takes away the sin of the world!"

John 1:29

Facilitator's Comment on the Verse:

Jesus is the Lamb of God who came to live the perfect life that you and I cannot live and be examined in our place.

Facilitator's Closing Comment:

Don't miss next time Jesus is going to make a public statement that is still raising eyebrows to this day. A statement He is willing and able to back up and prove by His actions.

Questions your group *might* have:

Remember: *Keep your group on track! If you find a question is more disruptive than beneficial, graciously thank them for their question and tell them you look forward to talking about it one-on-one.*

1. What about Mary?	**Pg. 121**
2. Questions about Jesus.	**Pg. 122**

1. What about Mary?

In the "Lamb of God" many statements are made about Mary. (Mary was a sinner, she needed a Savior, Mary had other kids, etc.) Each one of these clear, Biblical truths were respectfully and sensitively woven into the episode. Our intention in every episode was never to attack any denomination, church or religion, but always to study what the Bible teaches and measure everything by the Word of God.

In your Bible Study, always refer your students back to the Bible. When a position or opinion is voiced that contradicts what the Bible says, then we must gently point out to the questioner that he or she must choose whether or not they will base their convictions on what God says in His Word, or what is being taught by another mortal human being. Urge them read the Word and look to the Bible for answers.

Recommended Resources: (The first article is a good overview and the rest are dealing with specific questions about Mary.)

What does the Bible say about Mary? Pg. 307

Was Mary perpetually a virgin? Pg. 309

Is Mary the Mother of God? Pg. 310

Is Mary the Co-Redemptrix? Pg. 311

What is Mariolatry? Pg. 313

Is it wrong to say the Hail Mary? Pg. 314

2. Questions about Jesus:

Patiently deal with every individual's questions. Take time out to engage in one-on-one conversations with those who are seeking answers. A complete and full understanding of Who Jesus truly is, is absolutely vital to an understanding of the Gospel. Encourage each one in your group to truly search the Scriptures, grapple with these questions and investigate for themselves what the Bible says. Even if they are still hesitant to accept the fact that Jesus is God, urge them to start reading the Gospels. Encourage them to note carefully what Jesus does, says, and who He Himself claims to be.

The next episode "Messiah" will include more information regarding Jesus' deity.

Recommended Resources:

Why was Jesus "God in the flesh"? Pg. 316

Did the writers of the New Testament just copy from mythology? Pg. 214

Doesn't the Bible teach that God cannot be a man? Pg. 318

Isn't it blasphemy to say God has a Son? Pg. 265 - from EveryStudent

Isn't it blasphemy to say that God has a Son? Pg. 266 - from GotQuestions

These last two articles are written specifically with Muslims in mind, but are an excellent read for anyone with questions regarding this topic.

TE☩ELESTAI

CHAPTER 8

MESSIAH

Pre Bible Study Checklist:

❏ Have extra Bibles and pens on hand.

❏ Have chocolates for prizes for anyone who memorized the verse.

❏ Pray for each participant to come and be open to God's Word and His Spirit.

❏ Be familiar with the Synopsis.

❏ Be familiar with the questions and dynamics of how the Group Discussion will flow.

Synopsis of the Episode:

In Messiah, Jesus publicly announces His identity, chooses twelve disciples and begins to minister to the people. Jesus demonstrates His supernatural power over the spirit world, the physical world, over sickness, and even death. Jesus' miracles are the evidence given to back up His claims to be the Messiah as well as God Himself. As Jesus reaches out to people of all social and racial backgrounds, He embraces the rejected and touches the untouchable. Jesus displays incredible love and compassion like none the world has ever seen.

Greeting

❏ Note the attendance.

❏ Verse and chocolates.

❏ Brief open discussion of their Bible reading or articles.

Watch Episode 8 - *Messiah*

Jesus Chooses 12 Disciples:

After Jesus' baptism and temptation He chose 12 men to accompany Him. These men were known as disciples, a word which simply means "learner". If you or I would have designated disciples, we would have probably appointed men who had fame, wealth, and power, people who were respected in all of society. Jesus didn't do that. Jesus sees people differently than we do. Some of the men that Jesus chose as disciples were common fishermen. One was a zealot, a member of a political party that opposed the Romans, and yet another man worked for the Romans as a tax collector! As Jesus reached out across all social, ethnic, and racial barriers, His disciples were willing to leave everything in order to follow Him.

Jesus Proclaims Himself the Messiah:

Jesus began to teach on the Sabbath in synagogues. (**Luke 4:14-15**) Synagogues were buildings in which the Israelites, or Jews, met to worship God. Different men took turns reading passages, and explaining them from God's Word. **Luke 4:16-17** tells us that while Jesus was at the synagogue in Nazareth, He selected a prophecy that had been written over 700 years earlier. (**Isaiah 61:1-2**) It was a prophecy concerning the Anointed One, the Messiah. (**Luke 4:18-19**) After reading this, the eyes of everyone in the room were on Him; what He said next astounded them: *"Today this scripture is fulfilled in your hearing."* (**Luke 4:21**) Jesus proclaimed that He was the fulfillment of that prophecy; He was the Anointed One they had been waiting for! Jesus announced that He was the Messiah.

Miracles Authenticated Jesus' Claim:

Perhaps you may be thinking, "Well, anyone can claim to be the Messiah, and anyone can say they're God, but is there any proof?" As you examine Jesus' life in the four biographies written about Him, you will find that Jesus did phenomenal things that no ordinary human being could do; these are called "miracles." Never once did Jesus use His supernatural power for His own personal comfort. Rather, these miracles were evidence given to back up His claim that He was the Messiah. **John 10:24-25** records that Jesus asserted that the miracles He performed authenticated His message, and proved to the watching world that Jesus was who He claimed to be.

Power and Authority over Demons:

Jesus' life was characterized by a divine power and authority over the spirit world. The Bible tells of instances where demons have caused muteness, blindness or even insanity. Demons have caused people to mutilate themselves, live like uncontrollable animals, or kill themselves.

We are first given a glimpse of Jesus' power over demons in a town called Capernaum, at a meeting in their synagogue. (**Mark 1:23-24**) The demon knew that because Jesus was the Holy One, He had the power to destroy him. When the man possessed by the demon cried out, Jesus gave orders to the the demon, "Be quiet!" (**Mark 1:25**) Then, as the entire synagogue watched in astonishment, Jesus commanded the evil spirit, (**Mark 1:25-27**) *"Come out of him!"* The people were astounded that Jesus Himself had the power to make the demon obey. Jesus did not have to call out to a higher power, or perform some ceremony to try to appease or manipulate the demon. Jesus had absolute power and authority over demons. He was fulfilling the prophecies that the Messiah would proclaim freedom for the prisoners and release the oppressed.

Power Over Sickness

Another most prominent aspect of Jesus' ministry was His power over sickness. **Matthew 15:30-31** says, *"Great crowds came to Him, bringing the lame, the blind, the crippled, the mute and many others, and laid them at His feet; and He healed them."* This power over sickness was one more proof that Jesus was indeed the promised Messiah. **Matthew 8:16-17** reports that Jesus, *"…[H]ealed all the sick. This was to fulfill what was spoken through the prophet Isaiah: 'He took up our infirmities and carried our diseases.'"*

Incredible Compassion and Love:

Jesus healed men, women, young, and old. They were not crowds to Jesus. Each person had a face and each face had a name, and He knew each one. Jesus reached out to the needy, the hurting and the outcast. He demonstrated a love and compassion like none the world has ever seen. Once, a man with leprosy, an incurable, infectious disease, came to Jesus and begged Jesus to heal Him. Unlike the others, Jesus did not run from him, nor did he recoil in disgust. Rather, **Mark 1:41** says, *"Filled with compassion, Jesus reached out his hand and touched the man."* Immediately, the man was completely healed! Jesus came to embrace the rejected, to heal the broken, and to touch the untouchable.

Jesus Feeds over 5000

Once, when Jesus was surrounded by a large crowd, **Mark 6:34** says that, *"…[H]e had compassion on them, because they were like sheep without a shepherd. So he began teaching them many things."* **Mark 6:35-38** goes on to recount that later that day Jesus asked His disciples to give the crowd something to eat. Jesus then directed them to go out amongst the crowd and see how much food was there. Two disciples came back and gave Jesus five loaves of bread and two fish.

"Taking the five loaves and the two fish and looking up to heaven, He gave thanks and broke the loaves. Then He gave them to His disciples to set before the people. He also divided the two fish among them all." (**Mark 6:41**) Afterward, *"...[T]he disciples picked up twelve basketfuls of broken pieces of bread and fish."* (**Mark 6:43**) that were leftover! *"The number of those who ate was about five thousand men, besides women and children."* (**Matthew 14:21**)

"After the people saw the miraculous sign that Jesus did, they began to say, 'Surely this is the Prophet who is to come into the world.'" (**John 6:14**) God had promised that the Messiah would be a prophet. (**Deuteronomy 18:18**) The prophet Moses had come to give them the words of God and set them free. As the fulfillment to this prophecy, Jesus had also come to give them the very words of God and set them free from the powers of sin, death, and hell.

Power over Death:

In **Revelation 1:18** Jesus said, *"I hold the keys of death."* Jesus demonstrated this power over death on several occasions. He had complete power over death itself. Once, when Jesus was nearing the city of Nain, **Luke 7:12** says, *"...[A] dead person was being carried out - the only son of his mother, and she was a widow."* This widow was heartbroken over the loss of her son, but Jesus had come to bring hope to the hopeless. *"When the Lord saw her, His heart went out to her and He said, 'Don't cry.' He went up and touched the bier, and those carrying it stood still. He said, 'Young man, I say to you, get up!' The dead man sat up and began to talk, and Jesus gave him back to his mother."* (**Luke 7:13-15**)

The One who had breathed life into the first man in the Garden, had now spoken life into this dead man. Those in the funeral procession, *"...were all filled with awe and praised God. 'A great prophet has appeared among us,' they said. 'God has come to help His people.'"* (**Luke 7:16**) Indeed, God had come; just as the Scriptures had foretold: *"...[T]hey will call Him Emmanuel – which means, 'God with us.'"* (**Matthew 1:23**)

Power over the Physical World:

One thing the disciples soon realized was that Jesus had complete power and authority over everything in the physical world. **John 6** describes for us a terrifying storm that the disciples faced alone. The disciples went ahead in their boat and left Jesus behind on a mountainside to spend time alone in prayer with the Father. That night the disciples battled the wind and the waves and only made it halfway across the lake. They were exhausted and without hope.

In the middle of the storm they looked up and *"...[T]hey saw Jesus approaching the boat, walking on the water; and they were terrified. But He said to them, 'It is I; don't be afraid.' Then they were willing to take Him into the boat, and immediately the boat reached the shore where they were heading."* (**John 6:19-21**) *"Then those who were in the boat worshiped Him, saying, 'Truly you are the Son of God.'"* (**Matthew 14:33**)

The disciples realized only God can calm a storm. Only God can give orders to the wind and the waves. Only God can walk on water. Only God is worthy of our worship.

Jesus is God:

As you examine the four biographies written about Jesus, you will find that his life demonstrated that He was in fact God. In the Old Testament, when God described Himself to His people, He used such terms as: King, Judge, Light, Rock, Redeemer, Creator, the Giver of Life, the One who Speaks with Divine Authority, and the One who has the Ability to Forgive Sins. In the New Testament, every single one of these terms is applied to Jesus!

Jesus said in **John 14:7**, *"If you really know Me, you will know my Father as well."* In **John 10:30** Jesus said, *"I and the Father are one."* In **John 8:58** Jesus proclaimed He was eternal. In **Matthew 28:18** Jesus affirmed that He was all-powerful, and in **Matthew 28:20** Jesus declared that He was all-present. Jesus: 1) claimed to be God, 2) had the attributes of God and, 3) accepted worship as God.

Who do you say I am?

One day Jesus asked His disciples a question. He said: *"'Who do the crowds say I am?'"* (**Luke 9:18**) The disciples answered that the crowds had various opinions as to Jesus' identity. This is true to this day. People still discuss the identity of Jesus. Jesus made the question more personal when he asked his disciples: *"'But what about you? Who do you say I am?'"* (**Matthew 16:15**) Jesus knew that every individual would have to choose whether or not they would believe Jesus' claims.

You also must make this decision. Who do you believe that Jesus is? If you need to, take more time to study the eyewitness, biographical accounts of Jesus' life found in the Bible. As you study Jesus' claims, and the miracles authenticating His claims, you also must come to a conclusion. Peter, one of Jesus' closest disciples, had no doubt as to who Jesus was. In light of all the overwhelming evidence he had witnessed in Jesus' life, *"Simon Peter answered, 'You are the Christ, the Son of the living God.'"* (**Matthew 16:16**)

Group discussion time: Personal & Relevant

1. Divide into groups of 3-5 people.
2. Distribute the topics listed below, giving a topic to each group to discuss. *(If you have more than 3 groups, just repeat the topics.)*
3. Allow the groups ten minutes to discuss their topic and record their answer in their Study Guide.
4. After ten minutes, have everyone come back together again.
5. Ask each group to choose a representative to read their group's answer. Encourage everyone to take notes in their Study Guide as the other groups share the answers to their topics.
6. After "Topic One's" answers are shared, read the "Summary" for Topic One before moving on to Topic Two and so on.

Topic One: Fact or fiction?

Question: Are the Gospel accounts of Jesus historical or mythical? In order to determine this, analyze the following list:

A Truly Historical Document would make mention of:

Place a checkmark beside the statements that are true:

❑ **Events** that are verifiable historically or archaeologically.

❑ **Places** that are verifiable historically or archaeologically.

❑ **People** that are verifiable historically or archaeologically.

Based on the criteria above, do you think the Gospel records of Jesus are historical? *Why or why not?*

_____

_____

> **Facilitator's Summary:** The biographical accounts of Jesus that we have in the four Gospels are eyewitness accounts circulated within the lifetimes of the people they were writing about. In other words, you could hop on your camel and investigate the facts and question the eye witnesses yourself!
>
> They documented the names of *real* rulers and cities, in *real* time periods. The miracles they recounted happened to *real* people in *real* locations. Some of the events described had hundreds if not thousands of eyewitnesses!

Now, maybe you're thinking, *"If all of these things really did happen historically, then we should be able to read about these events in other historical records."* You're absolutely right! The truth is other historians outside of the Bible did write about these events! Take time out to read the articles mentioned in your Study Guide and examine the evidence for yourself:

Is There Proof Jesus Existed? (Biblical and Extra-Biblical) Pg. 219

Historical Proof Outside of the Bible for Jesus' Existence. Pg. 221

Topic Two: Hanging out

Question: What type of people would you expect a high-profile, popular, miracle working, religious leader to spend time with? What type of people did Jesus spend time with? What does that tell you about who Jesus wanted to relate to? *Popular? Rich? Religious?*

_____

_____

Facilitator's Summary: If you have not already done so, I would encourage you to begin reading the Bible today and discover more about Jesus. He will blow your mind. He broke all the social taboos of that day. It made no difference to Jesus whether the person He spoke with was a lawyer, a beggar or a soldier from the enemy occupying forces! He touched lepers, held children and accepted dinner invitations from people with questionable reputations.

He always spoke the truth uncompromisingly and courageously. As you read, take special note of Jesus' love and compassion as well as the life He offers. Realize that this same Jesus wants to have a relationship with you as well.

Topic Three: Who exactly is Jesus?

Question: Who did Jesus claim to be? Is there evidence in Jesus' life to back up His claim? If so, mention at least 3 examples that support His claim.

Did He claim to be a great moral teacher? A good person? Messiah? God?

_____

_____

> **Facilitator Summary:** Jesus claimed to be the Messiah. He also claimed to be God. Either Jesus was lying, or He was telling the truth. As you examine His life, you must make a choice.
>
> In his book *Mere Christianity*, the late C.S. Lewis said:
>
> > " *I am trying here to prevent anyone saying the really foolish thing that people often say about Him: I'm ready to accept Jesus as a great moral teacher, but I don't accept his claim to be God. That is the one thing we must not say. A man who was merely a man and said the sort of things Jesus said would not be a great moral teacher… Either this man was, and is, the Son of God, or else a madman or something worse. You can shut him up for a fool, you can spit at him and kill him as a demon or you can fall at his feet and call him Lord and God, but let us not come with any patronizing nonsense about His being a great human teacher. He has not left that open to us. He did not intend to.*"
>
> In Your Study Guide you can read Jesus' claims again. As you read Jesus' words, grapple with the question that each one of us must answer. It was the question that Jesus Himself asked His followers, "Who do *you* say that I am?"

Watch Episode 8 -"What does this mean for you?"

1. Jesus' miracles were evidence for you.

"Jesus' life was characterized by supernatural power. These miracles were the evidence given to back up His claims to be the Messiah, the Son of God. Jesus showed absolute power over the spirit world, the physical world, over sickness and even death itself. Jesus' miracles authenticated His message providing evidence for you to trust Him."

2. Jesus reaches out to you.

"Jesus reached out to people across all social, racial, and ethnic barriers. They were not crowds to Jesus; each person had a face and each face had a name and His offer of life was the same to all. Jesus' offer of life is the same today. He is reaching out to you.

3. You must consider Jesus' claims.

"Jesus claimed to be the Messiah and to be the divine Son of God. These claims were never met with neutral reactions. Jesus confronted people with what they believed. He knew each person would have to choose whether or not to believe His claims. As you study the eye witness accounts, you too must consider Jesus's claims and choose whether to believe them or reject them."

Closing Checklist:

- ❏ "Does anyone have any questions?" (Either as a group or one on one.)
- ❏ Encourage them to jot any questions or comments during the week.
- ❏ Encourage them to read the Bible and articles contained in their Study Guide. (See list below)

Read it for yourself:	
Luke 4:16-21	Jesus announces He is the fulfillment of their prophecies, their Messiah.
John 10:24,25	Jesus says His miracles are the evidence for the fact He is the Messiah the Son of God.
Mark 1:25-27	Jesus casts the demon out of the man.
Matthew 15:30,31	Jesus heals all the sick.
Luke 7:12-16	Jesus raises the dead.
Matthew 14:23	The disciples worship Jesus as God.
Matthew 16:15,16	Who do you say I am?

Dig Deeper	
These are not cleverly invented stories, but eyewitness accounts.	**II Peter 1:16-21**
Is there Proof Jesus existed? (Biblical and Extra-Biblical)	**Pg. 219** (Study Guide 151)
Historical Proof outside of the Bible for Jesus' Existence.	**Pg. 221** (Study Guide 153)

*Ask Someone to read the Verse out loud from their Study Guide.

Memorize this:

"Jesus answered, 'I am the way, the truth and the life. No one comes to the Father except through Me."
John 14:6

Facilitator's Comment on the Verse:

Jesus left no room for doubt as to Who He was claiming to be and what He was offering. He came offering life and salvation. This verse we are going to memorize is one of His most famous and important statements.

Facilitator's Closing Comment:

Don't miss next Bible Study! We will listen in on a heart-to-heart conversation with Jesus as He explains some of the most important truths about eternity and the life He offered.

TETELESTAI

CHAPTER 9

SALVATION

Pre Bible Study Checklist:

❏ Have extra Bibles and pens on hand.

❏ Have chocolates for prizes for anyone who memorized the verse.

❏ Pray for each participant to come and be open to God's Word and His Spirit.

❏ Be familiar with the Synopsis.

❏ Be familiar with the questions and dynamics of how the Group Discussion will flow.

❏ Glance through the *"Questions Your Group Might Have"* located at the end of this lesson.

Synopsis of the Episode:

In Salvation, Jesus explains that in order for the people to be able to receive the eternal life He offers, they need to repent and believe in Him alone. Their own good works cannot save them. In a heart-to-heart conversation with a man named Nicodemus, Jesus explains that just as Moses lifted up the snake in the desert, He too would be lifted up so that all who believe in Him would not perish but have eternal life. Salvation explains that rejecting this eternal life is the same as choosing eternal death. A sobering look at the reality of eternal death is given in the story of the rich man and Lazarus. Jesus pleads with the people to believe in Him and receive His life.

Greeting

❏ Note the attendance.

❏ Verse and chocolates.

❏ Brief open discussion of their Bible reading or articles.

Watch Episode 9 - *Salvation*

The Words of Eternal Life:

People came to Jesus not only because of what He did, but also because of what He *said*. People were attracted to Him not only because of His power to heal, but also because of His promises to *save*. Jesus had come to save them from eternal punishment. Jesus had come as the Messiah in order to save all of humanity from sin and death. Jesus always spoke the truth courageously and lovingly. Because of this, some people rejected Him; while others, like His disciples, told Him, *"…'You have the words of eternal life.'"* (**John 6:68**)

The Kingdom of God is Near:

Jesus was their long-awaited King, the Messiah, and His kingdom would never end. (**Mark 1:14-15**) To be a part of the kingdom of God, was to be able to live forever, to have eternal life. Jesus further explained that in order to be a part of His kingdom and have this eternal life, two things were needed. Jesus said: *"…[R]epent and believe the good news!"* (**Mark 1:15**)

The Need to Repent:

Repent means to change your mind. You see, the people thought that they were good enough to be accepted by God because of their good works and religious ceremonies. The Pharisees were a religious group of men who devotedly sought after eternal life, but they had wrongly put their confidence in *themselves*. They thought that because of their good works, their ancestry, and all their religious rituals, that they would be guaranteed eternal life. Jesus wanted all people, whether or not they were Pharisees, to realize their works were inadequate and that they were sinners who needed a Savior.

You Must be Born Again:

Nicodemus, himself a Pharisee, was one such man who began to realize that Jesus had come to be their Savior. (**John 3:1**) *"He came to Jesus at night…"* (**John 3:2**) During their conversation, Jesus told Nicodemus, he could not earn eternal life by anything he did. (**John 3:3**) There was only one way to enter the Kingdom of Heaven, being born again. Nicodemus must have been shocked! According to Jesus, all of Nicodemus' plans for earning eternal life and entering into God's kingdom were worthless.

New Spiritual Life:

"Jesus answered, 'I tell you the truth, no one can enter the kingdom of God unless he is born of water and the Spirit.'" (**John 3:4-5**) When Jesus used the phrase "born of water," He was referring to physical birth. Jesus was

telling Nicodemus that his physical birth was not enough; Nicodemus needed another birth, one that came from the Spirit of God. Jesus further explained in **John 3:6** that you receive physical life from a physical person, but only the Spirit of God can birth in you spiritual life. No amount of good works, religious ceremonies or following rules can produce this life of God within a person. Only the Spirit of God can give someone this new Life.

Just as Moses Lifted up the Snake:

"How can this be?" Nicodemus asked. (**John 3:9**) In order to answer Nicodemus' question, Jesus referred to an event that had taken place in Israel's history during their desert travels. When the people had rebelled against Him, God sent venomous snakes among them. But when the people cried out for deliverance, God told Moses to make a snake and place it on a pole. Whenever anyone looked at the snake, God gave them life. (**Numbers 21:4-9**) Jesus told Nicodemus, *"Just as Moses lifted up the snake in the desert, so the Son of Man must be lifted up, that everyone who believes in Him may have eternal life."* (**John 3:14-15**)

Sin Condemns us to Death:

Just as the snakebite caused the people to die, so too, the sin within us condemns us to death, for the payment for sin is death. No amount of good works or religious ceremonies can reverse the effects of our fatal condition. In the desert, God did not force His healing upon anyone. In the same way, Jesus did not force anyone to accept His offer of life. Each person would have to choose whether or not they would believe in Him. Jesus explained to Nicodemus, *"For God so loved the world that He gave His one and only Son, that whoever believes in Him shall not perish but have eternal life."* (**John 3:16**)

Just Believe:

Believe? Was Jesus really telling Nicodemus to just believe? Was that all that was required of him in order to gain entrance into Heaven? It seemed too easy. Surely God demanded more.

What does God require for entrance into Heaven? How would you answer if someone asked you, "What must I do to get to Heaven?" Be a good citizen? Help the poor? Do good works? Pray? Fast? Take part in religious ceremonies or even pilgrimages? What does God require?

When Jesus was asked to give a list of the works that God required, read how He answered in **John 6:29**. Jesus said the only thing that God asks you and me to do is to *believe* in the One God has sent: Jesus.

You can be Declared Righteous:

(**John 3:17**) Jesus came to save, not to condemn people; their sins already condemned them! God wants to offer us forgiveness and make us completely acceptable to Him. When God declares someone righteous that means their sins are completely forgiven, and they are fully acceptable to God. All who believe in Jesus as the Messiah and Christ will be declared righteous. (**Romans 3:22**) Jesus explained to Nicodemus that, *"Whoever believes in Him is not condemned, but whoever does not believe stands condemned already because he has not believed in the name of God's one and only Son."* (**John 3:18**)

One Way to Eternal Life:

Believe or reject Jesus. Receive eternal life or continue in a condition of being eternally condemned for your sins. This was the choice that God was offering. In **John 8:24** Jesus earnestly warned the people that if they didn't believe He was who He claimed to be, the Messiah who had come to save them, then they would eternally die because of their sins. There was only one way to be saved. In **Genesis 6-8**, because of all the wickedness and violence that had filled the earth, God sent a global flood. Just as the ark had been the only way to escape the flood, God has sent Jesus as the only way to escape being judged for our sins. All who refuse to come to Jesus to be saved are rejecting life.

To Reject Life is to Choose Death:

To reject life is to choose death. Jesus was offering *eternal* life. If you reject eternal life, you are choosing eternal death. In **Luke 16**, Jesus described the horrors of eternal death. In this chapter, he told of two men and their final destinies. One of them was a poor, sick and lonely beggar named Lazarus. The other was the rich man at whose gate Lazarus lay. Rich and poor alike, all people are faced with the decision of where they will spend their eternity. Lazarus and the rich man were both sinners, yet Lazarus had repented and chosen to believe God's Word. The rich man, however, had not.

Heaven or Hell:

Luke 16 says the time came when both of these men died. In the same way, that time will come for each one of us. Whether rich or poor, young or old, the time will come for every person on earth to die. And **Hebrews 9:27** says, *"…[M]an is destined to die once, and after that to face judgment…"* Each person is only given one life. Once that life is over, that person will go to spend eternity in either Heaven or Hell.

According to the Bible, these two places are not allegorical or imaginary. Rather, they are two very real and distinct locations. Heaven is a place of comfort and joy in the presence of God, but Hell is a place of torment and agony, separated from God forever. Lazarus died and was taken to Heaven with Abraham. (**Luke 16:22**)

Like Lazarus, when Abraham had been alive on earth, he had believed in God and was declared righteous, completely forgiven, and fully accepted by God. (**Luke 16:22-23**)

The rich man did not go to Hell because he was rich, just as Lazarus did not go to Heaven because he was poor. Actually **Genesis 13** tells us that Abraham was an extremely wealthy man…. and he went to heaven! You see, things like fame, power and money do not follow you or effect you after you die. The reason the rich man went to Hell was because he had not repented; he had not believed in God's Word. During his lifetime he had rejected and ignored God.

Eternal Destinies are Sealed at Death:

In agony he cried out: *"Father Abraham, have pity on me and send Lazarus to dip the tip of his finger in water and cool my tongue, because I am in agony in this fire."* (**Luke 16:24**) Throughout the Scriptures God has made it clear that once a person dies, his eternal destiny is sealed. (**Luke 16:26**) Life with God is forever and those who have chosen God will live with Him for all of eternity. Those who have chosen to reject God, however, will be separated from Him forever. Eternal life is as permanent as eternal death. Those who are in Hell can never leave.

God's Word Convinces us to Believe:

The rich man could not bear the thought of his brothers also coming to Hell. (**Luke 16:27-28**) He begged Lazarus to go back to earth and warn them. He hoped that this would convince them to repent and believe God's Word.[25] Abraham knew that if the brothers had rejected God's Word, not even someone coming back from the dead would convince them. (**Luke 16:31**) You see, it is God's Word that convinces us to believe the truth. While the brothers were still alive, they had an opportunity to listen to God's Word and believe. You and I also have this opportunity, to hear the Word of God and put our trust in what He says while we are still alive, and before it is too late.

The Final Passover:

After three years of healing and teaching, Jesus began to head towards Jerusalem. Peter and John were to prepare for the Passover celebration. (**Luke 22:8**) Each year, the Jews went to Jerusalem in order to celebrate the Passover, the time when God had delivered them from slavery in Egypt. Among other observances of the day, one of the most important things they did was to sacrifice a lamb that was then roasted and served at the meal. During the meal, they recalled how God told His people that at midnight the angel of death was to go throughout the land and strike down the firstborn son of every household. On that night, it had not mattered

---

[25] Moses and the Prophets: Another way of describing God's Word.

whether a person was good or bad, rich or poor; there was only one thing that determined whether the firstborn son lived or died. God had told them, *"[W]hen I see the blood, I will pass over you."* (**Exodus 12:13**)

A Greater Deliverance was at Hand:

As they gathered to celebrate the first Passover, the disciples did not realize that an even greater deliverance was at hand. As Jesus took some bread and broke it, He told his disciples that this was the way in which His body would be broken for them. (**Luke 22:19**)

"In the same way, after the supper He took the cup, saying, 'This cup is the new covenant in my blood, which is poured out for you.'" (**Luke 22:20**) At that first Passover long ago, it had been the blood of the lamb that had been shed so that the firstborn son might live. Now Jesus was telling them that *His* own blood was going to be poured out for them, as their Lamb, as their substitute, in order to give them eternal life.

You see, that first Passover had been a picture illustrating and pointing to the death of Jesus Christ. The greatest deliverance was about to take place, one in which men, women and children from all nationalities would be delivered from their bondage to sin and rescued from the punishment of eternal death. Jesus had come in order to pay the ultimate price for our *Salvation*.

Group discussion time: Personal & Relevant

1. Divide into groups of 3-5 people.
2. Distribute the topics listed below, giving a topic to each group to discuss. *(If you have more than 3 groups, just repeat the topics.)*
3. Allow the groups ten minutes to discuss their topic and record their answer in their Study Guide.
4. After ten minutes, have everyone come back together again.
5. Ask each group to choose a representative to read their group's answer. Encourage everyone to take notes in their Study Guide as the other groups share the answers to their topics.
6. After "Topic One's" answers are shared, read the "Summary" for Topic One before moving on to Topic Two and so on.

Topic One: What does God require?

Question: If you were to conduct a survey asking random people in a crowd, "What are the works that God requires for entrance into Heaven?" What are the different responses that people might give?

_____

_____

Questions: What answer did _Jesus_ give to this same question? Which answer is correct? *See **John 6:28,29**

_____

_____

Facilitator Summary: Contrary to what people might imagine, when asked this question, Jesus did _not_ give them a list of things they had to _do_. The text says, "_Then they asked Him, 'What must we do to do the works God requires?' Jesus answered, 'The work of God is this: 'to believe in the One He sent.'_ " (**John 6:28,29**) Jesus asked them to simply believe in Him. Remember Adam and Eve's attempt to deal with their own sin? While we think that clothing made out of leaves is ridiculous and obviously not a long term solution, our own attempts to deal with our own sin are the same: they are woefully inadequate!

In fact, when we as sinners try to impress God who is all-holy, our good deeds look like, '..._filthy rags..._" to Him! (**Isaiah 64:6**) This is why Jesus didn't give them a list of how to attain their salvation. **John 3:17** says, "_God did not send His Son into the world to condemn the world, but to save the world through Him._" Jesus was sent into the world to save us because we cannot save ourselves. He simply asks us to believe in Him.

Topic Two: "Just as Moses lifted up the snake in the desert..."

Question: In His conversation with Nicodemus as Jesus described the life He came to offer, He referred to an event in Israel's history. "_Just as Moses lifted us the snake in the wilderness, so the Son of Man must be lifted up, that everyone who believes may have eternal life in Him._" (**John 3:14,15**) What do you think Jesus was trying to get across to Nicodemus?

Facilitator Summary: Just as the snakebite was fatal, we too have a fatal condition: our sins condemn us to death. Just as it was impossible for the Israelites to produce a remedy for the snakebite, we cannot in our own effort save ourselves. There is ONE remedy, that is to trust in Jesus Christ to give you life.

Just as the healing was for anyone who was bitten, God offers life to all. In **John 3:14,15** Jesus said, "*Just as Moses lifted up the snake in the wilderness, so the Son of Man must be lifted up, that everyone who believes may have eternal life in Him.*"

Trusting in Jesus is the only way that sinners condemned to death can reverse the effect of sin and have eternal life.

*Note: There might be people in your group unfamiliar with the narrative of the bronze snake and having a hard time making the connections to Christ. Do not worry about over explaining. It will become clearer after the crucifixion.

Topic Three: Passover Lamb

Question: Earlier we saw John the Baptist identify Jesus as the Lamb of God. Now during the Passover feast, when the lambs were sacrificed, Jesus talked about His own body being broken; with His own blood being poured out for the forgiveness of sins. What similarities do you see between Jesus and the lamb sacrificed at Passover?

> **Facilitator Summary:** The Lamb had to be perfect with no defects; Jesus is perfect and has fully pleased God. He is our perfect Lamb. On that night there was only way to escape death: the blood of the lamb that had been shed. Jesus now said His own blood was about to be shed, as our substitute, so that we might have life.

Watch Episode 9 -"What does this mean for you?"

I. You cannot earn eternal life.

"Jesus told the people that in order to have eternal life they needed to repent, or change their minds. The people had wrongly thought they would be accepted by God because of their good works, but Jesus explained that there was only one way to have eternal life: being born again. The Spirit of God is the only One who can give someone this new life. No amount of rules, religious ceremonies, fasts or pilgrimages are enough. You need to repent, change your mind by realizing that no matter how good you are, you cannot earn eternal life. Like Nicodemus, you also need this new spiritual life that only God can give you."

2. The only thing you must do is believe in Jesus Christ.

"Jesus told Nicodemus that whoever believed in Him would have eternal life. Jesus explained that just as Moses lifted up the snake in the desert, He too would be lifted up. In the desert, those who were dying from the snakebite had only to believe what God said and look and they would have life. You are like those who were dying in the desert because your sin condemns you to death. In order to be saved, the only thing that God requires is for you to believe in His Son, Jesus Christ, and you will have eternal life."

3. God wants you to go to Heaven.

"God has planned eternal life to be in a real and wonderful place of comfort and joy called Heaven. All those who believe in Jesus Christ will enjoy the presence of God forever. But, all who refuse to come to Jesus to be saved are rejecting eternal life and choosing eternal death. Eternal death is separation from God forever in a real place of torment and agony called Hell. God wants you to go to Heaven. He desires you to be saved and not perish."

4.   Jesus came to be your Passover Lamb.

"Jesus and his disciples gathered to celebrate the passover. At the first passover long ago in Egypt, it had been the blood of the lamb that had been shed so that the firstborn son might live. But now, Jesus was explaining that His body would be broken for you. And that His own blood was going to be poured out. Jesus came to be your Passover Lamb, to be your substitute, so that you could have eternal life."

Closing Checklist:

- ❏   "Does anyone have any questions?" (Either as a group or one on one.)
- ❏   Encourage them to jot any questions or comments during the week.
- ❏   Encourage them to read the Bible and articles contained in their Study Guide. (See list below)

Read it for yourself:	
Mark 1:14,15	Jesus tells the people to repent and believe.
John 3:1-18	Jesus tells Nicodemus how to have eternal life.
John 6:28,29	What are the works God requires?
Luke 16:19-31	Lazarus and the rich man die.
Luke 22:19,20	Jesus celebrates the Passover.

Dig Deeper	
Jesus says He is the way, the truth, and the life	**John 14:6**
God does not want anyone to perish.	**II Peter 3:9**
How could a loving God send people to Hell?	**Pg. 224** (Study Guide 156)
Life now, life then, life after death?	**Pg. 226** (Study Guide 158)

*Ask Someone to read the verse out loud from their Study Guide.

Memorize this:

"*For God so loved the world that He gave His one and only Son, that whoever believes in Him shall not perish but have eternal life.*" **John 3:16**

Facilitator's Comment on Verse:

The verse for today is probably the most famous verse in the entire Bible. You may already know it. If you have never memorized this verse, now is your chance. God in His love gave us Jesus. He doesn't want anyone to perish. All He asks us to do is believe in Jesus and He will give us eternal life.

Facilitator's Closing Comment:

Today, we saw that people were attracted to Jesus not only because of His power to heal, but because of His promise to save. He told them that in order to rescue them He would have to pour out His blood for them. How is that going to all work out? Don't miss next time!

Questions your group *might* have:

Remember: *Keep your group on track! If you find a question is more disruptive than beneficial, graciously thank them for their question and tell them you look forward to talking about it one on one.*

1. **Isn't Hell symbolic?**	**Pg. 144**
2. **How could a loving God send anyone to Hell?**	**Pg. 144**
3. **Isn't it narrow-minded to say that it's ONLY through Jesus that you can go to Heaven and have eternal life?**	**Pg. 145**

1. Isn't Hell Symbolic?

Hell is a tragic and sobering subject. While it is true that the description of Hell in **Luke 16** might be symbolic, you must understand the nature of symbols in the Bible. Many times when God uses symbolic language to describe something, it means that the nature of what is described is so hard for our minds to comprehend that God has to use symbols or imagery to represent a greater reality. In the book of Revelation, God's voice is compared to "rushing waters". God's voice is not literally a rushing water, but the gravity and power of His voice is compared to a pounding waterfall. If the words in the description of Hell are symbolic, then it it only means they are symbolic of a greater reality than what is described. They are not symbolic of *nothingness*.

2. How could a loving God send anyone to Hell?

God does not want anyone to perish. (**II Peter 3:9**) He has sent Jesus into the world not to condemn but to save. God offers us eternal life but He does not force us.

Encourage your friend to check out the excellent resources below:

Recommended Resources:

How could a loving God send people to Hell? Pg. 224

Life now, life then, life after death? Pg. 226

3. Isn't it narrow-minded to say that it's ONLY through Jesus that you can go to Heaven and have eternal life?

The issue is that it is not *me*. I am not making this claim. *Jesus* is. He said, "*I am the way, the truth and the life. No one comes to the Father except through Me.*" (**John 14:6**) The nature of truth is that it is absolute. Jesus says "I am truth." Either He is or He isn't.

Here is a very helpful article that shows why *Christ*'s claims are unique among all other religions.

Recommended Resource:

Connecting with the Divine. Pg. 320 (A comparison of a few major world religions)

CHAPTER 10

IT IS FINISHED

Pre Bible Study Checklist:

❑ Have extra Bibles and pens on hand.

❑ Have chocolates for prizes for anyone who memorized the verse.

❑ Pray for each participant to come and be open to God's Word and His Spirit.

❑ Be familiar with the Synopsis.

❑ Be familiar with the questions and dynamics of how the Group Discussion will flow.

❑ Glance through the *"Questions Your Group Might Have"* located at the end of this lesson.

Synopsis of the Episode:

In the episode It is Finished, the Eternal Story of Redemption comes to the climax. The promised Savior, Jesus, fulfills countless prophecies as He is betrayed, tried illegally, flogged and crucified. When Barabbas, the guilty prisoner, is set free and the innocent Jesus is condemned, a striking picture is painted of the condition of humanity. Upon the cross, Jesus, the Lamb of God, takes the condemnation of our sins as our Substitute and then proclaims, "It is Finished," Tetelestai, in Greek. Jesus accomplishes all that is required to restore the broken relationship between God and man. The curtain in the tabernacle is rent in two, providing access to God for all who will come. Three days later, death itself is defeated as Jesus rises from the dead, once again fulfilling the Scriptures and proving He is able to offer eternal life through Himself.

Greeting

❑ Note the attendance.

❑ Verse and chocolates.

❑ Brief open discussion of their Bible reading or articles.

Watch Episode 10- *It is Finished*

Eternal Plan of Salvation:

During the Passover meal, only Jesus fully understood what was going to happen as Judas, one of his twelve disciples, set into motion a series of events that had been part of God's plan from before time began. In the very first book of the Bible, in **Genesis 3:15**, God gave the very first promise concerning the Messiah. By saying that the Messiah's heel would be bruised, God foretold the fact that in the process of completely defeating Satan, that the Messiah Himself would suffer.

For the next thousands of years, God further described His Plan of Salvation, in countless, specific prophecies woven throughout the scriptures. King David foretold the Messiah's betrayal, mocking, crucifixion, the soldiers who would gamble for his clothing, and even some of the Messiah's last words. **(Psalm 22)** Daniel foretold the exact time that the Messiah would die. **(Daniel 9:25-26)** Isaiah wrote that the Messiah would be beaten, flogged, and led like a lamb to the slaughter. **(Isaiah 53)** And Zechariah wrote that they would look on the One they had pierced. **(Zechariah 12:10)** Every single one of these prophecies, and more, were about to be fulfilled by Jesus Christ.

The Time was Drawing Near:

After Jesus and His disciples celebrated the Passover feast together, they left Jerusalem and went to a garden where Jesus had frequently gone to pray. There, Jesus was experiencing deep sorrow because He knew that the time was drawing near in which He would die. **(Mark 14:34)** Now, this didn't take Jesus by surprise. In fact, on three separate occasions, Jesus had already patiently explained to his disciples everything that He was about to go through. **(Mark 10:33-34)** Jesus knew that He was about to face more than excruciating pain and death. Jesus was about to take all of the punishment for our sins upon Himself, and be cursed by God. This is what Jesus dreaded more than the physical pain and death that He was about to endure.

No Other Way:

Three times that night Jesus prayed, begging His Father that if there be any other way to resolve the problem of sin and rescue humanity – that He be spared from what He was about to endure. **(Mark 14:36)** But there was no other way. No religious system, no amount of good works, no pilgrimage, no ritual, no ceremony would ever be adequate. For all had sinned, and the payment for sin is death. Jesus knew that in order to rescue humanity, He would have to die.

Fulfilling God's Rescue Plan:

Judas, one of Jesus' twelve disciples, had been paid off by the religious leaders to betray Jesus and hand him over to them. (**Mark 14:43-46**) As they arrested Jesus, He proclaimed that everything that was happening, was happening in order to fulfill the Scriptures, the Word of God. (**Mark 14:48-49**) For Jesus was not leading a rebellion, but a rescue; a rescue planned before the creation of the world and foretold in the Scriptures.

Condemned as Worthy of Death:

After Jesus' arrest, His enemies proceeded to hold an illegal trial in the middle of the night. (**Mark 14:55-56**) Wanting to justify their hatred of Jesus, they procured false witnesses. Finally, "*[T]he high priest asked Him, 'Are you the Christ, the Son of the Blessed One?' 'I am,' said Jesus.*" (**Mark 14:61-62**) When Jesus claimed to be their Messiah, the Son of God, the chief priest responded, "'*You have heard the blasphemy. What do you think?' They all condemned Him as worthy of death.*" (**Mark 14:64**)

The Guilty One Set Free:

After separately questioning Jesus, both Herod and Pontius Pilate came to the same conclusion: Jesus was innocent. "*Now it was the governor's custom at the Feast to release a prisoner chosen by the crowd. At that time they had a notorious prisoner called Barabbas…*" (**Matthew 27:15-16**) Barabbas was in prison with the insurrectionists who had committed murder in a recent uprising. (**Matthew 27:17-26**) Finally, after trying in vain to reason with the multitude of Jesus' innocence, Pontius Pilate, "*…released Barabbas to them. But he had Jesus flogged, and handed him over to be crucified.*" (**Matthew 27:26**)

Barabbas was a murderer and a law-breaker, Jesus was the perfect Son of God. On that day, however, it was the guilty one who was released. The guilty one was set free and given life because an innocent One was condemned and sentenced to death. You see, as the prisoner set free, Barabbas unknowingly represented you and me. We have broken God's holy laws; we are guilty and condemned. Yet Jesus came in order to take our condemnation, that we might be set free. Jesus came to die so that we might live.

His Body was Broken:

Before Jesus was crucified, Pilate had him flogged. Flogging was extremely brutal. A whip was made from braided leather and contained metal balls that would strike the victim, causing deep contusions. Pieces of bone that had been woven into the leather, shredded the victim's flesh. Many people died just from the floggings. After the soldiers had also mocked and beat Jesus, they led Him out to be crucified. (**Mark 15:17-20**)

Jesus' Love Held Him There:

At nine o'clock in the morning, they stretched out the hands of a trembling Jewish carpenter. These were the hands that had healed lepers. These hands had reached out to sinners and outcasts, but now they were being pierced. Why? Couldn't Jesus have stopped them? Weren't these the hands of the One who had commanded death and demons? Weren't these the feet of the One who had walked on water? Yes, they were. Jesus could have stopped them, but He chose not to. Though they nailed him to a cross, His love for you and me would have held Him there. As the pain from nail-smashed nerves, the dizziness from blood loss, and the throbbing of dislocated joints ravaged His body, *"Jesus said, "Father, forgive them, for they do not know what they are doing."* (**Luke 23:34**)

The Worst of All Agonies:

"At the sixth hour darkness came over the whole land until the ninth hour." (**Mark 15:33**) Darkness covered the land for three hours, from noon, until three o'clock in the afternoon. After Jesus had been hanging on the cross for six hours, He faced the most indescribable pain of all. In incredible anguish, Jesus cried out, *"My God, my God, why have you forsaken me?"* (**Mark 15:34**) This spiritual separation was the worst of all agonies.
2 Corinthians 5:21 says, Jesus, who had no sin, took our sins upon Himself. God took the punishment for all of those sins, and poured it out upon His Son, Jesus. (**Isaiah 53:6**) **Isaiah 53:5** says, *"[H]e was crushed for our iniquities; the punishment that brought us peace was upon Him."*

Rejected so We Could be Accepted:

Note also that Jesus said "My God, my God" and not, "My Father, my Father". On the cross, Jesus was taking our place, and enduring the wrath of God in order to give guilty sinners like you and me the right to do the unthinkable: the right to call all-Holy God, "Father."

Tetelestai: It is Finished:

Then, knowing that all was now completed, Jesus cried out: *"...'It is finished.'"* (**John 19:30**) Just before Jesus died, He proclaimed one of the most important phrases in all of history, "It is finished." This phrase comes from the Greek word *tetelestai*. *Tetelestai* was also a word that meant fulfilled, carried out, and completed. Jesus had fulfilled the prophecies. He had carried out all the requirements of God's perfect Laws. Jesus had completed what God had commanded Him to do. It was finished!

Tetelestai: Paid in Full:

Tetelestai also meant "paid in full". In this sense, it was used as a legal term. When a debt had been fully met, it was declared "Tetelestai", paid in full. You see, you and I also have a debt that we need to pay. We are sinners, and God has declared that, "the payment for sin is death."(**Romans 6:23**) Jesus had come in order to pay our debt for us. Jesus fully paid for our sins. There is no more payment, there is no more punishment or sacrifice left for me or you to offer God for the forgiveness of our sins. It is finished, it is Tetelestai!

Complete Access to all-Holy God:

When Jesus shouted "Tetelestai" something extraordinary happened within the temple. Now remember, like the tabernacle, within the Temple a thick curtain blocked the access into the Most Holy Place. But when Jesus shouted "Tetelestai" – It is finished, "...*the curtain of the temple was torn in two from top to bottom.*" (**Matthew 27:51**) The blood of Jesus Christ, the Lamb of God, had been poured out for the sins of the world! Jesus was the final sacrifice. In this way, atonement was made not temporarily, but once and for all! God's punishment was turned away from us. The curtain that separated man from God was torn from top to bottom to show that now, because of the sacrifice of Jesus, guilty sinners like you and me could have complete access to the all-Holy God!

Jesus Was Dead:

To get the bodies off the crosses before the Sabbath, the soldiers had been ordered to break the legs of all those who were crucified. John, a disciple of Jesus, was there at the foot of the cross. **John 19:33-34** tell us that when Jesus' side was pierced, it brought forth blood and water. When Jesus died a collection of fluids built up in the membranes surrounding Jesus' lungs and heart. The soldier's spear most likely pierced Jesus' right side, puncturing those membranes, causing the flow of blood and water. Medical doctor, Alexander Metherell, states that, "There was absolutely no doubt that Jesus was dead."

An Empty Tomb:

After Jesus died, Joseph, a follower of Jesus, along with Nicodemus, obtained permission from Pilate to take His body. **Mark 15:46-47** says that they placed Jesus' body in a tomb cut out of rock. Yet, **Luke 24:1-6** records, "*On the first day of the week, very early in the morning, the women took the spices they had prepared and went to the tomb. They found the stone rolled away from the tomb, but when they entered, they did not find the body of the Lord Jesus. While they were wondering about this, suddenly two men in clothes that gleamed like lightning stood beside them. But the men said to them, "Why do you look for the living among the dead? He is not here; he has risen!"*

A Resurrected Messiah:

Romans 1:4 says that Jesus' resurrection proved that He was the son of God, the Messiah. Jesus' resurrection was also proof that He had defeated death. In **John 11:25**, Jesus claimed, "…*I am the resurrection and the life. He who believes in me will live, even though He dies…*" Through Jesus' resurrection, He could now offer what every human being longs for, the guarantee of eternal life even after death. Finally, Jesus' resurrection was the evidence that God had accepted the sacrifice of the innocent Lamb of God. It is finished: Tetelestai!

Group discussion time: Personal & Relevant

1. Divide into groups of 3-5 people.
2. Distribute the topics listed below, giving a topic to each group to discuss. *(If you have more than 3 groups, just repeat the topics.)*
3. Allow the groups ten minutes to discuss their topic and record their answer in their Study Guide.
4. After ten minutes, have everyone come back together again.
5. Ask each group to choose a representative to read their group's answer. Encourage everyone to take notes in their Study Guide as the other groups share the answers to their topics.
6. After "Topic One's" answers are shared, read the "Summary" for Topic One before moving on to Topic Two and so on.

Topic One: Barabbas and you

Question: If we were to compare ourselves to Barabbas, what do we have in common with him?

_____

_____

Facilitator Summary: The events that played out that day with Barabbas were a dramatic portrayal of what Jesus was doing on behalf of all humanity. Just as Barabbas was a guilty law breaker, we too have broken God's laws. Jesus came to be our Substitute, to be the innocent One taking the place of all those who are guilty. Just as Jesus died and Barabbas was released, the Innocent One came to be condemned in your place so that you could be set free!

Topic Two: It is finished

Question: If someone asked, "What are the worst things you have ever done?", it would be too humiliating to list. Instead, list below the sins that plague humanity in general. *Pornography, drugs, hate...*

_____

Question: Read **Isaiah 53:5**. At the moment of the crucifixion, what did God do with your sins? *Your sins and the sins of the entire world.* When you think about what He did, what are your thoughts and feelings?

*Hint: Transgressions and iniquities are words that mean "sin."

_____

Question: Why did Jesus say, "It is Finished"? How does that phrase impact your life?

_____

_____

Facilitator Summary: Remember when we talked about the movie of your life? God is really recording every word, every action and even the intentions of your heart. **Romans 3:23** says, *"For all have sinned and fall short of the glory of God."*

Isaiah 53:5 says that all of your sins were placed on Jesus. Picture all of your failures, every word, every thought, every time you've sinned against God. All of those sins were placed on Jesus. Then God took the punishment that we deserve and He poured it out on Jesus as if Jesus had committed those sins. Jesus took the punishment in our place.

On the cross He didn't shout, "Almost! Now, you only have a little left to do in order to earn your way to Heaven." No! Jesus shouted, "It is finished!" The Bible clearly emphasizes, Jesus fully paid for your sins! There's nothing left for you to pay for! He did it all!

Every single sacrifice in the Old Testament had been pointing to this moment. Every time an innocent one died in the place of the one who was guilty, that was a picture of Jesus, the Lamb of God dying in our place. The righteous One for the unrighteous.

*For more, read I **Peter 3:18** - the righteous for the unrighteous, the innocent One in the place of those who were guilty.*

Topic Three: Access to God

Question: Why was there a Curtain separating people from entering into the Most Holy Place? *What did the Curtain remind the people of?*

_____

Question: Why was the Curtain torn from top to bottom when Jesus died on the cross?

_____

Facilitator Summary: At the moment that Adam and Eve sinned, their relationship with God was broken. The Curtain reminded everyone that sin separated them from God. No one was allowed into God's holy presence or they would die.

Now, with the curtain ripping, God dramatically showed us that a relationship with God is possible for everyone. Because of the sacrifice of Jesus, we can have access to God!

Closing Statement about the Resurrection:

Jesus told his followers the proof that He truly was the Messiah would be when they killed Him, three days later, He would rise from the dead. (**John 2:19-22**) I'd like to encourage each one of you to read the article in your Study Guide about proofs of the resurrection.

Jesus said in **John 11:25**, *"I am the resurrection and the life. The one who believes in Me will live, even though they die…."*

Watch Episode 10 -"What does this mean for you?"

1. Barabbas is a picture of you.

"Barabbas was guilty and deserved to be condemned. Yet Jesus was innocent, and deserved to be set free. On that day however, Barabbas was released, but Jesus was flogged and handed over to be crucified. You see, Barabbas is a picture of you, You also are guilty before God and deserve to be punished. Yet God gave His innocent Son to be condemned, so that you could be set free."

2. Jesus completely paid for your sins.

"The payment for sin is death. On the cross, God laid each one of your sins upon Jesus. God punished Him by pouring out His wrath on Jesus. Right before Jesus died, he shouted: "Tetelestai". Which means, 'It is Finished!' He was proclaiming that He had done everything necessary to pay for your sins. That means there is nothing left for you to do. There are no more sacrifices you must offer. There are no good works to fulfill. Jesus has completely paid for your sins."

3. You can have access to God.

"In the temple there was a thick curtain that blocked the access into the Most Holy Place. Only once a year did one man go behind the curtain into God's presence. But when Jesus shouted, "Tetelestai: it is finished"; the curtain that separated mankind from God was torn from top to bottom to show that because of Jesus' sacrifice, now you can have access to God."

4. Jesus offers eternal life to you.

"During Jesus' ministry, some of His critics had demanded He give them a miraculous sign to prove His authority. Jesus had told them that the final sign that would prove who He was would be this; when they had killed Him three days later He would rise from the dead. Jesus' resurrection is the proof that He is who He claimed to be; the Son of God, the Messiah. Jesus' resurrection demonstrates that His words can be trusted, and that He can truly offer eternal life to you."

Closing Checklist:

- ❏ "Does anyone have any questions?" (Either as a group or one on one.)
- ❏ Encourage them to jot any questions or comments during the week.
- ❏ Encourage them to read the Bible and articles contained in their Study Guide. (See list below)

Read it for yourself:

Mark 10:33,34	Jesus explains to his disciples how He will be betrayed, killed, and raise to life.
Mark 14:32-64	Jesus is betrayed and tried by the religious leaders.
Matthew 27:15-26	Jesus is condemned; Barabbas is released.
Mark 15:17-20	Jesus is flogged and mocked.
Luke 23:34	Jesus prays, "Father forgive them…"
John 19:30	Jesus proclaims, "It is finished!"
Matthew 27:51	The Curtain in the temple is torn.
John 19:33,34	Jesus' heart is pierced.
Mark 14:46,47	Jesus is buried in the tomb.
Luke 24:1-6	The women find the empty tomb.

Dig Deeper

Jesus died for our sins once and for all.	**I Peter 3:18**
Jesus had no sins and yet was punished in our place.	**II Corinthians 5:21**
Why did Jesus have to die?	**Pg. 230** (Study Guide 162)
Why should I believe in the resurrection?	**Pg. 234** (Study Guide 166)
Beyond Blind Faith	**Pg. 239** (Study Guide 171)

*Ask someone to read the verse from their Study Guide.

Memorize this:

"For the wages of sin is death, but the gift of God is Eternal Life in Christ Jesus our Lord."   **Romans 6:23**

Facilitator's Comment on Verse:

The payment for our sins is death. God did not tell us, "In order to pay for your sins: say prayers, give to the poor, fast, etc." No. The payment for our sins is *death*. Jesus Christ, however, came and paid that price in our place, and died the death that we deserved. He then offers us eternal life as a gift if we will only believe in Him. This is a very powerful verse. I hope each one of your will memorize it. We will talk more about this verse next time.

Facilitator's Closing Comment:

We are going to see more about the resurrection of Jesus next time, when Jesus Himself shows up to His disciples. We'll also see how this whole Story fits together, and what all this means for *you*. Don't miss it! It's our last Episode!

Questions your group *might* have:

Remember: *Keep your group on track! If you find a question is more disruptive than beneficial, graciously thank them for their question and tell them you look forward to talking about it one on one.*

1. Why did Jesus Have to Die?	**Pg. 158**
2. Veracity of the Resurrection	**Pg. 158**
3. Could Jesus Have Only Fainted on the Cross?	**Pg. 158**

1. Why did Jesus have to die?

A good article to recommend to your participants that will help complement everything they have heard in the episode and serve to further help the pieces fall into place:

Why did Jesus have to die? Pg. 230

2. Veracity of the resurrection

There are excellent resources to read more about the Resurrection of Jesus Christ written by Josh McDowell, Lee Strobel, Gary Habermas and many others. Take this investigation seriously. This was Jesus' ultimate proof substantiating all of His claims. You can start by reading the following articles:

Recommended Resources:

Why should I believe in the resurrection? Pg. 234

Is Jesus Dead? Pg. 326

Beyond Blind Faith Pg. 239

3. Could Jesus have only fainted on the cross?

He was scourged and beaten beyond recognition, then nailed to a cross. On the cross, the eyewitnesses said He died. The Romans stabbed Jesus in the heart to make sure He was, in fact, dead.
He was wrapped in pounds of ointment and linens and placed in a sealed tomb. Jesus was most definitely dead.

Recommended Resource:

Could Jesus have survived the crucifixion? Pg. 328

CHAPTER 11

ETERNAL LIFE

Pre Bible Study Checklist:

- ❑ Have extra Bibles and pens on hand. **Especially for the questionnaire at the end!**
- ❑ Have chocolates for prizes for anyone who memorized the verse.
- ❑ Pray for each participant to come and be open to God's Word and His Spirit.
- ❑ Be familiar with the Synopsis.
- ❑ Consider having soft background music to play while they are filling out the Final Questionnaire at the end.

Synopsis of the Episode:

Eternal Life is a very personal episode that journeys back through the themes of each episode in *Tetelestai*. Each foundational concept is pieced together from the series. Far from being theoretical concepts, as each point from the Eternal Story of Redemption is reviewed, inescapable application to the person watching this series is made. This is YOUR story. He came for YOU.

Greeting

- ❑ Note the attendance.
- ❑ Verse and chocolates.
- ❑ Brief open discussion of their Bible reading or articles.

Watch Episode 11 - *Eternal Life*

God's Eternal Plan of Salvation:

The disciples were both amazed and overwhelmed. (**Luke 24:36-39**) They had so many questions. They were certain Jesus was their Messiah who would reign forever. But they couldn't understand why He had allowed Himself to be crucified. Jesus explained to His disciples how His death and resurrection were God's Plan to rescue humanity, defeat Satan, and restore their broken relationship with God. As Jesus explained the Scriptures to them, they realized that from the very beginning, God had been writing His Eternal Story. (**Luke 24:44-45**) As we go over some of these Scriptures together, I hope that you also will understand and believe God's Plan of Salvation.

You were Created for a Relationship with God:

God, who is eternal, all-powerful, all-knowing, and all-present, created the heavens and the earth. In this perfect world, God created the first man and woman in His image, so that they might have a relationship with Him. You and I were also created for a relationship with God, created to enjoy His love. God, however, does not force us to love and obey Him, for real love is only love if it is a choice. God told Adam and Eve not to eat fruit from the Tree of the Knowledge of Good and Evil, or they would surely die. If they were to reject God, they would be choosing death.

Sin Brings Separation Between You and God:

Satan, an angel who had rebelled against God, came to the Garden as a snake in order to deceive Adam and Eve into doubting God's Word and His love. Adam and Eve chose to listen to Satan's lies, and disobeyed God. At that moment, sin entered the world. Sin is anything that goes against the perfect character of God. God is holy, which means He is completely pure, with nothing evil in Him. Adam and Eve's sin brought separation between them and God.

The Deliverer would Restore the Broken Relationship:

Driven by their shame, guilt, and fear, Adam and Eve tried in vain to resolve the problem of their sin in their own strength. Just as Adam and Eve's leaf clothes did not take away their shame and guilt, you and I cannot resolve the problem of our sin. God in His love, promised them that one day a Deliverer would be born without a human father. This Son would crush Satan's power over them, restoring the broken relationship between God and humanity.

You were Born a Sinner:

Adam and Eve had to leave the Garden. Adam's sin was passed down to each one of his descendants. You and I are born sinners, separated from God. The sin within the heart of every person is the cause for all of the suffering and evil in the world today.

God Desires a Relationship with You:

But God's desire was still for a relationship with humanity. Those who wanted this relationship, like Noah and his family, were still sinners but because they believed God they were made righteous. Their sins were forgiven by God. Tragically though, the rest of the world wanted nothing of God's forgiveness. As people rejected God, they became increasingly evil and corrupt.

The Ark - Pictured the One Way to be Saved through Jesus:

Because God is holy and must punish sin, a judgment of flood waters would be sent upon the earth. In His mercy, God provided one way to be saved; this was a picture of the salvation God offers only through Jesus. In the same way, our sins deserve judgment. If we reject Jesus, we are just like those who refused to enter the ark and died in the Flood. By rejecting Jesus you are rejecting the only way to be saved. Just as those who entered the ark lived, God in His love provided Jesus as the only way for you and me to live and escape His judgment.

The Deliverer would be a Descendant of Abraham:

After the Flood, Noah's descendants spread out over the earth. It was during the lifetime of Noah's son, Shem, that Abraham was born. God told Abraham that He was leading him to a land that would be his possession. God promised Abraham that His family would become a great nation through whom all people on earth would be blessed; for the Deliverer would come from this nation. Even though he and his wife Sarah were elderly and barren, Abraham put his faith in what God said. Because of Abraham's faith, God declared Abraham to be righteous, with all his sins forgiven.

Like the Ram - God Provided Jesus as a Substitute for You:

God gave Abraham and Sarah their son, Isaac. In a divine test, God asked Abraham to offer Isaac as a sacrifice to Him. God had promised that a nation, and the Deliverer, would come through Isaac. Although Abraham did not understand, he obeyed. As they journeyed up the mountain, Abraham told Isaac that God Himself would provide a lamb for the sacrifice. Because of our sin, you and I are also condemned to death. But God Himself intervened. Just as God provided a ram to be killed in Isaac's place, God provided Jesus as a substitute for you and me. Jesus died in the place of a world condemned to death.

Like the Passover Lamb - Jesus is Our Perfect Lamb

Isaac had a son named Jacob, whose name was changed to Israel. Israel's twelve sons formed the nation through which the Deliverer would come. During a famine, Israel's family went to live in Egypt. Many years later, the Israelites were enslaved.

In a remarkable series of events, God chose Moses to lead His people. The time had come for God to free the Israelites from their oppression. When God sent ten plagues upon Egypt, He displayed His power as the one true God who would rescue His people from slavery. He was also displaying a picture of the way He would powerfully rescue you and me from slavery to sin and death. You see, during the tenth plague there was only one way for the firstborn son to to escape certain death: a perfect lamb, without blemish, had to be killed in the place of the son, and its blood sprinkled on the doorposts of the home. Jesus was our perfect Lamb. His shed blood is the only way for you and me to escape eternal death.

Jesus can set You Free from Bondage to Sin and Death:

When God miraculously freed the slaves from the hand of their oppressors and brought them to safety, it was a picture of what God wants to do for you and me. We can be set free from our bondage to sin and death through the blood of Jesus shed for you and me on the cross.

The Law Reveals We Need Jesus to Rescue Us:

Before bringing the Israelites into the land He had promised to their ancestor Abraham, God led them to Mt. Sinai. There, God gave them the Ten Commandments. Because God is Holy, completely pure, with nothing evil in Him, God requires perfect obedience to His laws. God's standards go far beyond mere outward conformity. His standards deal with our words and even our deepest thoughts. The people, however, were sinners and disobeyed God's laws over and over again. We also, are like the Israelites; we too, have disobeyed God's commandments. Just as a mirror reveals imperfections, God's laws reveal the sinfulness of our hearts. They help us realize how much we need Jesus to rescue us from our sins, and restore our broken relationship with God.

Jesus' Blood Turns God's Punishment Away from You:

The Ten Commandments were placed in a golden box called the Ark of the Covenant, which was located in the Most Holy Place of the Tabernacle. Access into the Most Holy Place was blocked by an immense, richly ornamented curtain. This was to show that because God is holy, our sin separates us from Him. Only once a year did God allow the High Priest behind the curtain and into His presence, but never without the blood of the sacrifice. Inside the Ark of the Covenant were God's holy laws that show our complete sinfulness, and how much we deserve condemnation and death. Above the Atonement cover, was the presence of God. When God looked down, instead of seeing the laws that condemn, He chose to see the blood of the innocent one. In the same way, the laws that condemn you and me are covered by the blood of Jesus, in order to turn God's punishment away from us.

Jesus was Lifted Up to Give You Eternal Life:

Years later when the Israelites rebelled against God in the desert, a judgment of venomous snakes was sent upon the people. It was impossible for anyone bitten to produce a remedy to reverse the poison; the bite was fatal. God in His mercy, however, provided a way for all those who were bitten to be healed. All they had to do was believe what God said, look at the bronze snake, and they would be given life. Just as Moses lifted up the bronze snake in the desert, Jesus was lifted up, so that all who put their faith in Him will not perish but be given eternal life.

Messiah - Title for the Deliverer:

Those who eagerly awaited the arrival of the Deliverer began to refer to Him as the "Anointed One" or the "Messiah". Throughout Israel's history, God gave His people numerous prophecies describing who the Messiah would be, and what the Messiah would do.

Jesus Did Not have a Human Father:

Hundreds of years after these prophecies were given, God sent the angel Gabriel to announce to a virgin that she would give birth to the Messiah who would be called Jesus. Just as God had promised to Adam and Eve, the Messiah would not have a human father, for He would be the 'Son of God'. This good news of great joy was for all people. The Son of God, the One who had spoken the stars into existence, had taken on human form. Just as it had been prophesied, *"The virgin will conceive and give birth to a Son and they will call Him Immanuel, which means God with us."* (**Matthew 1:22**)

Jesus Perfectly Obeyed God's Laws:

When Jesus was about thirty years old, God sent John the Baptist to prepare the people's hearts for the Messiah. John told the people that they needed to repent, to change their minds, and admit they were sinners who needed a Savior. At Jesus' baptism God announced that His Son, Jesus, was the One who pleased Him. Jesus was the only One who perfectly obeyed God's laws and did not sin.

Jesus Came to be Examined in Your Place:

Jesus demonstrated this when He had total victory over Satan's temptations. Jesus lived the perfect sinless life that you and I cannot live, in order to be our perfect substitute. Just as the lambs for the sacrifice were examined instead of the sinner, Jesus came to be examined in our place. He came to be, *"The Lamb of God who takes away the sins of the world!"* (**John 1:29**)

Jesus is the Promised Messiah:

After His baptism, Jesus openly proclaimed that He was the Messiah they had been waiting for. To back up this claim, Jesus demonstrated supernatural power and authority over the spirit world as He fulfilled the prophecies that said the Messiah would proclaim freedom for the prisoners and release the oppressed. Jesus also"...*healed all the sick. This was to fulfill what was spoken through the prophet Isaiah: 'He took up our infirmities and carried our diseases."* (**Matthew 8:16-17**) Jesus had power over death itself. As Jesus reached out to the needy, the hurting and the outcasts, He demonstrated love like nothing the world has ever seen.

Jesus is God:

When his disciples were caught in a terrifying storm, Jesus came to them walking on the water, and brought total peace to the storm. The disciples realized that only God could walk on water. Only God could instantly calm the wind and the waves, and only God is worthy of our worship. In light of all they had seen and heard in Jesus' life, many like Peter, came to the conclusion that Jesus was the Messiah, the Son of God.

You Cannot Save Yourself - Only Jesus Can:

As the Messiah, Jesus spoke of the eternal life that He offered. Jesus told the people they needed to repent, change their minds. The people had wrongly thought they would be accepted by God because of their good works. Like Nicodemus, they needed to realize that their failure to obey all of God's laws condemned them to eternal death. They could not save themselves through their own efforts. This is why Jesus had come.

When Jesus and his disciples gathered to celebrate the Passover, Jesus told them that *His* own blood was going to be poured out. Jesus had come to be the Passover Lamb. His death would be the only way to rescue the world. No religious system, no pilgrimage, or good works the people tried to offer God, would ever be sufficient. For all had sinned, and the payment for sin is death. Jesus had come to make that payment.

Tetelestai - Jesus is the Final Sacrifice:

All of history had been pointing to this moment. The One who could calm a raging sea, allowed Himself to be taken by an angry mob. The Innocent One was tried and condemned, so that the guilty ones could be released and set free. Jesus was crushed for our iniquities. The punishment that brought us peace was upon Him. The Sinless One had lived the life that you and I could not live; then He died the death that we deserve. Just as God had provided a substitute for Isaac; just as the blood of the Passover lamb had been poured out: every single sacrifice had been pointing to this moment. On the cross, Jesus poured out His blood for the sins of the world! The Enemy's power was crushed. Jesus shouted: *Tetelestai*! It is Finished! Jesus was the final sacrifice! Our sins were paid in full. At that moment, the veil in the temple was torn in two; the way to God was opened! The broken relationship between sinful man and Holy God could be restored.

Jesus Offers Eternal Life to all who Believe:

On the third day, Jesus rose again, just as the Scriptures had foretold. The sacrifice of the innocent Lamb of God had been accepted. Jesus had completely conquered death! Through Jesus' resurrection, He now offers eternal life to all who believe.

A Glimpse of Eternal Life:

We are given a glimpse of this eternal life in the book of Revelation. In Heaven, there will be people from every tribe, language, people and nation worshipping Jesus and thanking Him for having died in their place to give them Eternal Life. (**Revelation 5:9**) They will be a part of His Eternal Kingdom where Jesus, the Messiah, will reign forever.

It is No Accident You are Hearing this Message Today:

It is no accident that you are hearing this message today. Do you realize how much God loves you? He created you to have a relationship with Him. This relationship is only possible through Jesus Christ. Jesus said in **John 14:6**: *"I am the way, the truth and the life. No one comes to the Father except through Me."* **Romans 6:23** says, *"For the wages of sin is death, but the gift of God is eternal life in Christ Jesus our Lord."*

Grace - Favor we do not Deserve: Will You Accept it?

You see, because of your sin, what you deserve is death, but Jesus has already come and paid the price for your sins, so that He can give you eternal life. This is what the Bible calls "grace". Grace is "favor that we do not deserve". By providing Jesus as the sacrifice for our sins, God has shown us His grace, His favor that we do not deserve.

In order to receive this grace, God says all we need is faith. Faith is believing that what God says is true. **Ephesians 2:8-9** says, *"...it is by grace you have been saved through faith and this is not from yourselves, it is the gift of God, not by works, so that no one can boast."* When you believe that what God says is true - that Jesus is the final sacrifice for your sins and that He has risen again - then you will receive eternal life as a gift. It's free. You don't have to pay for it. Jesus has already paid the ultimate price for your rescue. The only thing you need to do is accept it!

Personal Questionnaire: What do *you* believe?

Facilitator's Instructions:

Open your Study Guide to the Questionnaire, "What do _you_ believe?"

1. This for you to fill out by yourself.
2. This is not for discussing with others. We will do that next week.
3. This is your time alone with God.

A few words about this Questionnaire:

This is <u>not</u> a test, and you will not be graded. This is chance for <u>you</u> to face your own heart and honestly ask yourself, *"Now what? In light of all I have heard, what do I really believe?"*

Some of you may have already faced these questions within your own heart long ago and you already know what you believe. Are you prepared to share that with others? Take advantage of this moment to organize your thoughts and put into words the reasons for the hope that you have!

* Feel free to make photo-copies or print a copy of the Questionnaire "What do you believe?" for anyone in your group who does not have a Study Guide.

What do you believe?

Instructions: Fill this out honestly from your heart. Unlike all of the group discussions in this Bible Study, this isn't time to talk and formulate answers as a group. It's a quiet time to fill out what *you* believe.

This is a chance to examine your own heart in light of all you have studied in God's Word. If you already have a relationship with Jesus, then see this time as a chance to articulate what you believe in preparation to share this hope with others.

Take as much space as you need to fill out your answers.

1. Do you consider yourself to be a sinner? *(Please explain)*

   _____

   _____

   _____

2. What does God say the payment for sin is?

   _____

   _____

   _____

3. If you were having a conversation with someone, and that person told you, *"I don't believe Jesus is God. I think He was only a wise teacher, a good man, and an example to follow."* How would you respond?

   _____

   _____

   _____

4. If God says that the "wages [or payment] for sin is death" but Jesus was not a sinner, then why did He die and rise again?

    _____

    _____

    _____

5. Do you think you're going to Heaven?

    o   If I've been good enough and God thinks I deserve it, then I guess I will.

    o   No, I think I've sinned too many times.

    o   I think so, but many times I'm afraid I'm not going to Heaven.

    o   Absolutely yes! I have no doubts!

    o   Other:

    _____

    _____

    _____

6. If you were to die today and stand before God and He were to ask you, "Why should I let you into Heaven?" What would you say? *(Please explain)*

    _____

    _____

    _____

7. After finishing this Bible Study:

    o   I believe Jesus is the Messiah who died and rose again to pay for my sins.

    o   I'm not sure what to believe. I have questions about:

    _____

    _____

    _____

Closing Checklist:

- ❑ "Does anyone have any questions?" (Either as a group or one on one.)
- ❑ Encourage them to jot any questions or comments during the week.
- ❑ Encourage them to read the Bible and articles contained in their Study Guide. (See list below)

Read it for yourself:

Romans 3:23	Each one of us is a sinner. We cannot measure up to God's standards, we fall short.
John 3:16	God loved us so much that He sent His Son. Whoever believes in Him is not condemned but given eternal life.
Romans 6:23	The payment for sin is death. The gift that God gives us is eternal life through Jesus.
Ephesians 2:8,9	This gift God gives us is by grace which means that it cannot be earned by anything that we do.

Dig Deeper

Jesus died for our sins once and for all.	**I Peter 3:18**
Jesus had no sins and yet was punished in our place.	**II Corinthians 5:21**

*Ask someone to read the verse out loud from their Study Guide.

Memorize this:

"This is love: not that we loved God, but that He loved us and sent His Son as an atoning sacrifice for our sins." **John 4:10**

Facilitator's Comment on the Verse:

This verse is the heart of the Eternal Story of Redemption. It is the Story of the God who passionately loves humanity and pays the ultimate price for our rescue. God sent Jesus to be an atoning sacrifice. Remember: Atonement is the turning aside of God's punishment. We deserved to be punished for our sins. Jesus Christ came to take our punishment in our place. He was the final sacrifice.

Facilitator's Closing Comment:

Don't miss next week! We're going to examine each one of these questions in light of the answers that God gives in His Word.....And we're also having our party![26] Don't miss it!

Questions?

Encourage everyone to jot down their questions and bring them next week.

---

[26] Obviously, having a party is optional but we highly recommend making the conclusion of this series a celebration!

CHAPTER 12

WHAT DO *YOU* BELIEVE?

Pre Bible Study Checklist:

- ❏ Have extra Bibles and pens on hand. **ABSOLUTELY CRUCIAL TODAY!**
- ❏ Have chocolates for prizes for anyone who memorized the verse.
- ❏ Pray for each participant to come and be open to God's Word and His Spirit.
- ❏ Read through the Entire Bible Study. You might want to highlight areas you know someone might struggle with.

Synopsis of the Bible Study:

Pray through the best way to conduct today's Bible Study. For many people, this lesson is actually the most important lesson in the series. As seekers take time out to examine the Scriptures and face these paramount questions squarely, this is often when they make a decision for Christ. Other times, individuals who have gone to church all their lives go through these verses and suddenly realize for the first time the reality, simplicity, and power of the Gospel.

Greeting

- ❏ Note the attendance.
- ❏ Verse and chocolates.
- ❏ Brief open discussion of their Bible reading or articles. Don't get sidetracked into talking about things that might be discussed as you work your way through the Bible Study.

Instructions for the Facilitator:

1. Take turns reading the Questions and Answers out loud.[27]

2. Look up all the main verses that are marked "Read". (Other verses provided are optional and included as a valuable reference for further Study.)

   This is absolutely essential! Resist the urge to skip the verses and "get to the talking". The power is in the Word of God.[28] It may feel time consuming or laborious to help people who are unfamiliar with the Bible find a Bible passage, but it is critical. They will not always have you around, but if they have a Bible and can see the verses for themselves, you have led them to the most pivotal and powerful arguments for belief. The verses they hold in their hands will be more significant and outlive the impact you as an individual can have on them.

3. Guide the Discussions. Keep people focused. Don't get sidetracked.

4. They already "know it all" ?

   Keep encouraging them to see this time as a time of preparation to share with others! This will help equip them to clearly articulate their faith.

5. Help people feel at ease.

   People don't always feel comfortable sharing their inner thoughts or fears. Don't brush over questions that you might be tempted to skip thinking, "Oh, no one in our group thinks that!" By carefully covering every topic in this Questionnaire out loud, regardless of whether or not you think it's necessary, you are safeguarded from having a hidden, unvoiced fear go unanswered.

The following questions and their accompanying answers are included here exactly as they are seen in the Study Guide:

---

1. Do you consider yourself to be a sinner?

Read: Romans 3:23 -

This verse says we are all sinners and that we've fallen short of God's glory, which means we don't reach His standard.

---

[27] Obviously this can be adapted to whatever works best for your situation. Sometimes people are not comfortable reading out loud.

[28] Hebrews 4:12,13

1. *You were born a sinner.*

   Adam's sin was passed down to each of us (**Romans 5:12**) which means every single one of us was already born a sinner (**Psalm 51:5**) The Bible says that anyone who claims they don't have sin is a liar. (**I John 1:8**)

2. *You've broken God's holy laws.*

   God gave us His holy laws (**Exodus 20:1-17**) but because we are sinners, we are incapable of keeping them perfectly. (**James 2:10**) God's laws help us recognize how sinful we are and how much we need the Savior. (**Romans 3:20**)

2. What does God say the payment for sin is?

Read: Romans 6:23a.

The wages, or payment, for sin is death.

1. *After death we will give account to God.*

   Each one of us has one life to live. After death we will stand before God in judgment. (**Hebrews 9:27**) All of our actions, words and thoughts are recorded by God in the books being written about our life. We will be judged by these books. (**Revelation 20:12**)

2. *Separation from God is eternal.*

   If we are not rescued from our sins, then after we die, we will face eternal separation from God in the lake of fire. (**Luke 16:22-31**)

3. If you were having a conversation with someone and that person told you, *"I don't believe Jesus is God. I think He was only a wise teacher, a good man, and an example to follow."* How would you respond?

Read: John 1:1-3,14 - Jesus is God. Jesus came down to earth as a human in order to be our Savior.

Read: Philippians 2:6-11 - Even though Jesus was in fact God, He came to the earth to die on the cross for our sins.

1. Jesus claimed to be God.

In **John 10**, the religious leaders told Jesus they were going to kill Him for claiming to be God. If they had been misinterpreting Jesus, then at this time Jesus would have said, *"Oh, no, you misunderstood Me! I wasn't claiming to be God!"* but Jesus did not say that! They had not misunderstood His actions and words. He was, in fact, stating He was God! (**John 10:30-33**)

*See also: **John 8:24, 28; 56, 59; 18:5**; - Jesus repeatedly used the term "I Am." (God's name for Himself in **Exodus 3:14**.) **John 14:6-10** - Jesus claims to be the only way to Heaven and also claims to be One with the Father. Jesus describes Himself as the "first and the last" ,(**Revelation 1:17,18**) a term that is used by God in **Isaiah 44:6**. (See also **Revelation 22:13-16**)*

2. Jesus had the attributes of God.

Jesus has the titles of God:

In the Old Testament, some of God's titles are: King, Judge, Light, Rock, Redeemer, Creator[29], the Giver of life, the One who speaks with divine authority and the One who has the ability to forgive sins[30]. In the New Testament, every single one of these terms is applied to Jesus!

Jesus has the characteristics of God[31]:

*Jesus is Eternal (**John 8:58**) Jesus is All-powerful (**Matthew 28:18**) Jesus is All-present. (**Matthew 28:20**)*

Jesus is referred to as God:

*The prophecy about the Messiah who would be a Son who was given, a child who was born. This child would be called "Mighty God" (**Isaiah 9:6**) The angel said Jesus would be called "God with us." (**Matthew 1:23**) God the Father refers to His Son Jesus as "God" (**Hebrews 1:8,9**) Jesus is described as the "fullness of Deity in bodily form." (**Colossians 2:9**)*

---

[29] In the Old Testament it says God made the world alone by His power. In the New Testament it says Jesus made the world because He is God and the exact representation of His Being. (Isaiah 44:24;/ Hebrews 1:2,3; John 1:1-3) See also: Isaiah 45:12,18; Colossians 1:15-17

[30] Matthew 9:1-8 - When Jesus claimed to be able to forgive sins, the religious leaders rightly realized that He was claiming to do something only God can do.

[31] For the sake of brevity, only these are mentioned but the list could be much more extensive. (Jesus is Holy. Jesus is sinless. Jesus is perfectly loving and perfectly just. Etc.

*Thomas, Jesus' disciple, upon seeing the risen Jesus and His nail marked hands exclaims, "My Lord and my God! " - Again, if Jesus were not God; He would have said, "Whoah! Wait a second Thomas, I'm not God," but Jesus accepted Thomas's statement and his worship. (**John 20:27-28**)*

3. Jesus accepted worship as God.

When Jesus calmed the storm, His disciples worshipped Him proclaiming, "Truly, you are the Son of God!" Worship of anyone other than God is strictly forbidden in the Bible. If Jesus were merely a man, if He were only a good teacher or a prophet, He would have instantly rebuked them for worshipping Him. Jesus did not rebuke them; He accepted their worship of Him as God. (**Matthew 14:32,33**)

In scenes the book of Revelation gives us of Heaven, we see both Jesus and the Father being worshipped and given the same glory and honor. (**Revelation 5:13**)[32]

4. If the Bible says the "wages [or payment] for sin is death" and Jesus was not a sinner, then why did He die?

Read: Romans 6:23 - The payment was death. We are sinners; we deserved to die. However, Jesus came to die *in our place.*

Read: Isaiah 53:5,6 - Our sins were placed on Jesus; He was punished in our place in order to give us forgiveness.

1. Jesus died as our Substitute.

Just as the lambs were examined before sacrifice to see if they were acceptable, Jesus is our perfect Lamb who came to be our substitute! (**John 1:29**) He lived the perfect life we could not live and then died the death that we deserved.

Just as Jesus was condemned and Barabbas was set free, Jesus took our condemnation so that we might be given life! God allowed the innocent One, or righteous One, to die in the place of the guilty ones, or the unrighteous. (**I Peter 3:18; II Corinthians 5:21**)

*For more, see also: **Romans 5:8** - Jesus died for us while we were sinners.*

---

[32] Angels do not ever accept worship, because they know that worship is for God alone. *(Rev. 22:8,9)*

2. Jesus died to be the final sacrifice for our atonement.

Jesus came to be the final sacrifice for our sins and took our punishment. (**Romans 3:25**) Atonement is the turning aside of God's punishment. God's punishment was forever turned away from us because of trusting in the blood of Jesus as what paid for my sins rather than trusting in our own efforts.

*For more: Jesus death fulfilled the Scriptures. (**I Corinthians 15:3,4; Mark 14:48-49**)*

*Without the shedding of blood there can be no forgiveness. (**Hebrews 9:22**) Jesus' blood frees us from our sins. (**Revelation 1:5b**)*

---

5. Do you think you're going to Heaven?

❏ If I've been good enough and God thinks I deserve it, then I guess I will.

Read: James 2:10 - Even if you've done a "good job" keeping God's commands, breaking even *one* of His commands condemns you! God is Holy, which means He is completely pure with no evil in Him. God does not demand a *good try*. He demands *perfection*.

1. *None of us are "good enough."*

We have all sinned and our sins separate us from God. [33] When we try to resolve the problem of our sin in our own strength, we are just like Adam and Eve making clothing from leaves in the Garden. Our attempts to remedy our situation are inadequate.

Our efforts for dealing with the sin in our life (trying to balance out the bad things we do with good things) are not enough. Our "good works" we offer God are like filthy rags in comparison to God's holiness! (**Isaiah 64:6**)

2. *If we got what we "deserved," we would get eternal death.*

God's Word is very clear on the payment for sin. We are sinners and we deserve death![34]

When we begin to understand 1) God's holiness 2) Our sinfulness 3) The seriousness of sin and 4) The payment God requires, then we realize *We do not want what we deserve!*

---

[33] See number 1 for more on sin.

[34] See number 2.

3. *Salvation is not through "good works"*

When Jesus was asked what the works were that God required, He didn't give them a list of things to do. Jesus didn't say: fasts, pilgrimages, prayers, church attendance, baptism, don't smoke, don't drink, etc. Instead, Jesus told them God required only one thing: *to believe in Him.* (**John 6:28,29**)

Read: Ephesians 2:8,9 - Grace means favor we do not deserve. We cannot earn our salvation by our own good works. All we can do is believe what God has said and accept the life He offers.

*See also: **Galatians 2:16** and **Romans 11:6***

---

5. Do you think you're going to Heaven? (cont.)
❏   No, I've sinned too many times.

Read: John 3:14-17 - God did not come to condemn you but to save you!

God reaffirms that He sent Jesus in order to save a sinful world, not condemn it. On the cross, Jesus took all of our condemnation.

All God asks us to do is believe in Jesus and He will give us eternal life, just as God offered life to all of the Israelites in the desert. When the Israelites were bitten by venomous snakes in the wilderness, God offered complete healing to all people, if they would only believe what He said. God did not say, "Those of you who are good may be healed; those of you who have been very bad are going to die from the snakebite!" In the same way, Jesus Christ came to save you.[35]

1. Jesus' Blood was enough for you!

This thief on the cross was mostly likely a murderer who had committed heinous crimes to be given the sentence of crucifixion, yet when He believed in Jesus, Jesus said to Him, "Today you will be with me in paradise." There is no sin that is too great to be forgiven by the blood of Jesus! (**Luke 23:42-43**)

---

[35] Just as there was only one way to be healed in the desert, the same is true with the eternal life God offers through Jesus. Rejection of Jesus, is a rejections of the only way to be saved.

2. God will not hold your sins against you!

On the cross Jesus shouted, "It is finished[36]!" Jesus had completely accomplished all that was necessary for our salvation. He completely paid for our sins and fulfilled all the requirements of God. Your sins cannot condemn you any longer! (**John 19:30**) The Bible says when God forgives your sins, He removes them as far as the east is from the west. (**Psalm 103:11,12**)

3. Humility or arrogance?

Sometimes we think we are being humble by saying, "I don't think He can save me." In reality however, it is arrogance to look at the Lamb of God and say, "I don't think Your death was sufficient."

---

5. Do you think you're going to Heaven? (cont.)
❏ I think so, but many times I'm afraid I'm not going to Heaven.

---

1. Is your name in the Book of Life? Read **Revelation 20:12,15** for what God says about this.

If you believe in Christ:

If you believe in Jesus Christ then your sins are paid for by Jesus. Because He took your punishment, you are forgiven.[37] Because Jesus has already been judged and condemned in your place, there is no longer any judgment against you! God has given you life! (**Romans 8:1**) When you die, you will be welcomed into God's presence, because your name has been recorded in the Book of Life.

If you reject Christ:

If you do *not* believe in Jesus Christ and *do not* accept His death in your place, then your name will *not* be written in the Book of Life. You will still be under the condemnation of your sins because you did not accept that Christ be judged in your place. (**John 3:36**)

---

[36] Tetelestai in the Greek.

[37] See number 4, "Jesus died as our Substitute" and "Jesus died to be the final sacrifice for our atonement.""

Books will be opened and you will be judged according to what is recorded in the books about your life.[38] If your life is examined by a Holy God, He will give you a just and holy sentence - only what you deserve. The problem is, what you will *deserve* is death.[39]

2. If you believe in Christ, nothing can separate you from God's love!

Read: Romans 8:1; 31-39

You are completely forgiven. No condemnation can be against you. Nothing can separate you from the love of God that is poured out to you because of Jesus!

---

5. Do you think you're going to Heaven? (cont.)

❏ Absolutely yes! I have no doubts!

God wants you to have certainty! Read **John 5:24** and **1 John 5:13**.

God promises in His Word that you can have the assurance of going to Heaven. If you believe in Jesus then you have crossed over from death to life! You can know for a fact that you have eternal life!

---

6. If you were to die today and stand before God and He were to ask you, "Why should I let you into Heaven?" What would you say?

A question each person must answer:

The Bible says, "*death is the destiny of everyone; the living should take this to heart.*" (**Ecclesiastes 7:2**) It was intrinsically important for you to answer this question in your own words because each one of us will have to stand before God someday.

In the busyness of life and the pressures of our day to day schedule, many times we don't take time out to consider the most important question of all: What will happen after I die? Where will I go? Am I prepared?

---

[38] See number 2, "After death we will give account to God."

[39] See number 5 "What we deserve is death."

7. After finishing this Bible Study:

❏ I'm not sure what to believe. I would like to know more. I have a lot of questions.

If you are still searching and still have unanswered questions, I urge you to continue pursuing the Truth. Continue examining the claims of Jesus Christ.

Talk to your Bible Study leader, get in contact with Light in Action or one of the other ministries that would love to assist you on this journey. Ask God to reveal Himself to you. Don't stop your investigation before coming to a conclusion!

7. After finishing this Bible Study: (cont.)

I believe that Jesus Christ is the Messiah who died for my sins in my place and rose again.

❏ I was already a believer:

We pray that you have fallen more deeply in love with the One who gave His life for you and that your faith has been strengthened!

Pray that God will give you a renewed boldness for sharing the message of God's love with others! We challenge you to next lead a Bible Study yourself! It doesn't matter whether you start a big group or invite just your neighbor next door, the fact is God has given us the most important message and told us to share the message of eternal life with those who have never heard!

7. After finishing this Bible Study: (cont.)

I believe that Jesus Christ is the Messiah who died for my sins in my place and rose again.

❏ I believe now.

Maybe as you studied through *Tetelestai* you understood for the first time the message of the Bible and why God sent His Son, Jesus, into the world to die for our sins! You have just made the decision that impacts your eternal destiny, you have chosen LIFE, the life that God offers you through His Son, Jesus. Life that will never end! Welcome to His Family!

Instructions for Facilitator:

Consider going around the room and having each person pray thanking God for having sent His Son, Jesus, to die for them.

What are they looking at?

On the following page you will see a copy of how the Study Guide concludes, so that you can be aware of what page your group is looking at and be able to interact accordingly.

We'd love to hear Your Feedback!

What was your experience using *Tetelestai*? Do you have any questions or comments? Let us know how we can make the Facilitator Guide better! We'd love to hear from you! You'll find our contact information on the following page.

We'd love to hear from you!

If you were strengthened in your faith or became a believer in Jesus Christ after studying *Tetelestai*, the Light in Action team would love to hear from you! You can write to us at the following addresses:

Light in Action Team:	
E-mail	Tetelestai@lightinaction.org
Address	Light in Action 1104 El Sonoro Dr. Sierra Vista, AZ, 85635

You can also connect with any of the following ministries below. Let them know you watched *Tetelestai*. They would love to answer your questions and assist you in your journey with God.

Chat with Someone or Ask Questions:	
Talk to Someone Live	**Call:** 888-NeedHim (888-633-3446) **Chat Online:** www.chataboutJesus.com
Ask a Question	www.gotquestions.org
Ask a Question	www.everystudent.com
Free Bible Study to help you grow in your relationship with God.	https://www.everystudent.com/features/followup.html

Study Guide Appendix

The Appendix that accompanies the Study Guide is included here for you as well.

WHY YOU CAN BELIEVE THE BIBLE

It is the history of the Bible that makes it unique among 'sacred texts.' See who wrote the Bible, how its reportive style is backed by archaeology and historians...

History of the Bible - Who wrote the Bible?

The Bible was written over a span of 1500 years, by 40 writers. Unlike other religious writings, the Bible reads as a factual news account of real events, places, people, and dialogue. Historians and archaeologists have repeatedly confirmed its authenticity.

Using the writers' own writing styles and personalities, God shows us who He is and what it's like to know Him. There is one central message consistently carried by all 40 writers of the Bible: God, who created us all, desires a relationship with us. He calls us to know Him and trust Him.

The Bible not only inspires us, it explains life and God to us. It does not answer *all* the questions we might have, but enough of them. It shows us how to live with purpose and compassion. How to relate to others. It encourages us to rely on God for strength, direction, and enjoy His love for us. The Bible also tells us how we can have eternal life.

Multiple categories of evidence support the historical accuracy of the Bible as well as its claim to divine authorship. Here are a few reasons you can trust the Bible.

Archaeology confirms the Bible's historical accuracy.

Archaeologists have consistently discovered the names of government officials, kings, cities, and festivals mentioned in the Bible -- sometimes when historians didn't think such people or places existed. For example, the Gospel of John tells of Jesus healing a cripple next to the Pool of Bethesda. The text even describes the five porticoes (walkways) leading to the pool. Scholars didn't think the pool existed, until archaeologists found it forty feet below ground, complete with the five porticoes.[1]

The Bible has a tremendous amount of historical detail, so not everything mentioned in it has yet been found through archaeology. However, not one archaeological find has conflicted with what the Bible records.[2]
In contrast, news reporter Lee Strobel comments about the *Book of Mormon*: "Archaeology has repeatedly failed to substantiate its claims about events that supposedly occurred long ago in the Americas. I remember writing to the Smithsonian Institute to inquire about whether there was any evidence supporting the claims of

Mormonism, only to be told in unequivocal terms that its archaeologists see 'no direct connection between the archaeology of the New World and the subject matter of the book.'" Archaeologists have never located cities, persons, names, or places mentioned in the *Book of Mormon*.[3]

Many of the ancient locations mentioned by Luke in the Book of Acts in the New Testament, have been identified through archaeology. "In all, Luke names thirty-two countries, fifty-four cities and nine islands without an error."[4]

Archaeology has also refuted many ill-founded theories about the Bible. For example, a theory still taught in some colleges today asserts that Moses could not have written the Pentateuch (the first five books of the Bible), because writing had not been invented in his day. Then archaeologists discovered the Black Stele. "It had wedge-shaped characters on it and contained the detailed laws of Hammurabi. Was it post-Moses? No! It was pre-Mosaic; not only that, but it was pre-Abraham (2,000 B.C.). It preceded Moses' writings by at least three centuries."[5]

Archaeology consistently confirms the historical accuracy of the Bible.

Chart listing some of the major archaeological finds:

ARCHAEOLOGICAL FIND	SIGNIFICANCE
Mari Tablets	Over 20,000 cuneiform tablets, which date back to Abraham's time period, explain many of the patriarchal traditions of Genesis.
Ebla Tablets	Over 20,000 tablets, many containing law similar to the Deuteronomy law code. The previously thought fictitious five cities of the plain in Genesis 14 (Sodom, Gomorrah, Admah, Zeboiim, and Zoar) are identified.
Nuzi Tablets	They detail customs of the 14th and 15th century parallel to the patriarchal accounts such as maids producing children for barren wives.

WHY YOU CAN BELIEVE THE BIBLE

ARCHAEOLOGICAL FIND	SIGNIFICANCE
Black Stele	Proved that writing and written laws existed three centuries before the Mosaic laws.
Temple Walls of Karnak, Egypt	Signifies a 10th century B.C. reference to Abraham.
Laws of Eshnunna (ca. 1950 B.C.); Lipit-Ishtar Code (ca. 1860 B.C.); Laws of Hammurabi (ca. 1700 B.C.)	Show that the law codes of the Pentateuch were not too sophisticated for that period.
Ras Shamra Tablets	Provide information on Hebrew poetry.
Lachish Letters	Describe Nebuchadnezzar's invasion of Judah and give insight into the time of Jeremiah.
Gedaliah Seal	References Gedaliah is spoken of in 2 Kings 25:22.
Cyrus Cylinder	Authenticates the Biblical description of Cyrus' decree to allow the Jews to rebuild the temple in Jerusalem (see 2 Chronicles 36:23; Ezra 1:2-4).
Moabite Stone	Gives information about Omri, the sixth king of Israel.
Black Obelisk of Shalmaneser III	Illustrates how Jehu, king of Israel, had to submit to the Assyrian king.
Taylor Prism	Contains an Assyrian text which details Sennacherib's attack on Jerusalem during the time of Hezekiah, king of Israel.

PAST CHARGES BY CRITICS	ANSWERED BY ARCHAEOLOGY
Moses could not have written the Pentateuch because he lived before the invention of writing.	Writing existed many centuries before Moses.
Abraham's home city of Ur does not exist.	Ur was discovered. One of the columns had the inscription "Abram."
The city built of solid rock called "Petra" does not exist.	Petra was discovered.
The story of the fall of Jericho is a myth. The city never existed.	The city was found and excavated. It was found that the walls tumbled in the exact manner described by the biblical narrative.
The "Hittites" did not exist.	Hundreds of references to the amazing Hittite civilization have been found. One can even get a doctorate in Hittite studies at the University of Chicago.
Belshazzar was not a real king of Babylon; he is not found in the records.	Tablets of Babylonia describe the reign of this coregent and son of Nabonidus.

The Bible today is the same as what was originally written.

Some people have the idea that the Bible has been translated "so many times" that it has become corrupted through stages of translating. That would probably be true if the translations were being made from other translations. But translations are actually made directly from original Greek, Hebrew and Aramaic source texts based on thousands of ancient manuscripts.

The accuracy of today's Old Testament was confirmed in 1947 when archaeologists found "The Dead Sea Scrolls" along today's West Bank in Israel. "The Dead Sea Scrolls" contained Old Testament scripture dating

1,000 years older than any manuscripts we had. When comparing the manuscripts at hand with these, from 1,000 years earlier, we find agreement 99.5% of the time. And the .5% differences are minor spelling variances and sentence structure that don't change the meaning of the sentence.

Regarding the New Testament, it is humanity's most reliable ancient document. All ancient manuscripts were written on papyrus, which didn't have much of a shelf life. So people hand copied originals, to maintain the message and circulate it to others.

Few people doubt Plato's writing of "The Republic." It's a classic, written by Plato around 380 B.C. The earliest copies we have of it are dated 900 A.D., which is a 1,300 year time lag from when he wrote it. There are only seven copies in existence. Caesar's "Gallic Wars" were written around 100-44 B.C. The copies we have today are dated 1,000 years after he wrote it. We have ten copies.

When it comes to the New Testament, written between 50-100 A.D, there are more than 5,000 copies. All are within 50-225 years of their original writing. Further, when it came to Scripture, scribes (monks) were meticulous in their copying of original manuscripts. They checked and rechecked their work, to make sure it perfectly matched. What the New Testament writers originally wrote is preserved better than any other ancient manuscript.

We can be more certain of what we read about Jesus' life and words, than we are certain of the writings of Caesar, Plato, Aristotle and Homer.

A comparison of the New Testament to other ancient writings:

Author	Book	Date Written	Earliest Copies	Time Gap	# of Copies
Homer	*Iliad*	800 B.C.	c. 400 B.C.	c. 400 yrs.	643
Herodotus	*History*	480-425 B.C.	c. A.D. 900	c. 1,350 yrs.	8
Thucydides	*History*	460-400 B.C.	c. A.D. 900	c. 1,300 yrs.	8

Author	Book	Date Written	Earliest Copies	Time Gap	# of Copies
Plato		400 B.C.	c. A.D. 900	c. 1,300 yrs.	7
Demosthenes		300 B.C.	c. A.D. 1100	c. 1,400 yrs.	200
Caesar	*Gallic Wars*	100-44 B.C.	c. A.D. 900	c. 1,000 yrs.	10
Tacitus	*Annals*	A.D. 100	c. A.D. 1100	c. 1,000 yrs.	20
Pliny Secundus	*Natural History*	A.D. 61-113	c. A.D. 850	c. 750 yrs.	7
New Testament		A.D. 50-100	c. A.D. 114 (portions) c. A.D. 200 (books) c. A.D. 325 (complete N.T.)	c. +50 yrs. c. 100 yrs. c. 225 yrs.	5366

More reasons to trust the gospel accounts of Jesus.

Four of the writers of the New Testament each wrote their own biography on the life of Jesus. These are called the four gospels, the first four books of the New Testament. When historians try to determine if a biography is reliable, they ask, "How many other sources report the same details about this person?"

Here's how this works. Imagine you are collecting biographies of President John F. Kennedy. You find many biographies describing his family, his presidency, his goal of putting a man on the moon, and his handling of the Cuban Missile Crisis. Regarding Jesus, do we find multiple biographies reporting similar facts about his life? Yes.

Here is a sampling of facts about Jesus, and where you would find that fact reported in each of their biographies.

	Matthew	Mark	Luke	John
Jesus was born of a virgin	1:18-25	-	1:27, 34	-
He was born in Bethlehem	2:1	-	2:4	-
He lived in Nazareth	2:23	1:9, 24	2:51, 4:16	1:45, 46
Jesus was baptized by John the Baptist	3:1-15	1:4-9	3:1-22	-
He performed miracles of healing	4:24, etc.	1:34, etc.	4:40, etc.	9:7
He walked on water	14:25	6:48	-	6:19
He fed five thousand people with five loaves and two fish	14:7	6:38	9:13	6:9
Jesus taught the common people	5:1	4:25, 7:28	9:11	18:20
He spent time with social outcasts	9:10, 21:31	2:15, 16	5:29, 7:29	8:3
He argued with the religious elite	15:7	7:6	12:56	8:1-58
The religious elite plotted to kill him	12:14	3:6	19:47	11:45-57
They handed Jesus over to the Romans	27:1, 2	15:1	23:1	18:28
Jesus was flogged	27:26	15:15	-	19:1

He was crucified	27:26-50	15:22-37	23:33-46	19:16-30
He was buried in a tomb	27:57-61	15:43-47	23:50-55	19:38-42
Jesus rose from the dead and appeared to his followers	28:1-20	16:1-20	24:1-53	20:1-31

Two of the gospel biographies were written by the apostles Matthew and John, men who knew Jesus personally and traveled with him for over three years. The other two books were written by Mark and Luke, close associates of the apostles. These writers had direct access to the facts they were recording. At the time of their writing, there were still people alive who had heard Jesus speak, watched him heal people and perform miracles.

So the early church readily accepted the four gospels because they agreed with what was already common knowledge about Jesus' life.
Each of the gospels of Matthew, Mark, Luke and John, read like news reports, factual accountings of the days' events, each from their own perspective. The descriptions are unique to each writer, but the facts are in agreement.

Sample of what is presented in one of the Gospels...

The Gospels are presented as matter-of-fact, "this is how it was." Even reports of Jesus doing the miraculous are written without sensationalism or mysticism. One typical example is the account in Luke, chapter 8, where Jesus brings a little girl back to life.

Notice the details and clarity in its reporting:

Then a man named Jairus, a ruler of the synagogue, came and fell at Jesus' feet, pleading with Him to come to his house because his only daughter, a girl of about twelve, was dying.

As Jesus was on his way, the crowds almost crushed Him. And a woman was there who had been subject to bleeding for twelve years, but no one could heal her.

She came up behind Him and touched the edge of his cloak, and immediately her bleeding stopped.

"Who touched me?" Jesus asked. When they all denied it, Peter said, "Master, the people are crowding and pressing against you." But Jesus said, "Someone touched me; I know that power has gone out from me."

WHY YOU CAN BELIEVE THE BIBLE

Then the woman, seeing that she could not go unnoticed, came trembling and fell at his feet. In the presence of all the people, she told why she had touched Him and how she had been instantly healed. Then He said to her, "Daughter, your faith has healed you. Go in peace."

While Jesus was still speaking, someone came from the house of Jairus, the synagogue ruler. "Your daughter is dead," he said. "Don't bother the teacher any more." Hearing this, Jesus said to Jairus, "Don't be afraid; just believe, and she will be healed."

When He arrived at the house of Jairus, He did not let anyone go in with Him except Peter, John and James, and the child's father and mother. Meanwhile, all the people were wailing and mourning for her. "Stop wailing," Jesus said. "She is not dead but asleep." They laughed at Him, knowing that she was dead.
But He took her by the hand and said, "My child, get up!" Her spirit returned, and at once she stood up. Then Jesus told them to give her something to eat. Her parents were astonished, but He ordered them not to tell anyone what had happened.

Like other accounts of Jesus healing people, this has a ring of authenticity. If it were fiction, there are portions of it that would have been written differently. For example, in a fictional account there wouldn't be an interruption with something else happening. If it were fiction, the people in mourning would not have laughed at Jesus' statement; get angry maybe, be hurt by it, but not laugh. And in writing fiction, would Jesus have ordered the parents to be quiet about it? You would expect the healing to make a grand point. But real life isn't always smooth. There are interruptions. People do react oddly. And Jesus had his own reasons for not wanting the parents to broadcast this.

The best test of the Gospels' authenticity is to read it for yourself. Does it read like a report of real events, or like fiction? If it is real, then God has revealed Himself to us. Jesus came, lived, taught, inspired, and brought life to millions who read His words and life today. What Jesus stated in the gospels, many have found reliably true: "I have come that they might have life, and have it more abundantly." (John 10:10)

Here's why the gospels were written.

In the early years after Jesus' death and resurrection there was no apparent need for written biographies about Jesus. Those living in the Jerusalem region were witnesses of Jesus and well aware of his ministry.[6]
However, when news of Jesus spread beyond Jerusalem, and the eyewitnesses were no longer readily accessible, there was a need for written accounts to educate others about Jesus' life and ministry.

If you would like to know more about Jesus, this article will give you a good summary of his life: Beyond Blind Faith. Pg. 239

How the books of the New Testament were determined.

The early church accepted the New Testament books almost as soon as they were written. It's already been mentioned that the writers were friends of Jesus or His immediate followers, men to whom Jesus had entrusted the leadership of the early church. The Gospel writers Matthew and John were some of Jesus' closest followers.

Mark and Luke were companions of the apostles, having access to the apostles' account of Jesus' life. The other New Testament writers had immediate access to Jesus as well: James and Jude were half-brothers of Jesus who initially did not believe in Him. Peter was one of the 12 apostles. Paul started out as a violent opponent of Christianity and a member of the religious ruling class, but he became an ardent follower of Jesus, convinced that Jesus rose from the dead.

The reports in the New Testament books lined up with what thousands of eyewitnesses had seen for themselves. When other books were written hundreds of years later, it wasn't difficult for the church to spot them as forgeries. For example, the Gospel of Judas was written by the Gnostic sect, around 130-170 A.D., long after Judas' death. The Gospel of Thomas, written around 140 A.D., is another example of a counterfeit writing erroneously bearing an apostle's name.

These and other Gnostic gospels conflicted with the known teachings of Jesus and the Old Testament, and often contained numerous historical and geographical errors.[7] In A.D. 367, Athanasius formally listed the 27 New Testament books (the same list that we have today). Soon after, Jerome and Augustine circulated this same list. These lists, however, were not necessary for the majority of Christians. By and large, the whole church had recognized and used the same list of books since the first century after Christ.

As the church grew beyond the Greek-speaking lands and needed to translate the Scriptures, and as splinter sects continued to pop up with their own competing holy books, it became more important to have a definitive list.

Historians confirm what the Bible says about Jesus.

Not only do we have well-preserved copies of the original manuscripts, we also have testimony from both Jewish and Roman historians.

The gospels report that Jesus of Nazareth performed many miracles, was executed by the Romans, and rose from the dead. Numerous ancient historians back the Bible's account of the life of Jesus and his followers: Cornelius Tacitus (A.D. 55-120), an historian of first-century Rome, is considered one of the most accurate historians of the ancient world.[8] An excerpt from Tacitus tells us that the Roman emperor Nero "inflicted the most exquisite tortures on a class...called Christians. ...Christus [Christ], from whom the name had its origin, suffered the extreme penalty during the reign of Tiberius at the hands of one of our procurators, Pontius Pilatus...."[9]

Flavius Josephus, a Jewish historian (A.D. 38-100), wrote about Jesus in his *Jewish Antiquities*. From Josephus, "we learn that Jesus was a wise man who did surprising feats, taught many, won over followers from among Jews and Greeks, was believed to be the Messiah, was accused by the Jewish leaders, was condemned to be crucified by Pilate, and was considered to be resurrected."[10]

Suetonius, Pliny the Younger, and Thallus also wrote about Christian worship and persecution that is consistent with New Testament accounts.

Even the Jewish *Talmud,* certainly not biased toward Jesus, concurs about the major events of his life. From the *Talmud,* "we learn that Jesus was conceived out of wedlock, gathered disciples, made blasphemous claims about himself, and worked miracles, but these miracles are attributed to sorcery and not to God."[11]

This is remarkable information considering that most ancient historians focused on political and military leaders, not on obscure rabbis from distant provinces of the Roman Empire. Yet ancient historians (Jews, Greeks and Romans) confirm the major events that are presented in the New Testament, even though they were not believers themselves.

Does it matter if Jesus really did and said what is in the Gospels?

Yes. For faith to really be of any value, it must be based on facts, on reality. Here is why. If you were taking a flight to London, you would probably have faith that the jet is fueled and mechanically reliable, the pilot trained, and no terrorists are on board. Your faith, however, is not what gets you to London. Your faith is useful in that it got you on the plane. But what actually gets you to London is the integrity of the plane, pilot, etc. You could rely on your positive experience of past flights. But your positive experience would not be enough to get that plane to London. What matters is the object of your faith -- is it reliable?

Is the New Testament an accurate, reliable presentation of Jesus? Yes. We can trust the New Testament because there is enormous factual support for it. This article touched on the following points: historians concur, archaeology concurs, the four Gospel biographies are in agreement, the preservation of document copies is remarkable, there is superior accuracy in the translations. All of this gives a solid foundation for believing that what we read today is what the original writers wrote and experienced in real life, in real places.

John, one of the writers, sums it up well, "Now Jesus did many other signs in the presence of the disciples, which are not written in this book; but these are written so that you may believe that Jesus is the Christ, the Son of God, and that by believing you may have life in His name."[12]

Footnotes: (1) Strobel, Lee. *The Case for Christ* (Zondervan Publishing House, 1998), p. 132. (2) The renowned Jewish archaeologist, Nelson Glueck, wrote: "It may be stated categorically that no archaeological discovery has ever controverted a biblical reference." cited by McDowell, Josh. (3) Strobel, p. 143-144. (4) Geisler, Norman L. *Baker Encyclopedia of Christian Apologetics* (Grand Rapids: Baker, 1998). (5) McDowell, Josh. *Evidence That Demands a Verdict* (1972), p. 19. (6) See Acts 2:22, 3:13, 4:13, 5:30, 5:42, 6:14, etc. (7) Bruce, F.F. *The Books and the Parchments: How We Got Our English Bible* (Fleming H. Revell Co., 1950), p. 113. (8) McDowell, Josh. *The New Evidence that Demands a Verdict* (Thomas Nelson Publishers, 1999), p. 55. (9) Tacitus, A. 15.44. (10) Wilkins, Michael J. & Moreland, J.P. *Jesus Under Fire* (Zondervan Publishing House, 1995), p. 40. (11) Ibid. (12) John 20:30,31

Used with Permission from EveryStudent

https://www.everystudent.com/features/bible.html

WHAT ARE SOME EXCITING DISCOVERIES IN BIBLICAL ARCHAEOLOGY?

Answer: Biblical archaeology is the science of investigating and recovering remains of past cultures that can validate, or at least shed new light on, the biblical narrative. Biblical archaeology involves the study of architecture, language, literature, art, tools, pottery and many other items that have survived the ravages of time. For almost two hundred years, those who study biblical archaeology have been working in the Middle East in their quest to recover the past. There have been thousands of archaeological finds that have advanced the study greatly, but some are more significant than others. Some of these finds have been the Dead Sea Scrolls, the Tel Dan Inscription, the Caiaphas Ossuary, the Crucified Man, the Ketef Hinnom Amulets, the House of God Ostracon, and the Pilate Inscription. Let's briefly look at each one of these to see why they are significant.

Dead Sea Scrolls: One of the most important finds in the field of biblical archaeology is the discovery of the Dead Sea Scrolls in 1947 in the Qumran area on the northwest shore of the Dead Sea. There are approximately 900 documents and fragments that comprise the find. The scrolls predate A.D. 100 and include a complete copy of the book of Isaiah. The significance of the find is the age of the documents and the astonishing lack of variants to documents that have been most trustworthy such as the Masoretic Text, Codex Vaticanus and the Codex Sinaiticus. The vast majority of the variants (about 99 percent) are punctuation or spelling errors. Incredibly, none of the variants changed the meaning of the text, nor did they contain any significant theological differences. This gives us the assurance that the text we have today in our Bible is the same as the early church had two thousand years ago. No other secular manuscripts can make the same claim.

Tel Dan Inscription: This stone tablet contains an inscription that is the first reference to the Davidic dynasty outside of the Bible. It was erected by Hazael, king of Aram, which is present-day Syria. The inscription makes reference to a military victory and corresponds to the biblical account in 2 Chronicles 22. This inscription dates to the 9th century B.C., thus giving us accurate dating to the Davidic dynasty as well verifying its existence. This is the only extra-biblical reference to the House of David that has been discovered to date.

Caiaphas Ossuary: An ossuary is a stone or pottery box in which the remains of a deceased person are buried (an ancient casket). The Caiaphas Ossuary bears the inscription "*Yeosef bar Qafa*" and is dated to the second temple period. Yeosef (Joseph) was the son of Caiaphas. This verifies that there was a high priest at the time of Jesus and his name was Caiaphas. Caiaphas was the priest that presided over the false trial of Jesus (Matthew 26:57-67).

Crucified Man: This is the remains of a full skeleton of a man crucified in the first century. The foot bone contains a bent crucifixion nail. There have been those that argued that the crucifixion of Christ was a hoax because that was not a form of capital punishment in Christ's time. These remains verify that crucifixion was being done and that the crucifixion of Jesus was done exactly as outlined in the biblical narrative.

Ketef Hinnom Amulets: In 1979, two silver scrolls that were worn as amulets were found in a tomb at Ketef Hinnom, overlooking the Hinnom Valley, where they had been placed around the 7th century B.C. The delicate process of unrolling the scrolls while developing a method that would prevent them from disintegrating took three years. Brief as they are, the amulets rank as the oldest surviving texts from the Hebrew Bible. Upon unrolling the amulets, biblical archaeologists found two inscriptions of significance. One is a temple priest blessing from the book of Numbers: "The Lord bless you and protect you. The Lord make his face to shine upon you and be gracious to you. The Lord lift up his countenance to you and give you peace" (Numbers 6:24-26). The other is the tetragrammaton *YHWH*, the name of the Lord, from which we get the English *Jehovah*. The amulets predate the Dead Sea Scrolls by 500 years and are the oldest known example of the Lord's name in writing.

House of God Ostracon: Ostraca—writings on pottery—are common finds in archaeological digs. The House of God Ostracon was found in Arad, a Canaanite city in the Negev. Over 100 pieces of ostraca were found and have been dated to the early part of the 6th Century BC. Of significance are the references to the temple in Jerusalem and to names of people that are recorded in Scripture. This not only helps to date the temple, but it verifies the existence of people listed in the biblical text.

Pilate Inscription: This stone tablet was found in Caesarea on the Mediterranean coast. The tablet was found in the theater of Caesarea and bears an inscription mentioning the name of Pontius Pilate the procurator of Judea, and the Tiberium, which was an edifice built in honor of the Emperor Tiberius by Pilate. There has been much written to discredit the biblical narrative in regard to the existence of Pilate; this tablet clearly says that it was from "Pontius Pilate, Prefect of Judea" and verifies that he was a person that lived during the time of Jesus, exactly as written in the biblical narrative.

These finds are interesting from an educational point of view and do validate the historical accuracy of the Bible. But for the believer, finds like these should add nothing to our understanding of the importance or credibility of the Bible. The Bible is the written Word of God, inerrant and infallible and was God-breathed to human writers and is useful for edifying and teaching believers in the ways of God: "All Scripture is God-breathed and is useful for teaching, rebuking, correcting and training in righteousness, so that the man of God may be thoroughly equipped for every good work" (2 Timothy 3:16-17). The Bible needs no corroborative evidence to verify its truth, but it is interesting to note that no scientific or archaeological find has ever disproven a single word of Scripture, and many, many findings have attested to its historical and scientific accuracy.

Recommended Resource: The Popular Handbook of Archaeology and the Bible by Geisler & Holden

---

Used with Permission from GotQuestions

https://www.gotquestions.org/biblical-archaeology.html

WHO IS THE DEVIL?

A brief description of the devil. Who is he? And is he a threat to you?

In cartoons and comics, the devil appears as a cute, benign tempter, pushing you to do something that's fun or a little bit wrong. In reality however, Satan is anything but cute.

Who is the devil? He is not God's counterpart, because God has no equal, no opposite. God has always existed, and everything else that exists now, including angels, were created by God.

The devil (sometimes referred to as Satan or Lucifer) is an angel who rebelled against God. He is the enemy not only of God, but also of humankind, relentless in his mission: to kill, destroy, or enslave us. We're warned, "...be watchful. Your adversary the devil prowls around like a roaring lion, seeking someone to devour."[1]

The devil's power is laughable compared to the power of God. Yet, he is a real threat to humans, and has the capacity to ruin a person's life.

Satan has one primary tactic: to deceive us. He seeks to deceive entire nations, the world, and individuals. He twists and distorts what is true, and there is power in his lies.

Dr. Neil Anderson made an astute observation. He said the Bible describes Satan in three ways:
- The tempter
- The accuser
- The father of lies

Dr. Anderson noted, "If I were to tempt you, you would know it. If I were to accuse you, you would know it. But if I were to deceive you, you wouldn't know it. The power of Satan is in the lie. If you remove the lie you remove the power."

In what ways does the devil lie?

Here are just a few examples.

God created Adam and Eve with free will to choose and make decisions, just like humans can today. The Garden of Eden contained perhaps hundreds of fruit-bearing trees. The only instruction God gave to Adam and Eve was to not eat from one particular tree. It was a straightforward instruction to follow. Just don't eat from that one tree or you will die. Simple enough.

Yet Satan persuaded Eve, "You will not surely die." That's the initial lie. Now he lies further, "You will not surely die. For God knows that when you eat of it your eyes will be opened, and you will be like God, knowing good and evil."[2]

Satan deceived Eve, convincing her that God was withholding something wonderful from them, that this fruit would make them like God. And wouldn't that be a good thing? The problem was, it wasn't true. Adam and Eve believed Satan's lie, rather than what God told them, leading to horrible consequences. That's exactly how the devil operates. He distorts the truth in order to harm the person.

How the Devil Accuses God

Satan's greatest desire is to keep people far away from God. He will seek to either cause you to deny God's existence or to slander, lie about God's character. Here's an example.

God repeatedly affirms his love for us. "I have loved you with an everlasting love, therefore I have continued my faithfulness to you."[3] "...not that we loved God, but that he loved us..."[4] "See what kind of love the Father has given to us..."[5] "For God so loved the world that He gave His only Son, that whoever believes in Him should not perish, but have eternal life."[6]

But what does Satan say? "God doesn't love you. Look at all the problems you have. If God loved you, you wouldn't have these problems." Sounds convincing.

Yet all people face problems. It's part of life. What Satan neglects to tell you is that if you have a relationship with God and depend on Him, God can lead you through those problems. You do not need to shoulder or solve them on your own. God can give you wisdom and real strength in the midst of those problems. Not only that, but He says while we face difficulties, "...my peace I give to you..."[7] Why? Because the person knows that God can be trusted.

Without God, a person is described as "without hope in this world." That is not God's desire for anyone.

How the Devil Accuses You

Not only does Satan try to deceive you about God's goodness, but Satan also slanders you to God. Satan did this with a man named Job. Satan said if Job suffered, then Job would curse God to His face, which Job never did. Satan seeks to undermine you and condemn you before God.

But not only that. Satan turns his slander and condemnation toward you.

He convinces you, "God wouldn't want you. You could never be holy enough. Look at all the junk in your life, all the ways you've failed, the things you do, the addictions you have. God would never accept you or want you. You'd never make it."

Again, all lies. God is very clear that none of us need to become "good" in order to be accepted by God, nor to become sinless in order to maintain that relationship with God.

Jesus said of Satan, "He was a murderer from the beginning...there is no truth in him. When he lies, he speaks out of his own character, for he is a liar and the father of lies."[8] The contrast between the devil and God is stunning. Jesus said, "The thief comes only to steal and kill and destroy. I came that they may have life and have it abundantly."[9] Jesus says of those who believe in Him, "If you abide in my word...you will know the truth, and the truth will set you free."[10]

Instead of being deceived by Satan, there is an opportunity to know what God says is true about Himself, about your life, about relationships. While Satan would like you to be enslaved by his deception, God wants you to know what's true, to be free and experience real life.

In addition to being a liar and an accuser, Satan, through his lies, tempts people toward slavery and addictions. "Oh go ahead. One more won't hurt you. No one will find out. You're not really hurting anyone. And you'll feel so much better."

How to Deal with Satan

If you decide to begin a relationship with God, you will still be tempted by Satan. You still have free will, making whatever decision you'd like to make. However, in many situations you would also know what's true and be less likely to give in to Satan's lies, less likely to feel helpless, confused or fearful. Further, God offers His help.

We're told, "The temptations in your life are no different from what others experience. And God is faithful. He will not allow the temptation to be more than you can stand. When you are tempted, He will show you a way out so that you can endure."[11]

Who is Satan? A tempter, slanderer, and liar. His intent is to keep people isolated from God, so they will listen only to Satan, joining in his rebellion and experiencing destruction. Nothing he says about God or your life is true.

God desires a relationship with you and for you to experience His love. He created you not to live in darkness and confusion, but to know what's true. Jesus said, "I am the light of the world. Whoever follows Me will not walk in darkness, but will have the light of life."[12]

Footnotes: (1) 1Peter 5:8 (2) Genesis 3:4,5 (3) Jeremiah 31:3 (4) 1John 4:10 (5) 1John 3:1 (6) John 3:16 (7) John 14:27 (8) John 8:44 (9) John 10:10 (10) John 8:31 (11) 1Corinthians 10:13 (12) John 8:12

Used with Permission from EveryStudent

https://www.everystudent.com/wires/devil.html

CAN THE FLOOD MENTIONED IN GENESIS BE PROVEN?

Is there evidence for the biblical account of a global flood?

Answer: The flood recorded in Genesis 6 cannot be proved with absolute certainty, but there is ample evidence to support the view that a global flood did occur. The Bible presents the flood as part of the early history of the world, yet there are certainly skeptics that will reject the evidence.

One evidence of the flood of Noah's day is the abundance of global flood stories found in a wide variety of cultures. Anthropologists have catalogued hundreds of ancient flood legends from all over the world. The ancient Babylonians, Native Americans, Australian Aboriginals, Aztecs, Romans, Greeks, Chinese, Mayans, Inuits, and many others recorded flood stories. Further, their stories share many similarities to the Genesis account, including an angry god and people who survived the flood in a boat.

A second area of evidence for the flood of Genesis 6 is physical evidence found on the earth's surface. For example, 75 percent of earth's land surface is comprised of sedimentary rock—rock that was washed away, dissolved in fluid, and redeposited elsewhere. Fossils are found in many of these sedimentary layers. It is common to find massive fossil graveyards consisting of jumbled, smashed, and contorted fossil remains that give the appearance of a large number of animals destroyed simultaneously by an incredible force.

A third area of evidence for the flood of Noah's day is the long-distance movement of various types of rock. For example, scientists have noted quartzites discovered more than 300 miles from their source in Oregon, a phenomenon no longer taking place today. The displaced minerals could be the result of what is spoken of in Psalm 104:6–8—the waters standing above the mountains and violently running down into the valleys.

A fourth line of evidence for the global flood is the presence of abundant fossil remains of marine life at the tops of every major mountain range in the world, including the Himalayas. What could have caused this phenomenon? A global flood in which water covered the tallest mountains could explain it. Genesis 7:18–19 notes that "the waters rose and increased greatly on the earth, and the ark floated on the surface of the water. They rose greatly on the earth, and all the high mountains under the entire heavens were covered." Scientists have yet to provide an adequate alternative theory for the abundance of fossilized marine life at high elevations.

The Bible itself serves as an additional line of support. Time and again, the history of the Bible has been validated through a variety of means. If Scripture is accurate in many other areas of history, why would its account of a global flood be disputed? Taken alongside the evidence from the various global flood narratives, abundant fossils, and high-elevation marine fossils, the Bible's account offers a plausible scenario for what took place during the time of Noah.

Recommended Resource: The Genesis Flood: The Biblical Record and Its Scientific Implications, 50th Anniversary Edition by Morris & Whitcomb

---

Used with Permission from GotQuestions

https://www.gotquestions.org/Genesis-flood-proven.html

IS THERE ACTIVITY OF DEMONIC SPIRITS
IN THE WORLD TODAY?

Answer: Ghosts, hauntings, séances, tarot cards, Ouija boards, crystal balls—what do they have in common? They are fascinating to many people because they seem to offer insight into an unknown world that lies beyond the limits of our physical existence. And to many, such things seem innocent and harmless.

Many who approach these subjects from non-biblical perspectives believe that ghosts are the spirits of dead people who, for whatever reason, have not gone on to the "next stage." According to those who believe in ghosts, there are three different kinds of hauntings: (1) residual hauntings (likened to video playbacks with no actual interaction with any spirits). (2) Hauntings by human spirits, whose natures are a combination of good and bad (but not evil). Such spirits may simply want to get a person's attention; others may be pranksters, but, in either case, they do not truly harm people. (3) Interaction with non-human spirits or demons. These entities can masquerade as human spirits, but they are harmful and dangerous.

When reading about ghosts and hauntings from non-biblical sources, remember that, just because an author may refer to the Bible or to Bible characters (such as Michael the archangel), it does not mean he approaches the subject from a biblical perspective. When no authority is given for an author's information, the reader has to ask himself, "How does he/she know this to be so? What is his/her authority?" For example, how does an author know that demons masquerade as human spirits? Ultimately, those who address such subjects from non-biblical sources must base their understanding on their own thoughts, the thoughts of others, and/or the experiences of the past. However, based on their own admission that demons are deceiving and can imitate benevolent human spirits, experiences can be deceiving! If one is to have a right understanding on this subject, he must go to a source that has shown itself to be accurate 100 percent of the time—God's Word, the Bible. Let's take a look at what the Bible has to say about such things.

1. The Bible never speaks of hauntings. Rather, it teaches that when a person dies, the spirit of that person goes to one of two places. If the person is a believer in Jesus Christ, his spirit is ushered into the presence of the Lord in heaven (Philippians 1:21-23; 2 Corinthians 5:8). Later, he will be reunited with his body at the resurrection (1 Thessalonians 4:13-18). If the person is not a believer in Christ, his spirit is put in a place of torment called hell (Luke 16:23-24).

Whether a person is a believer or an unbeliever, there is no returning to our world to communicate or interact with people, even for the purpose of warning people to flee from the judgment to come (Luke 16:27-31). There are only two recorded incidents in which a dead person interacted with the living. The first is when King Saul of Israel tried contacting the deceased prophet Samuel through a medium. God allowed Samuel to be disturbed long enough to pronounce judgment upon Saul for his repeated disobedience (1 Samuel 28:6-19). The second incident is when Moses and Elijah interacted with Jesus when he was transfigured in Matthew 17:1-8. There was nothing "ghostly" about the appearance of Moses and Elijah, however.

2. Scripture speaks repeatedly of angels moving about unseen (Daniel 10:1-21). Sometimes, these angels have interaction with living people. Evil spirits, or demons, can actually possess people, dwelling within them and controlling them (see Mark 5:1-20, for example). The four Gospels and the Book of Acts record several instances of demon possession and of good angels appearing to and aiding believers. Angels, both good and bad, can cause supernatural phenomena to occur (Job 1–2; Revelation 7:1; 8:5; 15:1;16).

3. Scripture shows that demons know things of which people are unaware (Acts 16:16-18; Luke 4:41). Because these evil angels have been around a long time, they would naturally know things that those living limited life spans would not. Because Satan currently has access to God's presence (Job 1–2), demons might also be allowed to know some specifics about the future, but this is speculation.

4. Scripture says Satan is the father of lies and a deceiver (John 8:44; 2 Thessalonians 2:9) and that he disguises himself as an "angel of light." Those who follow him, human or otherwise, practice the same deceit (2 Corinthians 11:13-15).

5. Satan and demons have great power (compared to humans). Even Michael the archangel trusts only God's power when dealing with Satan (Jude 1:9). But Satan's power is nothing compared to God's (Acts 19:11-12; Mark 5:1-20), and God is able to use Satan's evil intent to bring about His good purposes (1 Corinthians 5:5; 2 Corinthians 12:7).

6. God commands us to have nothing to do with the occult, devil worship, or the unclean spirit world. This would include the use of mediums, séances, Ouija boards, horoscopes, tarot cards, channeling, etc. God considers these practices an abomination (Deuteronomy 18:9-12; Isaiah 8:19-20; Galatians 5:20; Revelation 21:8), and those who involve themselves in such things invite disaster (Acts 19:13-16).

7. The Ephesian believers set an example in dealing with occult items (books, music, jewelry, games, etc.). They confessed their involvement with such as sin and burned the items publicly (Acts 19:17-19).

8. Release from Satan's power is achieved through God's salvation. Salvation comes through believing in the gospel of Jesus Christ (Acts 19:18; 26:16-18). Attempts to disentangle oneself from demonic involvement without salvation are futile. Jesus warned of a heart devoid of the Holy Spirit's presence: such a heart is merely an empty dwelling place ready for even worse demons to inhabit (Luke 11:24-26). But when a person comes to Christ for the forgiveness of sin, the Holy Spirit comes to abide until the day of redemption (Ephesians 4:30).

Some paranormal activity can be attributed to the work of charlatans. It would seem best to understand other reports of ghosts and hauntings as the work of demons. Sometimes these demons may make no attempt to conceal their nature, and at other times they may use deception, appearing as disembodied human spirits. Such deception leads to more lies and confusion.

God states it is foolish to consult the dead on behalf of the living. Rather, He says, "To the law and to the testimony!" (Isaiah 8:19-20). The Word of God is our source of wisdom. Believers in Jesus Christ should not be involved in the occult. The spirit world is real, but Christians do not need to fear it (1 John 4:4).

Recommended Resource: Unseen Realities: Heaven, Hell, Angels, and Demons by R.C. Sproul

---

Used with Permission from GotQuestions

https://www.gotquestions.org/demonic-activity.html

WHAT IS THE CHRISTIAN VIEW OF PSYCHICS / FORTUNE TELLERS?

Answer: The Bible strongly condemns spiritism, mediums, the occult, and psychics (Leviticus 20:27; Deuteronomy 18:10-13). Horoscopes, tarot cards, astrology, fortune tellers, palm readings, and séances fall into this category as well. These practices are based on the concept that there are gods, spirits, or deceased loved ones that can give advice and guidance. These "gods" or "spirits" are demons (2 Corinthians 11:14-15). The Bible gives us no reason to believe that deceased loved ones can contact us. If they were believers, they are in heaven enjoying the most wonderful place imaginable in fellowship with a loving God. If they were not believers, they are in hell, suffering the un-ending torment for rejecting God's love and rebelling against Him.

So, if our loved ones cannot contact us, how do mediums, spiritists, and psychics get such accurate information? There have been many exposures of psychics as frauds. It has been proven that psychics can gain immense amounts of information on someone through ordinary means. Sometimes by just using a telephone number through caller ID and an internet search, a psychic can get names, addresses, dates of birth, dates of marriage, family members, etc. However, it is undeniable that psychics sometimes know things that should be impossible for them to know. Where do they get this information? The answer is from Satan and his demons. "And no wonder, for Satan himself masquerades as an angel of light. It is not surprising, then, if his servants masquerade as servants of righteousness. Their end will be what their actions deserve" (2 Corinthians 11:14-15). Acts 16:16-18 describes a fortune teller who was able to predict the future until the apostle Paul rebuked a demon out of her.

Satan pretends to be kind and helpful. He tries to appear as something good. Satan and his demons will give a psychic information about a person in order to get that person hooked into spiritism, something that God forbids. It appears innocent at first, but soon people can find themselves addicted to psychics and unwittingly allow Satan to control and destroy their lives.

Peter proclaimed, "Be self-controlled and alert. Your enemy the devil prowls around like a roaring lion looking for someone to devour" (1 Peter 5:8). In some cases, the psychics themselves are deceived, not knowing the true source of the information they receive. Whatever the case and wherever the source of the information, nothing connected to spiritism, witchcraft, or astrology is a godly means of discovering information. How does God want us to discern His will for our life? God's plan is simple, yet powerful and effective: study the Bible (2 Timothy 3:16-17) and pray for wisdom (James 1:5).

Recommended Resource: The Truth Behind Ghosts, Mediums, and Psychic Phenomena by Ron Rhodes

---

Used with Permission from GotQuestions

https://www.gotquestions.org/psychics-Christian.html

MESSIANIC

PROPHECIES & FULFILLMENTS:

Messiah Would:	Prophecy Given:	Fulfillment:
Be born in Bethlehem	Mic. 5:2	Matt. 2:1-6; Lk. 2:1-20
Be born of a virgin	Is. 7:14	Matt. 1:18-25; Lk. 1:26-38
Be a descendant of David	Is. 9:7	Matt. 1:1
Flee to Egypt	Hos. 11:1	Matt. 2:13
Have a forerunner	Is. 40:3	Matt. 1:17; Lk 1: 16-17; Jn. 1:19-28
Be a prophet like Moses	Deut. 18:15, 18-19	Jn. 7:40
Enter Jerusalem on a donkey	Zech. 9:9	Matt. 21:1-9; Jn. 12:12-16
Be rejected by His own people	Is. 53:1, 3; Ps. 118:22	Matt. 26:3, 4; Jn. 12:37-43; Acts 4:1-12
Be betrayed by a friend	Ps. 41:9	Matt. 26:14-16, 47-50; Lk. 22:19-23
Be sold for 30 pieces of silver and the silver would be used to buy a field	Zech. 11:12-13	Matt. 26:14-15
Be tried and condemned	Is. 53:8	Lk. 23:1-25; Matt. 27:1,2
Be silent before His accusers	Is. 53:7	Matt. 27:12-14; Mk. 15:3-4; Lk. 23:8-10
Be struck and spat on by His enemies	Is. 50:6	Matt. 26:67; Matt. 27:30; Mk. 14:65

Messiah Would:	Prophecy Given:	Fulfillment:
Be mocked and insulted	Ps.22:7-8	Matt. 27:39-44; Lk. 23:11, 35
Suffer with criminals	Is. 53:12	Matt. 27:38; Mk.15:27-28; Lk. 23:32-34
Pray for His enemies	Is. 53:12	Matt. 27:38; Mk.15:27-28; Lk. 23:32-34
Be given vinegar and gall	Ps. 69:21	Matt. 27:34; Jn. 19:28-30
Have people gamble for His garments	Ps. 22:18	Matt. 27:35; Jn.19:23-24
Not have any bones broken	Ex. 12:46	Jn.19:31-36
Die as a sacrifice for sin	Is. 53:5-6, 8, 10-12	Jn. 1:29; 11:49-52; Acts 10:43; 13:38-39
Have His hands and feet pierced	Ps. 22:14, 16-17	Matt. 27:31; Mk. 15:20, 25
Be buried with the rich	Is. 53:9	Mk. 15:43-46
Be raised from the dead	Ps. 16:10	Acts 2:22-32; Matt. 28:1-10
Sit at God's right hand	Ps. 110:1	Mk. 16:19; Lk. 24:50-51

All of these prophecies and more were fulfilled by one man: Jesus Christ. Could this have happened by chance? Let's look at the mathematical probability of one man fulfilling just eight of these prophecies:

1. **He would be born in Bethlehem.**
2. **He would have a forerunner.**
3. **He would enter Jerusalem on a donkey.**
4. **He would be betrayed by a friend.**
5. **He would be sold for silver.**
6. **The silver would be used to buy a field.**
7. **He would be silent before His accusers.**
8. **He would be pierced before death.**

In their book *Science Speaks*[40], Peter W. Stoner and Robert C. Newman, S.T.M., Ph.D[41] write that the probability of these eight prophecies being fulfilled by one man is 1 in 10^{17}.

In order to help us visualize this statistic, they write:

"Suppose that we take 10^{17} silver dollars and lay them on the face of Texas. They will cover all of the state two feet deep. Now mark one of these silver dollars and stir the whole mass thoroughly, all over the state. Blindfold a man and tell him that he can travel as far as he wishes, but he must pick up one silver dollar and say that this is the right one.

What chance would he have of getting the right one? Just the same chance that the prophets would have had of writing these eight prophecies and having them all come true in any one man, from their day to the present time, providing they wrote using their own wisdom. Now these prophecies were either given by inspiration of God or the prophets just wrote them as they thought they should be. In such a case the prophets had just one chance in 10^{17} of having them come true in any man, but they all came true in Christ.[42] "

Author's Note:

The preceeding statistics were carefully reviewed by a committee of American Scientific Affiliation members and by the Executive Council of the same group. In his foreword to the book *Science Speaks*, H. Harold Hartzler, Ph.D wrote on behalf of the committee:

> *"The mathematical analysis included is based upon principles*
> *of probability which are thoroughly sound and Professor Stoner*
> *has applied these principles in a proper and convincing way."*

---

[40] Stoner, Peter W., M.S. and Newman, Robert C.S.T.M., Ph.D.; *Science Speak*, Moody Press, Chicago, 1976, Chapter 3

[41] Peter Stoner, June 16, 1888 - March 21, 1980
PETER W. STONER, M.S.:
Chairman of the Departments of Mathematics and Astronomy at Pasadena City College until 1953; Chairman of the Science Division, Westmont College, 1953-57; Professor Emeritus of Science, Westmont College; Professor Emeritus of Mathematics and Astronomy, Pasadena City College.
ROBERT C. NEWMAN, S.T.M., Ph.D.:
Ph.D. in Astrophysics, Cornell University, 1967; S.T.M., Biblical School of Theology, 1972; Associate Professor of Physics and Mathematics, Shelton College, 1968-71; Associate professor of New Testament, Biblical School of Theology, 1971-

[42] http://sciencespeaks.dstoner.net/ Online edition to the book *Science Speaks*, prepared by Don W. Stoner, grandson of Peter W. Stoner

IS JESUS A MYTH?

Is Jesus just a copy of the pagan gods of other ancient religions?"

Answer: There are a number of people claiming that the accounts of Jesus as recorded in the New Testament are simply myths borrowed from pagan folklore, such as the stories of Osiris, Dionysus, Adonis, Attis, and Mithras. The claim is that these myths are essentially the same story as the New Testament's narrative of Jesus Christ of Nazareth. As Dan Brown claims in *The Da Vinci Code*, "Nothing in Christianity is original."

To discover the truth about the claim that the Gospel writers borrowed from mythology, it is important to (1) unearth the history behind the assertions, (2) examine the actual portrayals of the false gods being compared to Christ, (3) expose any logical fallacies being made, and (4) look at why the New Testament Gospels are trustworthy depictions of the true and historical Jesus Christ.

The claim that Jesus was a myth or an exaggeration originated in the writings of liberal German theologians in the nineteenth century. They essentially said that Jesus was nothing more than a copy of popular dying-and-rising fertility gods in various places—Tammuz in Mesopotamia, Adonis in Syria, Attis in Asia Minor, and Horus in Egypt. Of note is the fact that none of the books containing these theories were taken seriously by the academics of the day. The assertion that Jesus was a recycled Tammuz, for example, was investigated by contemporary scholars and determined to be completely baseless. It has only been recently that these assertions have been resurrected, primarily due to the rise of the Internet and the mass distribution of information from unaccountable sources.

This leads us to the next area of investigation—do the mythological gods of antiquity really mirror the person of Jesus Christ? As an example, the *Zeitgeist* movie makes these claims about the Egyptian god Horus:

- He was born on December 25 of a virgin: Isis Mary

- A star in the East proclaimed his arrival

- Three kings came to adore the newborn "savior"

- He became a child prodigy teacher at age 12

- At age 30 he was "baptized" and began a "ministry"

- Horus had twelve "disciples"

- Horus was betrayed

- He was crucified

- He was buried for three days
- He was resurrected after three days

However, when the actual writings about Horus are competently examined, this is what we find:

- Horus was born to Isis; there is no mention in history of her being called "Mary." Moreover, "Mary" is our Anglicized form of her real name, Miryam or Miriam. "Mary" was not even used in the original texts of Scripture.
- Isis was not a virgin; she was the widow of Osiris and conceived Horus with Osiris.
- Horus was born during month of Khoiak (Oct/Nov), not December 25. Further, there is no mention in the Bible as to Christ's actual birth date.
- There is no record of three kings visiting Horus at his birth. The Bible never states the actual number of magi that came to see Christ.
- Horus is not a "savior" in any way; he did not die for anyone.
- There are no accounts of Horus being a teacher at the age of 12.
- Horus was not "baptized." The only account of Horus that involves water is one story where Horus is torn to pieces, with Isis requesting the crocodile god to fish him out of the water.
- Horus did not have a "ministry."
- Horus did not have 12 disciples. According to the Horus accounts, Horus had four demigods that followed him, and there are some indications of 16 human followers and an unknown number of blacksmiths that went into battle with him.
- There is no account of Horus being betrayed by a friend.
- Horus did not die by crucifixion. There are various accounts of Horus' death, but none of them involve crucifixion.
- There is no account of Horus being buried for three days.
- Horus was not resurrected. There is no account of Horus coming out of the grave with the body he went in with. Some accounts have Horus/Osiris being brought back to life by Isis and then becoming the lord of the underworld.

When compared side by side, Jesus and Horus bear little, if any, resemblance to one another.

Jesus is also compared to Mithras by those claiming that Jesus Christ is a myth. All the above descriptions of Horus are applied to Mithras (e.g., born of a virgin, being crucified, rising in three days, etc.).

But what does the Mithras myth actually say?

- He was born out of a solid rock, not from any woman.

- He battled first with the sun and then with a primeval bull, thought to be the first act of creation. Mithras killed the bull, which then became the ground of life for the human race.

- Mithras's birth was celebrated on December 25, along with winter solstice.

- There is no mention of his being a great teacher.

- There is no mention of Mithras having 12 disciples. The idea that Mithras had 12 disciples may have come from a mural in which Mithras is surrounded by the twelve signs of the zodiac.

- Mithras had no bodily resurrection. Rather, when Mithras completed his earthly mission, he was taken to paradise in a chariot, alive and well. The early Christian writer Tertullian did write about Mithraic cultists re-enacting resurrection scenes, but this occurred well after New Testament times, so if any copycatting was done, it was Mithraism copying Christianity.

More examples can be given of Krishna, Attis, Dionysus, and other mythological gods, but the result is the same. In the end, the historical Jesus portrayed in the Bible is unique. The alleged similarities of Jesus' story to pagan myths are greatly exaggerated. Further, while tales of Horus, Mithras, and others pre-date Christianity, there is very little historical record of the *pre-Christian* beliefs of those religions. The vast majority of the earliest writings of these religions date from the third and fourth centuries A.D. To assume that the *pre*-Christian beliefs of these religions (of which there is no record) were identical to their *post*-Christian beliefs is naive. It is more logical to attribute any similarities between these religions and Christianity to the religions copying Christian teaching about Jesus.

This leads us to the next area to examine: the logical fallacies committed by those claiming that Christianity borrowed from pagan mystery religions. We'll consider two fallacies in particular: the fallacy of the false cause and the terminological fallacy.

If one thing precedes another, some conclude that the first thing must have caused the second. This is the fallacy of the false cause. A rooster may crow before the sunrise every morning, but that does not mean the rooster *causes* the sun to rise. Even if pre-Christian accounts of mythological gods closely resembled Christ (and they do not), it does not mean they caused the Gospel writers to invent a false Jesus. Making such a claim is akin to saying the TV series *Star Trek* caused the NASA Space Shuttle program.

The terminological fallacy occurs when words are redefined to prove a point. For example, the *Zeitgeist* movie says that Horus "began his ministry", but the word *ministry* is being redefined. Horus had no actual "ministry"—

nothing like that of Christ's ministry. Those claiming a link between Mithras and Jesus talk about the "baptism" that initiated prospects into the Mithras cult, but what was it actually? Mithraic priests would place initiates into a pit, suspend a bull over the pit, and slit the bull's stomach, covering the initiates in blood and gore. Such a practice bears no resemblance whatsoever to Christian baptism—a person going under water (symbolizing the death of Christ) and then coming back out of the water (symbolizing Christ's resurrection). But advocates of a mythological Jesus deceptively use the same term, "baptism", to describe both rites in hopes of linking the two.

This brings us to the subject of the truthfulness of the New Testament. No other work of antiquity has more evidence to its historical veracity than the New Testament. The New Testament has more writers (nine), better writers, and earlier writers than any other existing document from that era. Further, history testifies that these writers went to their deaths claiming that Jesus had risen from the dead. While some may die for a lie they think is true, no person dies for a lie he knows to be false. Think about it—if you were threatened with crucifixion, as tradition says happened to the apostle Peter, and all you had to do to save your life was renounce a lie you had knowingly told, what would you do?

In addition, history has shown that it takes at least two generations to pass before myth can enter a historical account. That's because as long as there are eyewitnesses to an event, errors can be refuted and mythical embellishments can be exposed. All the Gospels of the New Testament were written during the lifetime of the eyewitnesses, with some of Paul's Epistles being written as early as A.D. 50. Paul directly appeals to contemporary eyewitnesses to verify his testimony (1 Corinthians 15:6).

The New Testament attests to the fact that in the first century, Jesus was not mistaken for any other god. When Paul preached in Athens, the elite thinkers of that city said, "'He seems to be a proclaimer of strange deities,'—because he was preaching Jesus and the resurrection. And they took him and brought him to the Areopagus, saying, 'May we know what this new teaching is which you are proclaiming? For you are bringing some strange things to our ears; so we want to know what these things mean'" (Acts 17:18–20, NASB). Clearly, if Paul were simply rehashing stories of other gods, the Athenians would not have referred to his doctrine as a "new" and "strange" teaching. If dying-and-rising gods were plentiful in the first century, why, when the apostle Paul preached Jesus rising from the dead, did the Epicureans and Stoics not remark, "Ah, just like Horus and Mithras"?

In conclusion, the claim that Jesus is a copy of mythological gods originated with authors whose works have been discounted by academia, contain logical fallacies, and cannot compare to the New Testament Gospels, which have withstood nearly 2,000 years of intense scrutiny. The alleged parallels between Jesus and other gods disappear when the original myths are examined. The Jesus-is-a-myth theory relies on selective descriptions, redefined words, and false assumptions.

Jesus Christ is unique in history, with His voice rising above all false gods as He asks the question that ultimately determines a person's eternal destiny: "Who do you say I am?" (Matthew 16:15).

Recommended Resource: The Case for the Real Jesus by Lee Strobel

---

Used with Permission from GotQuestions

https://www.gotquestions.org/Jesus-myth.html

HOW DO WE KNOW JESUS EVER REALLY LIVED?

Q: *"Are there any historical writings, other than the Bible, that prove that Jesus ever really lived?"*

Our A: Yes. Cornelius Tacitus (A.D. 55-120) was considered the greatest historian of ancient Rome. He wrote of Nero who "punished with the most exquisite tortures, the persons commonly called Christians, who were hated for their enormities. Christus [Christ], the founder of the name, was put to death by Pontius Pilate, procurator of Judea in the reign of Tiberius: but the pernicious superstition, repressed for a time, broke out again, not only through Judea where the mischief originated, but through the city of Rome also."[1]

Also, Flavius Josephus, a Jewish historian, (A.D. 38-100+) wrote about Jesus in his *Jewish Antiquities,* saying that Jesus was a wise man who did surprising feats, taught many, won over followers from among Jews and Greeks, that Jesus was believed to be the Messiah, was accused by the Jewish leaders, was condemned to be crucified by Pilate, and was considered to be resurrected.[2]

The existence of Jesus Christ is recorded not only by Josephus and Tacitus, but also by ancient writers such as Suetonius, Thallus, Pliny the Younger, and Lucian. And from the Jewish *Talmud,* "we learn that Jesus was conceived out of wedlock, gathered disciples, made blasphemous claims about himself, and worked miracles, but these miracles are attributed to sorcery and not to God."[3]

Thus, historians both favorable and unfavorable regarding Jesus did write about him. Also there were many historical writings about the early Christians.
For more historical sources, please see https://www.everystudent.com/features/bible.html#4

Note: Many people also have an internal source of confirmation that Jesus existed, and still exists today.

The Bible says that God by His Spirit bears witness of Christ (John 15:26) and convinces the world concerning Him (John 16:8-11). So it's possible for someone without access to ancient historical writings or the Bible to believe that Jesus was real.

A person can hear about Jesus from another source, and God can confirm it by His Spirit.

Footnotes: (1) *Annals* XV, 44 as quoted in *The New Evidence That Demands a Verdict* by Josh McDowell. See this book for other historical sources. (2) Noted in *Jesus Under Fire* by Michael J. Wilkins and J. P. Moreland, Zondervan Publishing. (3) Ibid.

Used with Permission from EveryStudent

https://www.everystudent.com/forum/historical.html

DID JESUS REALLY EXIST?

Is there any historical evidence of Jesus Christ?

Answer: Typically, when this question is asked, the person asking qualifies the question with "outside of the Bible." We do not grant this idea that the Bible cannot be considered a source of evidence for the existence of Jesus. The New Testament contains hundreds of references to Jesus Christ. There are those who date the writing of the Gospels to the second century A.D., more than 100 years after Jesus' death. Even if this were the case (which we strongly dispute), in terms of ancient evidences, writings less than 200 years after events took place are considered very reliable evidences. Further, the vast majority of scholars (Christian and non-Christian) will grant that the Epistles of Paul (at least some of them) were in fact written by Paul in the middle of the first century A.D., less than 40 years after Jesus' death. In terms of ancient manuscript evidence, this is extraordinarily strong proof of the existence of a man named Jesus in Israel in the early first century A.D.

It is also important to recognize that in A.D. 70, the Romans invaded and destroyed Jerusalem and most of Israel, slaughtering its inhabitants. Entire cities were literally burned to the ground. We should not be surprised, then, if much evidence of Jesus' existence was destroyed. Many of the eyewitnesses of Jesus would have been killed. These facts likely limited the amount of surviving eyewitness testimony of Jesus.

Considering that Jesus' ministry was largely confined to a relatively unimportant area in a small corner of the Roman Empire, a surprising amount of information about Jesus can be drawn from secular historical sources. Some of the more important historical evidences of Jesus include the following:

The first-century Roman Tacitus, who is considered one of the more accurate historians of the ancient world, mentioned superstitious "Christians" (from Christus, which is Latin for Christ), who suffered under Pontius Pilate during the reign of Tiberius. Suetonius, chief secretary to Emperor Hadrian, wrote that there was a man named Chrestus (or Christ) who lived during the first century (Annals 15.44).

Flavius Josephus is the most famous Jewish historian. In his Antiquities he refers to James, "the brother of Jesus, who was called Christ." There is a controversial verse (18:3) that says, "Now there was about this time Jesus, a wise man, if it be lawful to call him a man. For he was one who wrought surprising feats....He was [the] Christ...he appeared to them alive again the third day, as the divine prophets had foretold these and ten thousand other wonderful things concerning him." One version reads, "At this time there was a wise man named Jesus. His conduct was good and [he] was known to be virtuous. And many people from among the Jews and the other nations became his disciples. Pilate condemned him to be crucified and to die. But those who became his disciples did not abandon his discipleship. They reported that He had appeared to them three days after his crucifixion, and that He was alive; accordingly He was perhaps the Messiah, concerning whom the prophets have recounted wonders."

Julius Africanus quotes the historian Thallus in a discussion of the darkness which followed the crucifixion of Christ (Extant Writings, 18).

Pliny the Younger, in Letters 10:96, recorded early Christian worship practices including the fact that Christians worshiped Jesus as God and were very ethical, and he includes a reference to the love feast and Lord's Supper.

The Babylonian Talmud (Sanhedrin 43a) confirms Jesus' crucifixion on the eve of Passover and the accusations against Christ of practicing sorcery and encouraging Jewish apostasy.

Lucian of Samosata was a second-century Greek writer who admits that Jesus was worshiped by Christians, introduced new teachings, and was crucified for them. He said that Jesus' teachings included the brotherhood of believers, the importance of conversion, and the importance of denying other gods. Christians lived according to Jesus' laws, believed themselves to be immortal, and were characterized by contempt for death, voluntary self-devotion, and renunciation of material goods.

Mara Bar-Serapion confirms that Jesus was thought to be a wise and virtuous man, was considered by many to be the king of Israel, was put to death by the Jews, and lived on in the teachings of His followers.

Then we have all the Gnostic writings (The Gospel of Truth, The Apocryphon of John, The Gospel of Thomas, The Treatise on Resurrection, etc.) that all mention Jesus.

In fact, we can almost reconstruct the gospel just from early non-Christian sources: Jesus was called the Christ (Josephus), did "magic", led Israel into new teachings, and was hanged on Passover for them (Babylonian Talmud) in Judea (Tacitus), but claimed to be God and would return (Eliezar), which his followers believed, worshipping Him as God (Pliny the Younger).

There is overwhelming evidence for the existence of Jesus Christ, both in secular and biblical history. Perhaps the greatest evidence that Jesus did exist is the fact that literally thousands of Christians in the first century A.D., including the twelve apostles, were willing to give their lives as martyrs for Jesus Christ. People will die for what they believe to be true, but no one will die for what they know to be a lie.

Recommended Resource: The Case for the Real Jesus by Lee Strobel

---

Used with Permission from GotQuestions

https://www.gotquestions.org/did-Jesus-exist.html

HOW CAN A LOVING GOD SEND PEOPLE TO HELL?

Q: "I'm trying to understand how God who is love can send people to be in hell. What's the thought behind going to hell?"

Our A: Here are some things to consider:

(1) **God has given all people enough evidence to know that He exists.**

"...What may be known about God is plain to them [people], because God has made it plain to them. For since the creation of the world God's invisible qualities – His eternal power and divine nature – have been clearly seen, being understood from what has been made, so that men are without excuse."[1]

"The heavens declare the glory of God; the skies proclaim the work of his hands."[2]

(2) **Nonetheless, some people choose not to know Him.**

"They exchanged the truth of God for a lie, and worshiped and served created things rather than the Creator."[3]

"The fool has said in his heart, 'there is no God.'"[4]

"We all, like sheep, have gone astray, each of us has turned to his own way."[5]

(3) **People have been given free will. They can seek God and begin a relationship with Him, or reject God. Whatever people choose, their decision continues after they die.**

Eternal life is life with God, eternally. And Jesus was clear that eternal life is gained by believing in Him. It is a relationship with God that is unending.

"For God so loved the world that He gave His one and only Son, that whoever believes in Him shall not perish but have eternal life."[6]

"Whoever believes in the Son has eternal life…"[7]

"I am the resurrection and the life. He who believes in me will live, even though he dies."[8]

God wants all people to know Him. However, the Bible also reveals that God does not force people to choose Him. He allows people to reject Him. God is love, but God allows people to reject His love, and to remain separated from Him. Jesus said, "*I tell you the truth, whoever hears My word and believes Him who sent Me has eternal life and will not be condemned; he has crossed over from death to life.*" [9]

Footnotes: (1) Romans 1:19,20 (2) Psalms 19:1 (3) Romans 1:25 (4) Psalms 14:1 (5) Isaiah 53:6 (6) John 3:16 (7) John 3:36 (8) John 11:25 (9) John 5:24

Used with Permission from EveryStudent

https://www.everystudent.com/forum/punish.html

WHAT HAPPENS THEN?

Life now. Life then. Life after death?

Today maybe you're in college. Somewhere between the ages of 18 and 24. But what about Tomorrow?

You graduate. You get a job. You get married. You have children. You go through a few more jobs. You buy a house. Okay, THEN what?

You go to soccer games for your kids. You try to be a good parent and spouse. You watch your children go to the prom even though yesterday they were wearing diapers. You do and say the things your parents did and said, even though you vowed you never would.

You have a mid-life crisis or two. Your children graduate from college. You become a grandparent. Someone calls you grandma or grandpa. You live out your life in leisure, drawing income from a retirement fund. You take walks in the morning. You work in the garden. You read the newspaper.

You watch TV. You talk to your children and grandchildren on the phone. You travel.
Okay, THEN what?

Well, then someday you die. If you are fortunate, you live a relatively long life. Seventy to 90 years. If you don't get taken away prematurely by cancer or a car accident. But always, eventually, you die.

Death is the Tomorrow that awaits us all, the inevitable *Then* that none of us can escape.
But is that it? Is there anything more?

Someday you'll be just a corpse. They'll bury your body in the ground. Or burn your body and put your ashes in an urn. The big question is, *Will I cease after that? Will there still be a conscious ME somewhere? Is there really life after death?*

In truth, we probably all hope there is something that comes after. Maybe in the smallest recesses of our minds, we are planning on it.

What are we planning on? A life after death of some sort. Some call it paradise. Some call it heaven. Some also talk of hell.

Another thought that many people possess throughout life, often subconsciously, is: *I'm a basically good person. Therefore, I will get to go to heaven someday.*

Is that how it works?

Many people think they are "good enough" for heaven. It's an assumption we make. If we haven't robbed a bank, or murdered anyone, or cheated on our taxes, we think we're just the kind of folk God is looking for to populate His home. By golly, we are good enough.

At heaven's box office, we bought our ticket by being basically good people all throughout our lives. But what if that thinking is incorrect? THEN what? What a thing to have been wrong about! What a misfire!

If you think you're good enough for heaven, there are two things to consider:

(1) If heaven is a place of perfection[1], how can *anyone* be good enough?

Most of us would say we have a "skeleton in the closet." At least one. Something we hope no one ever finds out about us. A mistake in our past. A poor decision. A moment of weakness or stupidity that we'd rather not think about.

That's the extreme. But there are many other more common things we don't really want others to know or notice about us. It might be the "little white lies" we tell. Or how we talk behind someone's back. Or how we copy other people's homework. Or the unkind words we say to people. Or the unkind thoughts we have about people.

Much more than a one-time regrettable event, our lives, if we closely scrutinize them, show a pattern of wrongdoing. We often don't do what we believe to be right. And we often do what we believe is wrong.

All of us, even people whom we would call basically good, are also basically selfish and basically very imperfect.[2] Everything we do is seen by God.[3] So that means there's no fooling Him. He's perfectly aware of all the good we haven't done (and yet could have), as well as all the bad we've done. He even knows all of our thoughts and all of our motives.

Here's the second thing to consider if we think we're "good enough" for heaven:

(2) Is it possible to be a basically good person and still have rejected God?

Consider Ralph. He's a "good" person. He was ethical in his job. He never stole even a paper clip. He was a faithful father and husband. He provided for his children. He made sacrifices for them and for his wife (whom he never cheated on). He even gave money to many charities throughout his life.

But Ralph, though good in some sense, never "let God in". Many times in his life, Ralph sensed God's desire to come into his life. It was as if God were knocking on the door of Ralph's heart. But Ralph never opened that door. He always came up with some excuse not to. Ironically, one of the recurring excuses was, *I've been a good person all my life. I will go to heaven.*

Ralph wanted to go to heaven. Everyone does. But in reality, Ralph didn't want to know God. And he didn't stop to analyze the huge implications of that decision (the decision to keep God out).

Think about it. Heaven is God's home. If Ralph didn't want to know God during his life on Earth, why would Ralph want to know God in an afterlife? In other words, what Ralph didn't calculate is how much he would LOATHE heaven.

Heaven is a place where God is very present. It's likely that every aspect of heaven will remind one of God, constantly. What a horrible place for Ralph!

Ralph always assumed heaven would be a place of ultimate comfort. But he never considered how ultimately uncomfortable it would be for him, since he didn't want to know God or have a relationship with God. For Ralph, heaven would not be heaven, but rather a type of hell.

Would you let someone into your home even if you knew they didn't want to have anything to do with you? If you knew that everywhere they turned, they'd be reminded of you?

Many people are like Ralph. They want heaven, but they don't want God. And they don't realize that, under those circumstances, heaven would be an awful place to be.

Maybe the truth of the matter is that heaven is for people who know they're not good enough to be there -- but who nonetheless want to be there solely because God is there. They want to know God and be with Him forever. The life-after-death prize isn't heaven, but rather its Primary Occupant.

Do you want to know God? Do you want to learn how to become "good enough" for heaven? See Knowing God Personally.[43]

Go to the link in the footnotes to watch "Bulletproof Faith[44]"

Footnotes: (1) *"Nothing impure will ever enter it, nor will anyone who does what is shameful or deceitful."* (Revelation 21:27)

(2) *"No one is good – except God alone."* (Luke 18:19); more: Isaiah 53:6, Romans 3:10, Romans 3:23, James 2:10

(3) *"Nothing in all creation is hidden from God's sight. Everything is uncovered and laid bare before the eyes of him to whom we must give account."* (Hebrews 4:13); more: Matthew 10:26, 1 Corinthians 4:5

Used with Permission from EveryStudent

https://www.everystudent.com/journeys/then.html

WHY DID JESUS DIE?

The crucifixion of Jesus is a highly significant event for those who believe in Jesus. Here's what happened.

The religious leaders in Jerusalem arrested Jesus, charging Him with blasphemy for claiming to be God. They brought Jesus before the occupying Roman government for sentencing. Pilate, who had the final say, believed Jesus should be set free. But the crowds demanded that Jesus be put to death. "Crucify him! Crucify him!" The verdict: death by crucifixion, the Roman government's method of torture and death.

None of this was a surprise to Jesus. Many times, prior to His crucifixion, Jesus told His disciples that He was going to be arrested, beaten, crucified. He also said that three days after being buried he would come back to life. Jesus said He was laying down his life willingly, for the forgiveness of our sins.

However, the religious leaders were correct. Jesus was very clear about His deity. Jesus said He existed before the creation of the world,[1] that He had power to forgive sins,[2] and answer prayer[3] and grant eternal life.[4] He said to know Him was to know God.[5] To see Him was to see God.[6] To believe in Him was to believe in God. [7] To receive Him was to receive God.[8] To hate Him was to hate God.[9] And to honor Him was to honor God.[10] Jesus offered convincing proof for these statements.

Before Jesus' Crucifixion

For example, only weeks before His crucifixion, a close friend of Jesus' named Lazarus died. Jesus was in another town at the time, but mutual friends sent word to him. By the time Jesus arrived, Lazarus had been buried for four days. Jesus brought him back to life. There were many witnesses, and news spread quickly.

In town after town, Jesus healed every disease, every sickness. He fed crowds of 4,000 people who came to hear Him preach. Another time, 5,000 people. The religious authorities complained, "Look, the world has gone after Him,"[11] "If we let Him go on like this, everyone will believe in Him…"[12]

Jesus' death on the cross was not merely the natural consequences of His miracles and His statements. He was not at their mercy.

Jesus had already proved He had absolute power. In light of that, the whipping, thorns in His head, nails through His wrists and feet did not kill Him. Neither did the slow suffocation on the cross. Jesus could have stepped off the cross at any moment. This was the equivalent of someone bending over and putting their head under water, and choosing to deliberately drown when they had the power to raise their head at any moment. Jesus chose to die. Jesus said, "No one takes My life from Me. I lay it down of my own choosing."[13] He did so purposefully. It was planned. Intentional.

And here's why…

Why Did Jesus Die

To varying degrees, we act in ways that are opposed to God's ways. Just take a quick scan of the news on any given day…racism, murders, sexual abuse, lies, greed, corruption, terrorism, wars, etc. As people we have a great way of messing up our lives and the lives of others. God sees us as lost, blind and under His judgment for our ways. Think how sickened and grieved we are to hear that a 6-year-old girl is kidnapped from her family for sexual abuse. It's such an affront to our moral senses, that even those who oppose the death penalty might be tempted.

Well, *all* of our sin is an affront to a holy God. All of our sin grieves Him. We don't live up to our own standards, let alone His. When honest, we even disgust ourselves at times. So what would a perfectly holy God see?

God says that the penalty for sin is death.[14] This is why, in the Old Testament you see God instructing the Israelites to sacrifice a lamb once a year for the forgiveness of their sins. The lamb died in their place. But that was a temporary forgiveness. They had to do this each year. When Jesus came, the prophet John the Baptist said this about Jesus, "Behold, the lamb of God who takes away the sins of the world."[15]

Jesus came to take the penalty for humanity's sin, for our sin, in our place. Rather than us die and be permanently, eternally separated from God, Jesus paid for our sin on the cross, in order that we could be forever forgiven and have eternal life. This is exactly why Jesus came, as our Savior, to save us from God's judgment, condemnation and payment of our sin. Any sin you have ever committed, or will do, Jesus was aware of while hanging on the cross. Jesus took the punishment for our sins for us.

DaVinci's Last Supper

You've seen the famous painting by Leonardo da Vinci of the "Last Supper" with Jesus sitting at a long table and the disciples sitting next to him on both sides of him. Da Vinci was depicting the dinner that Jesus had with his disciples the night before he was arrested and crucified. At that "Last Supper" Jesus told His disciples that His blood would be "poured out for many for the forgiveness of sins."[16]

Jesus was beaten, whipped nearly to death with a metal or bone tipped "cat-o-nine-tails" torture device, then his wrists and feet nailed to a cross, then uprighted, where He hung until death. A spear was thrust into His side to confirm His death. Jesus, who knew no sin, paid for our sin on the cross. It's not fair. We didn't deserve for Him to take our place. Why would He do it?

We're told, "God shows His love toward us in this: while we were yet sinners, Christ died for us."[17]

Our Response to the Crucifixion of Jesus

What does he ask of us? To earn our forgiveness? No. We could never be worthy of what Jesus did for us. What He asks of us is simple...to believe in Him. He asks us to accept His death on our behalf, to accept His complete forgiveness as a free gift.

Oddly enough, many people don't want to do this. They want to try to earn their own salvation. Earn their own way into heaven. They want to show by their efforts that they are worthy of a relationship with God. Jesus said they will die in their sin and face judgment, because they reject what Jesus did for them. The disciple Peter said of Jesus, "everyone who believes in Him receives forgiveness of sins through His name."[18]

But not only forgiveness, also eternal life and a close, personal relationship with God now, in this life. It is all ours, because Jesus died on the cross for us. Jesus was not merely taking punishment for our sin. He was eliminating the wall that stood between us and God. He was offering far more than forgiveness. He was offering reconciliation, full acceptance, a full relationship with Him, so we could know His love for us.
This is like a wealthy billionaire not only cancelling the debt a person owes him, but then turning over his entire estate to the person who couldn't pay him back.

Eternal life, heaven, is a free gift: "For the payment for sin is death, but the gift of God is eternal life in Christ Jesus our Lord."[19]

Jesus came into the world to die for us, to provide a way for us to know Him intimately. It is our decision to receive the gift of a relationship with Him that He is offering us. Jesus summarized it this way, "I am the way, the truth, and the life; no one comes to the Father except through Me."[20]

His Offer to Us

Anyone who will invite Jesus into their lives and accept his free gift of forgiveness and eternal life, begins a never-ending relationship with Him.

After His crucifixion, they buried Jesus in a tomb and stationed a trained Roman guard of soldiers at His tomb. Why? Jesus had repeatedly said that three days after His burial, He would rise from the dead. It would prove everything He said about Himself. Three days later, the tomb was empty. Jesus then physically appeared to the disciples many times, to a crowd of 500, to individuals. Each of Jesus' disciples went throughout the world proclaiming Jesus' resurrection. Each one was martyred for it, in different locations from each other, so convinced of Jesus' identity.

It is our decision whether to accept the forgiveness He offers, by moving toward Him, asking Him to forgive us and enter our lives. John states it well in the Bible, "We have come to know and to believe the love that God has for us. God is love, and whoever abides in love abides in God, and God abides in him. By this is love perfected with us, so that we may have confidence for the day of judgment."[21]

Jesus explicitly stated, "Truly, truly, I say to you, whoever hears my word and believes Him who sent Me has eternal life. He does not come into judgment, but has passed from death to life."[22]

Jesus' prayer right before His death: "Righteous Father, though the world does not know you, I know you, and they [Jesus' followers] know that you have sent me. I have made you known to them, and will continue to make you known in order that the love you have for me may be in them and that I myself may be in them."[23]
Would you like to invite Jesus Christ into your life right now? Here is how you can.

"Jesus, I ask you to come into my life. Forgive my sin. Thank you for dying on the cross for me. Lead my life as you want. Thank you for coming into my life right now and giving me a relationship with you. Amen."

Footnotes: (1) John 17:24 (2) Matthew 9:6 (3) John 14:13,14 (4) John 5:24 (5) John 8:19 (6) John 12:45; 14:9 (7) John 12:44; 14:1 (8) Mark 9:37 (9) John 15:23 (10) John 5:23 (11) John 12:19 (12) John 11:48 (13) John 10:18 (14) Romans 6:23 (15) John 1:29 (16) Matthew 26:28 (17) Romans 5:8 (18) Acts 10:43 (19) Romans 6:23 (20) John 14:6 (21) 1John 4:16,17 (22) John 5:24 (23) John 17:25,26

Used with Permission from EveryStudent

https://www.everystudent.com/wires/whydid.html

"WHY SHOULD I BELIEVE IN CHRIST'S RESURRECTION?"

Answer: It is a fairly well-established fact that Jesus Christ was publicly executed in Judea in the 1st Century A.D., under Pontius Pilate, by means of crucifixion, at the behest of the Jewish Sanhedrin. The non-Christian historical accounts of Flavius Josephus, Cornelius Tacitus, Lucian of Samosata, Maimonides and even the Jewish Sanhedrin corroborate the early Christian eyewitness accounts of these important historical aspects of the death of Jesus Christ.

As for His resurrection, there are several lines of evidence which make for a compelling case. The late jurisprudential prodigy and international statesman Sir Lionel Luckhoo (of The Guinness Book of World Records fame for his unprecedented 245 consecutive defense murder trial acquittals) epitomized Christian enthusiasm and confidence in the strength of the case for the resurrection when he wrote, "I have spent more than 42 years as a defense trial lawyer appearing in many parts of the world and am still in active practice. I have been fortunate to secure a number of successes in jury trials and I say unequivocally the evidence for the Resurrection of Jesus Christ is so overwhelming that it compels acceptance by proof which leaves absolutely no room for doubt."

The secular community's response to the same evidence has been predictably apathetic in accordance with their steadfast commitment to methodological naturalism. For those unfamiliar with the term, methodological naturalism is the human endeavor of explaining everything in terms of natural causes and natural causes only. If an alleged historical event defies natural explanation (e.g., a miraculous resurrection), secular scholars generally treat it with overwhelming skepticism, regardless of the evidence, no matter how favorable and compelling it may be.

In our view, such an unwavering allegiance to natural causes regardless of substantive evidence to the contrary is not conducive to an impartial (and therefore adequate) investigation of the evidence. We agree with Dr. Wernher von Braun and numerous others who still believe that forcing a popular philosophical predisposition upon the evidence hinders objectivity. Or in the words of Dr. von Braun, "To be forced to believe only one conclusion… would violate the very objectivity of science itself."

Having said that, let us now examine several lines of evidence for Christ's resurrection.

The First Line of Evidence for Christ's resurrection

To begin with, we have demonstrably sincere eyewitness testimony. Early Christian apologists cited hundreds of eyewitnesses, some of whom documented their own alleged experiences. Many of these eyewitnesses willfully and resolutely endured prolonged torture and death rather than repudiate their testimony. This fact attests to their sincerity, ruling out deception on their part. According to the historical record (The Book of Acts 4:1-17; Pliny's Letters to Trajan X, 97, etc) most Christians could end their suffering simply by renouncing the faith. Instead, it seems that most opted to endure the suffering and proclaim Christ's resurrection unto death.

Granted, while martyrdom is remarkable, it is not necessarily compelling. It does not validate a belief so much as it authenticates a believer (by demonstrating his or her sincerity in a tangible way). What makes the earliest Christian martyrs remarkable is that they knew whether or not what they were professing was true. They either saw Jesus Christ alive-and-well after His death or they did not. This is extraordinary. If it was all just a lie, why would so many perpetuate it given their circumstances? Why would they all knowingly cling to such an unprofitable lie in the face of persecution, imprisonment, torture, and death?

While the September 11, 2001, suicide hijackers undoubtedly believed what they professed (as evidenced by their willingness to die for it), they could not and did not know if it was true. They put their faith in traditions passed down to them over many generations. In contrast, the early Christian martyrs were the first generation. Either they saw what they claimed to see, or they did not.

Among the most illustrious of the professed eyewitnesses were the Apostles. They collectively underwent an undeniable change following the alleged post-resurrection appearances of Christ. Immediately following His crucifixion, they hid in fear for their lives. Following the resurrection they took to the streets, boldly proclaiming the resurrection despite intensifying persecution. What accounts for their sudden and dramatic change? It certainly was not financial gain. The Apostles gave up everything they had to preach the resurrection, including their lives.

The Second Line of Evidence for Christ's resurrection

A second line of evidence concerns the conversion of certain key skeptics, most notably Paul and James. Paul was of his own admission a violent persecutor of the early Church. After what he described as an encounter with the resurrected Christ, Paul underwent an immediate and drastic change from a vicious persecutor of the Church to one of its most prolific and selfless defenders. Like many early Christians, Paul suffered impoverishment, persecution, beatings, imprisonment, and execution for his steadfast commitment to Christ's resurrection.

James was skeptical, though not as hostile as Paul. A purported post-resurrection encounter with Christ turned him into an inimitable believer, a leader of the Church in Jerusalem. We still have what scholars generally accept to be one of his letters to the early Church. Like Paul, James willingly suffered and died for his testimony, a fact which attests to the sincerity of his belief (see The Book of Acts and Josephus' Antiquities of the Jews XX, ix, 1).

The Third and Fourth Lines of Evidence for Christ's resurrection

A third line and fourth line of evidence concern enemy attestation to the empty tomb and the fact that faith in the resurrection took root in Jerusalem. Jesus was publicly executed and buried in Jerusalem. It would have been impossible for faith in His resurrection to take root in Jerusalem while His body was still in the tomb where the Sanhedrin could exhume it, put it on public display, and thereby expose the hoax. Instead, the Sanhedrin accused the disciples of stealing the body, apparently in an effort to explain its disappearance (and therefore an empty tomb). How do we explain the fact of the empty tomb? Here are the three most common explanations:

First, the disciples stole the body. If this were the case, they would have known the resurrection was a hoax. They would not therefore have been so willing to suffer and die for it. (See the first line of evidence concerning demonstrably sincere eyewitness testimony.) All of the professed eyewitnesses would have known that they hadn't really seen Christ and were therefore lying. With so many conspirators, surely someone would have confessed, if not to end his own suffering then at least to end the suffering of his friends and family. The first generation of Christians were absolutely brutalized, especially following the conflagration in Rome in A.D. 64 (a fire which Nero allegedly ordered to make room for the expansion of his palace, but which he blamed on the Christians in Rome in an effort to exculpate himself). As the Roman historian Cornelius Tacitus recounted in his Annals of Imperial Rome (published just a generation after the fire):

"Nero fastened the guilt and inflicted the most exquisite tortures on a class hated for their abominations, called Christians by the populace. Christus, from whom the name had its origin, suffered the extreme penalty during the reign of Tiberius at the hands of one of our procurators, Pontius Pilatus, and a most mischievous superstition, thus checked for the moment, again broke out not only in Judaea, the first source of the evil, but even in Rome, where all things hideous and shameful from every part of the world find their centre and become popular. Accordingly, an arrest was first made of all who pleaded guilty; then, upon their information, an immense multitude was convicted, not so much of the crime of firing the city, as of hatred against mankind. Mockery of every sort was added to their deaths. Covered with the skins of beasts, they were torn by dogs and perished, or were nailed to crosses, or were doomed to the flames and burnt, to serve as a nightly illumination, when daylight had expired." (Annals, XV, 44)

Nero illuminated his garden parties with Christians whom he burnt alive. Surely someone would have confessed the truth under the threat of such terrible pain. The fact is, however, we have no record of any early Christian denouncing the faith to end his suffering. Instead, we have multiple accounts of post-resurrection appearances and hundreds of eyewitnesses willing to suffer and die for it.

If the disciples didn't steal the body, how else do we explain the empty tomb? Some have suggested that Christ faked His death and later escaped from the tomb. This is patently absurd. According to the eyewitness testimony, Christ was beaten, tortured, lacerated, and stabbed. He suffered internal damage, massive blood loss, asphyxiation, and a spear through His heart. There is no good reason to believe that Jesus Christ (or any other man for that matter) could survive such an ordeal, fake His death, sit in a tomb for three days and nights without medical attention, food or water, remove the massive stone which sealed His tomb, escape undetected (without leaving behind a trail of blood), convince hundreds of eyewitnesses that He was resurrected from the death and in good health, and then disappear without a trace. Such a notion is ridiculous.

The Fifth Line of Evidence for Christ's resurrection

Finally, a fifth line of evidence concerns a peculiarity of the eyewitness testimony. In all of the major resurrection narratives, women are credited as the first and primary eyewitnesses. This would be an odd invention since in both the ancient Jewish and Roman cultures women were severely disesteemed. Their testimony was regarded as insubstantial and dismissible. Given this fact, it is highly unlikely that any perpetrators of a hoax in 1st Century Judea would elect women to be their primary witnesses. Of all the male disciples who claimed to see Jesus resurrected, if they all were lying and the resurrection was a scam, why did they pick the most ill-perceived, distrusted witnesses they could find?

Dr. William Lane Craig explains, "When you understand the role of women in first-century Jewish society, what's really extraordinary is that this empty tomb story should feature women as the discoverers of the empty tomb in the first place. Women were on a very low rung of the social ladder in first-century Israel. There are old rabbinical sayings that said, 'Let the words of Law be burned rather than delivered to women' and 'blessed is he whose children are male, but woe to him whose children are female.' Women's testimony was regarded as so worthless that they weren't even allowed to serve as legal witnesses in a Jewish court of law. In light of this, it's absolutely remarkable that the chief witnesses to the empty tomb are these women...Any later legendary account would have certainly portrayed male disciples as discovering the tomb - Peter or John, for example. The fact that women are the first witnesses to the empty tomb is most plausibly explained by the reality that - like it or not - they were the discoverers of the empty tomb! This shows that the Gospel writers faithfully recorded what happened, even if it was embarrassing. This bespeaks the historicity of this tradition rather than its legendary status." (Dr. William Lane Craig, quoted by Lee Strobel, The Case For Christ, Grand Rapids: Zondervan, 1998, p. 293)

In Summary

These lines of evidence: the demonstrable sincerity of the eyewitnesses (and in the Apostles' case, compelling, inexplicable change), the conversion and demonstrable sincerity of key antagonists- and skeptics-turned-martyrs, the fact of the empty tomb, enemy attestation to the empty tomb, the fact that all of this took place in Jerusalem where faith in the resurrection began and thrived, the testimony of the women, the significance of such testimony given the historical context; all of these strongly attest to the historicity of the resurrection. We encourage our readers to thoughtfully consider these evidences. What do they suggest to you? Having pondered them ourselves, we resolutely affirm Sir Lionel's declaration:

"The evidence for the Resurrection of Jesus Christ is so overwhelming that it compels acceptance by proof which leaves absolutely no room for doubt."

Recommended Resource: The Case for the Resurrection of Jesus by Gary Habermas

---

Used with Permission from GotQuestions

https://www.gotquestions.org/why-believe-resurrection.html

BEYOND BLIND FAITH

Who is Jesus? Is Jesus God? See what Jesus said about Himself, His equality with God, and what exactly Jesus did to prove it.

By Paul E. Little

It is impossible for us to know conclusively whether God exists and what He is like unless He takes the initiative and reveals Himself.

We must scan the horizon of history to see if there is any clue to God's revelation. There is one clear clue. In an obscure village in Palestine, 2,000 years ago, a Child was born in a stable. Today the entire world is still celebrating the birth of Jesus, and for good reason.

Did Jesus ever claim to be God?

We're told that "the common people heard him gladly." And, "He taught as One who had authority, and not as their teachers of the Law."[1]

It soon became apparent, however, that He was making shocking and startling statements about Himself. He began to identify Himself as far more than a remarkable teacher or prophet. He began to say clearly that He was God. He made his identity the focal point of His teaching. The all-important question he put to those who followed Him was, "Who do you say I am?" When Peter answered and said, "You are the Christ, the Son of the living God,"[2] Jesus was not shocked, nor did He rebuke Peter. On the contrary, He commended him!

Jesus frequently referred to "My Father", and His hearers got the full impact of his words. We are told, "The Jews tried all the harder to kill Him; not only was He breaking the Sabbath, but He was even calling God His own Father, making Himself equal with God."[3]

On another occasion He said, "I and My Father are One." Immediately the religious authorities wanted to stone Him. He asked them which of His good works caused them to want to kill Him. They replied, "We are not stoning you for any of these but for blasphemy, because you, a mere man, claim to be God."[4]

Look at His life.

As Jesus was healing a paralyzed man, Jesus said to him, "Son, your sins are forgiven you." The religious leaders immediately reacted. "Why does this fellow talk like that? He's blaspheming! Who can forgive sins but God alone?"

When Jesus was on trial for His life, the high priest put the question to Him directly: "Are you the Christ, the Son of the Blessed One?" "I am", said Jesus. "And you will see the Son of Man sitting at the right hand of the Mighty One and coming on the clouds of heaven." The high priest rendered the verdict. "Why do we need any more witnesses?" he asked. "You have heard His blasphemy."[5]

So close was Jesus' connection with God that He equated a person's attitude to himself with the person's attitude toward God. Thus, to know Him was to know God.[6] To see Him was to see God.[7] To believe in Him was to believe in God.[8] To receive Him was to receive God.[9] To hate Him was to hate God.[10] And to honor Him was to honor God.[11]

Possible explanations

"As we face the claims of Christ, there are only four possibilities. He was either a liar, mentally ill, a legend, or the Truth."

The question is, was He telling the truth?

Maybe Jesus lied when He said He was God. Perhaps He knew He was not God, but deliberately deceived His hearers. But there is a problem with this reasoning. Even those who deny His deity affirm that He was a great moral teacher. Jesus could hardly be a great moral teacher if, on the most crucial point of his teaching -- His identity -- He was a deliberate liar.

Another possibility is that Jesus was sincere but self-deceived. We have a name for a person today who thinks he is God. Mentally disabled. But as we look at the life of Christ, we see no evidence of the abnormality and imbalance we find in a mentally ill person. Rather, we find the greatest composure under pressure.

A third alternative is that His enthusiastic followers put words into His mouth He would have been shocked to hear. Were He to return, He would immediately repudiate them.

No, modern archeology verifies that four biographies of Christ were written within the lifetime of people who saw, heard and followed Jesus. These gospel accounts contained specific facts and descriptions confirmed by those who were eyewitnesses of Jesus. The early writing of the Gospels by Matthew, Mark, Luke and John, is why they gained such circulation and impact, unlike the fictional Gnostic gospels which appeared centuries later.

Jesus was not a liar, or mentally disabled, or manufactured apart from historical reality. The only other alternative is that Jesus was being consciously truthful when He said He was God.

What is the proof?

From one point of view, however, claims don't mean much. Talk is cheap. Anyone can make claims. There have been others who have claimed to be God. I could claim to be God, and you could claim to be God, but the question all of us must answer is, "What credentials do we bring to substantiate our claim?" In my case it wouldn't take you five minutes to disprove my claim. It probably wouldn't take too much more to dispose of yours.

But when it comes to Jesus of Nazareth, it's not so simple. He had the credentials to back up His claim. He said, "Even though you do not believe Me, believe the evidence of the miracles, that you may learn and understand that the Father is in Me, and I am in the Father."[12]

The life of Jesus - His unique moral character

His moral character coincided with His claims. The quality of His life was such that He was able to challenge His very enemies with the question, "Can any of you prove Me guilty of sin?"[13] He was met by silence, even though He addressed those who would have liked to point out a flaw in His character.

We read of Jesus being tempted by Satan, but we never hear of a confession of sin on His part. He never asked for forgiveness, though He told his followers to do so.

This lack of any sense of moral failure on Jesus' part is astonishing in view of the fact that it is completely contrary to the experience of the saints and mystics throughout the ages. The closer men and women draw to God, the more overwhelmed they are with their own failure, corruption, and shortcomings. The closer one is to a shining light, the more he realizes his need of a bath. This is true also, in the moral realm, for ordinary mortals.

It is also striking that John, Paul, and Peter, all of whom were trained from earliest childhood to believe in the universality of sin, all spoke of the sinlessness of Christ: "He committed no sin, and no deceit was found in His mouth."[14]

Even Pilate, who sentenced Jesus to death, asked, "What evil has He done?" After listening to the crowd, Pilate concluded, "I am innocent of this man's blood; see to it yourselves." The crowd relentlessly demanded Jesus be crucified (for blasphemy, claiming to be God). The Roman centurion who assisted in the crucifixion of Christ said, "Surely He was the Son of God."[15]

He cured the sick

Jesus constantly demonstrated His power and compassion. He made the lame to walk, the blind to see, and healed those with diseases. For example, a man who had been blind from birth. Everyone knew him as the familiar beggar who sat outside the temple. Yet Jesus healed him. As the authorities questioned the beggar about Jesus, he said, "One thing I do know. I was blind but now I see!" he declared. He was astounded that these religious authorities didn't recognize this Healer as the Son of God. "Nobody has ever heard of opening the eyes of a man born blind," he said.[16] To him the evidence was obvious.

His ability to control nature

Jesus also demonstrated a supernatural power over nature itself. He commanded a raging storm of high wind and waves on the Sea of Galilee to be calm. Those in the boat were awestruck, asking, "Who is this? Even the wind and waves obey Him!"[17] He turned water into wine, at a wedding. He fed a massive crowd of 5,000 people, starting with five loaves of bread and two fish. He gave a grieving widow back her only son by raising him from the dead.

Lazarus, a friend of Jesus', died and was buried in a tomb for four days already. Yet Jesus said, "Lazarus, come forth!" and dramatically raised him from the dead, witnessed by many. It is most significant that His enemies did not deny this miracle. Rather, they decided to kill Him. "If we let Him go on like this," they said, "everyone will believe in Him."[18]

Is Jesus God, as he claimed?

Jesus' supreme evidence of deity was His own resurrection from the dead. Five times in the course of His life, Jesus clearly predicted in what specific way He would be killed and affirmed that three days later he would rise from the dead.

Surely this was the great test. It was a claim that was easy to verify. It would either happen or not. It would either confirm His stated identity or destroy it. And significant for you and me, Jesus' rising from the dead would verify or make laughable statements such as these:

"I am the way, the truth, and the life; no one comes to the Father except through Me."[19] "I am the light of the world. He who follows Me will not live in darkness, but will have the light of life."[20] For those who believe in Him, "I give them eternal life..."[21]

So by his own words, He offers this proof, ""The Son of Man is going to be delivered into the hands of men, and they will kill Him. And when He is killed, after three days He will rise."[22]

What this would mean

> "Talk is cheap. Anyone can make claims. But when it comes to Jesus of Nazareth... He had the credentials to
> back up His claim."

If Christ rose, we know with certainty that God exists, what God is like, and how we may know Him in personal experience. The universe takes on meaning and purpose, and it is possible to experience the living God in this life.

On the other hand, if Christ did not rise from the dead, Christianity has no objective validity or reality. The martyrs who went singing to the lions, and contemporary missionaries who have given their lives while taking this message to others, have been poor deluded fools. Paul, the great apostle, wrote, "If Christ has not been raised, our preaching is useless and so is your faith."[23] Paul rested his whole case on the bodily resurrection of Christ.

Did Jesus prove He is God?

Let's look at the evidence for Jesus' resurrection.

Given all the miracles He had performed, Jesus easily could have avoided the cross, but He chose not to. Before His arrest, Jesus said, "I lay down my life that I may take it up again. No one takes it from Me, but I lay it down of my own accord...and I have authority to take it up again."[24]

During his arrest, Jesus' friend Peter tried to defend Him. But Jesus said to Peter, "Put your sword back into its place...Do you think that I cannot appeal to my Father, and He will at once send Me more than twelve legions of angels?"[25] He had that kind of power in heaven and on earth. Jesus went willingly to His death.

Jesus' crucifixion and burial.

Jesus' death was by public execution on a cross, a common form of torture and death, used by the Roman government for many centuries. The accusation against Jesus was for blasphemy (for claiming to be God). Jesus said it was to pay for our sin.

Jesus was lashed with a multi-cord whip having metal or bone fragmented ends. A mock crown of long thorns was beaten into His skull. They forced Him to walk to an execution hill outside of Jerusalem. They put Him on a wooden cross, nailing His wrists and feet to it. He hung there, eventually dying. A sword was thrust into His side to confirm His death.

The body of Jesus was taken from the cross, wrapped in mummy-like linens covered with gummy-wet spices. His body was placed in a solid rock tomb, where a very large boulder was rolled down to it, to secure the entrance.

Everyone knew that Jesus said He would rise from the dead in three days. So they stationed a guard of trained Roman soldiers at the tomb. They also affixed an official Roman seal to the outside of the tomb declaring it government property.

Three days later, the tomb was empty.

In spite of all this, three days later the boulder, formerly sealing the tomb, was found up a slope, some distance away from the tomb. The body was gone. Only the grave linens were found in the tomb, caved in, empty of the body.

It is important to note that both critics and followers of Jesus agree that the tomb was empty and the body missing. The earliest explanation circulated was that the disciples stole the body while the guards were sleeping. This makes little sense. This was an entire guard of highly trained Roman soldiers, and falling asleep on duty was punishable by death.

Further, each of the disciples (individually and separately from each other) were tortured and martyred for proclaiming that Jesus was alive, risen from the dead. Men and women will die for what they believe to be true, though it may actually be false. They do not, however, die for what they know is a lie. If ever a man tells the truth, it is on his deathbed.

Maybe the authorities moved the body? Yet they crucified Jesus to stop people from believing in Him. This also is a weak possibility. If they had Christ's body, they could have paraded it through the streets of Jerusalem. In one fell swoop they would have successfully smothered Christianity in its cradle. That they did not do this bears eloquent testimony to the fact that they did not have the body.

Another theory is that the women, distraught and overcome by grief, missed their way in the dimness of the morning and went to the wrong tomb. In their distress they imagined Christ had risen because the tomb was empty. But again, if the women went to the wrong tomb, why did the high priests and other enemies of the faith not go to the right tomb and produce the body?

"Men and women will die for what they believe to be true, though it may actually be false. They do not, however, die for what they know is a lie."

One other possibility is what some call "the swoon theory." In this view, Christ did not actually die. He was mistakenly reported to be dead, but had swooned from exhaustion, pain, and loss of blood, and in the coolness of the tomb, He revived. (One would have to overlook the fact that they put a spear in his side to medically confirm his death.)

But let us assume for a moment that Christ was buried alive and swooned. Is it possible to believe that He would have survived three days in a damp tomb without food or water or attention of any kind? Would He have had the strength to extricate Himself from the grave clothes, push the heavy stone away from the mouth of the grave, overcome the Roman guards, and walk miles on feet that had been pierced with spikes? It too makes little sense.

However, it wasn't the empty tomb that convinced Jesus' followers of His deity.

Not just the empty tomb.

That alone did not convince them that Jesus actually rose from the dead, was alive, and was God. What convinced them were the number of times that Jesus showed up, in person, in the flesh, and ate with them, and talked with them. Luke, one of the gospel writers, says of Jesus, "He presented Himself to them and gave many convincing proofs that He was alive. He appeared to them over a period of forty days and spoke about the kingdom of God."[26]

Is Jesus God?

All four of the gospel writers give accounts of Jesus physically showing up after His burial, obviously alive. One time that Jesus joined the disciples, Thomas, was not there. When they told him about it, Thomas simply wouldn't believe it. He flatly stated, "Unless I see the nail marks in His hands and put my finger where the nails were, and put my hand into His side, I will not believe it."

One week later, Jesus came to them again, with Thomas now present. Jesus said to Thomas, "Put your finger here; see My hands. Reach out your hand and put it into My side. Stop doubting and believe." Thomas replied, "My Lord and my God!" Jesus told him "Because you have seen Me, you have believed; blessed are those who have not seen and yet have believed."[27]

Your opportunity

Why did Jesus go through all of that? It was so we could know God now, in this life, by believing in Him. Jesus offers us a far more meaningful life, by being in a relationship with Him. Jesus said, "I came that they might have life, and have it abundantly."[28]

You can begin an intimate relationship with Him right now. You can begin to personally know God in this life on earth, and after death into eternity. Here is God's promise to us:

"For God so loved the world, that He gave his only Son, that whoever believes in Him should not perish but have eternal life."[29] Jesus took our sin on himself, on the cross. He chose to receive punishment for our sin, so that our sin would no longer be a barrier between us and Him. Because He fully paid for your sin, He offers you complete forgiveness and a relationship with Him.

Here is how you can begin that relationship. Jesus said, "Behold, I stand at the door [of your heart] and knock; if anyone hears my voice and opens the door, I will come into him."[30] Right now, you can invite Jesus Christ into your life. The words are not important. What matters is that you respond to Him, in light of what He has done for you, and is now offering you.

You could say to Him something like, "Jesus, I believe in you. Thank you for dying on the cross for my sins. I ask you to forgive me and to come into my life right now. I want to know you and follow you. Thank you for coming into my life and giving me a relationship with you, right now. Thank you."

Adapted from *Know Why You Believe* by Paul E. Little, published by Victor Books, copyright (c) 1988, SP Publications, Inc., Wheaton, IL 60187. Used by permission.

Footnotes: (1) Matthew 7:29 (2) Matthew 16:15-16 (3) John 5:18 (4) John 10:33 (5) Mark 14:61-64 (6) John 8:19; 14:7 (7) 12:45; 14:9 (8) 12:44; 14:1 (9) Mark 9:37 (10) John 15:23 (11) John 5:23 (12) John 10:38 (13) John 8:46 (14) 1 Peter 2:22 (15) Matthew 27:54 (16) John 9:25, 32 (17) Mark 4:41 (18) John 11:48 (19) John 14:6 (20) John 8:12 (21) John 10:28 (22) Mark 9:31 (23) 1 Corinthians 15:14 (24) John 10:18 (25) Matthew 26:52,53 (26) Acts 1:3 (27) John 20:24-29 (28) John 10:10 (29) John 3:16 (30) Revelation 3:20

Used with Permission from EveryStudent

https://www.everystudent.com/features/faith.html

Facilitator Guide Appendix

Facilitator Guide Appendix cont.

What Makes this Second Appendix Different from the First One?

The first appendix which is labeled, "Study Guide Appendix," is a copy of the Appendix found in *Tetelestai's Study Guide,* the student book for *Tetelestai.* It is important for you to know exactly what your students are being encouraged to read. The appendix contains various articles that will assist the student in the study of God's Word.

Whereas this second appendix, the "Facilitator Guide Appendix," is only found in your leader's guide and contains articles answering **specific questions from people of various socio-religious backgrounds.**

For example, you may be reaching out to a Muslim coworker who thinks the concept of God having a Son is blasphemy. We've included an article here that will help you know how to answer him or her biblically.

...Or you may have someone in your Bible Study who comes from an idolatrous culture, we've included extra material on how to help untangle the deception they have lived in by guiding him or her through the Scriptures.

IS THE BIBLE GOD'S WORD? OR HAS IT BEEN CHANGED, OR CORRUPTED OVER TIME?

Just as introduction, here are a few statements found in the Bible: "Until heaven and earth disappear, not the smallest letter, not the least stroke of a pen will by any means disappear, from the Law until everything has been accomplished."[1]

The Word of God will not disappear. Everything in it will be accomplished in its entirety till the very end. Again it states, "Heaven and earth will pass away but my words will never pass away."[2]

Also, "All scripture is God-breathed and useful for teaching, rebuking, correcting and training in righteousness."[3] All scripture is inspired by God.

And, "the grass withers and the flowers fall, but the Word of our God stands forever."[4]

We need to ask ourselves, "Is God able to protect His word? Is God able to fulfill these statements, that His word will never disappear, never go unfulfilled?"

Is God capable? Yes, of course. This is God's word to all people. Are we accusing God himself by saying that He was not able to protect it from being changed? Nothing has been changed. That is only a rumor. The Quran does not say the Bible has been changed. Just the opposite. It honors the Torah and the Bible. It mentions the Torah, and the "Zabur" (the Old Testament and Psalms) and the "Injil" (the New Testament) many times. When Islam began in the 6th century, 600 years after Jesus Christ, the Bible was accepted as true.

So, you might ask, has the Bible changed since the 6th century? No. All you have to do is compare today's Bible with a Bible written long ago. We can find complete Bibles, all the way back to 300 A.D., hundreds of years before the Quran. You can find one in the London Museum, in the Vatican, and many other places. If you compare today's Bible with the Bibles of 300 A.D., the Bible we have today is the same as then.

Did you know that there exists today nearly 25,000 hand-written copies of portions of the New Testament? As historians have compared these manuscripts, they have concluded that the New Testament we have today is at least 99.5% accurate to the original. No change. (The .5% differences refer to spelling, but no change in meaning.)

Also, you might be familiar with the more recent archeological findings of the Dead Sea Scrolls. These were found in caves of Qumran, just off the northwest corner of the Dead Sea. Researchers have compared the Bible we have today with what they found, and they remained highly similar, nearly 100% identical.

Don't let anyone tell you that the New Testament or the Bible has been changed from its original writing. That simply is not historically accurate. The Bible has not been changed.

Ok, but what about having four Gospels? Aren't those different Scriptures, different from each other?

Yes, there are four gospels: Matthew, Mark, Luke, and John, in the New Testament. These actually help show that the Bible has never been falsified. These are four witnesses, four accounts of Jesus' life, what He said, what He did.

Imagine if one or two, or let's say four people, witnessed a car accident on a corner of a street. And each one was asked to write up their account, their witness of the accident for the court. Do you think that each one would give the exact same description, exactly the same witness, word-for-word? Obviously not. Each one would write from his or her own perspective of what he or she saw. And that's what happened when each of these witnesses wrote their account, as eyewitnesses of Jesus.

For centuries judicial systems have involved witnesses. And, on very important matters, it cannot be one person's word against another's. Often, you need more than one witness. Here's a statement in the New Testament, quoting from the Old Testament, "Every matter must be established by the witness of two or three people."[5]

Not only are there four witnesses about Jesus who wrote the gospels, but there are many more witnesses. James, Paul, Jude, Peter, and others wrote the rest of the books in the New Testament.

John said, "[We write] what our eyes have seen, what our hands have touched."[6] They were eyewitnesses to Jesus. So they wrote what they saw.

What about all the languages that the Bible is written in, all the translations?

The Bible was written in Hebrew and Greek. Any Bible, no matter what year it was printed, is always a translation from the original Hebrew and Greek languages. (Bibles are never translated English to English, for example. They always start with the original text.)

There are some Bibles that are paraphrases, not translations. And they are identified as paraphrases. However, translations, are just that -- translating what the original Hebrew and Greek text states.

The Hebrew and Greek writings of the Bible have been translated into thousands of languages. Why? Because God wants every person in the world to know the good news of salvation.

And the Bible is not difficult to translate. There are portions of the Bible that are poetic (the Proverbs, the Song of Solomon, the Psalms). But the heart of the Bible itself is a very simple language that deals with our daily lives. It is not hard to translate. The fact that the Bible is a straightforward, simple account is another reason to trust the Bible.

Here's a true story.
"My son called me one day. He was in another country, in the middle of a big highway, in a car accident. His car was hit by another car, and was turned 180 degrees, landing in the middle of the highway, in the wrong direction. He said, 'Dad, I'm ok. But what do I do now?'

He's in trouble. He needed help. Well, do you think this is the time that I will send him a poetic message? A poem that I have memorized? No.

This is the time to simply say, 'John, here's what you need to do. You're in deep trouble and here is how to get out of it.' And that really is the heart of the Bible. Humanity is in trouble, heading for hell. For all have sinned and come short of the glory of God. And we need a simple message of salvation. The Bible tells us how we can be forgiven, how we can be brought into a close relationship with God that begins now and lasts eternally. It is a message that changes our lives.

Footnotes: (1) Matthew 5:18 (2) Matthew 24:35 (3) 2 Timothy 3:16 (4) Isaiah 40:8 (5) 2 Corinthians 13:1 (6) 1 John 1:1

Used with Permission from EveryStudent
https://www.everystudent.com/wires/jesusislam.html#1

IS THERE A GOD?

Does God exist? Here are six straightforward reasons to believe that God is really there.

By Marilyn Adamson

Just once wouldn't you love for someone to simply show you the evidence for God's existence? No arm-twisting. No statements of, "You just have to believe." Well, here is an attempt to candidly offer some of the reasons which suggest that God exists.

But first consider this. When it comes to the possibility of God's existence, the Bible says that there are people who have seen sufficient evidence, but they have suppressed the truth about God.[1] On the other hand, for those who want to know God if He is there, He says, "You will seek Me and find me; when you seek Me with all your heart, I will be found by you."[2] Before you look at the facts surrounding His existence, ask yourself, *If God does exist, would I want to know him?* Here then, are some reasons to consider...

1. The complexity of our planet points to a deliberate Designer who not only created our universe, but sustains it today.

Many examples showing God's design could be given, possibly with no end. But here are a few:

The Earth...its size is perfect. The Earth's size and corresponding gravity holds a thin layer of mostly nitrogen and oxygen gases, only extending about 50 miles above the Earth's surface. If Earth were smaller, an atmosphere would be impossible, like the planet Mercury. If Earth were larger, its atmosphere would contain free hydrogen, like Jupiter.[3] Earth is the only known planet equipped with an atmosphere of the right mixture of gases to sustain plant, animal and human life.

The Earth is located the right distance from the sun. Consider the temperature swings we encounter, roughly -30 degrees to +120 degrees. If the Earth were any further away from the sun, we would all freeze. Any closer and we would burn up. Even a fractional variance in the Earth's position to the sun would make life on Earth impossible. The Earth remains this perfect distance from the sun while it rotates around the sun at a speed of nearly 67,000 mph. It is also rotating on its axis, allowing the entire surface of the Earth to be properly warmed and cooled every day.

And our moon is the perfect size and distance from the Earth for its gravitational pull. The moon creates important ocean tides and movement so ocean waters do not stagnate, and yet our massive oceans are restrained from spilling over across the continents.[4]

Water...colorless, odorless and without taste, and yet no living thing can survive without it. Plants, animals and human beings consist mostly of water (about two-thirds of the human body is water). You'll see why the characteristics of water are uniquely suited to life: It has a wide margin between its boiling point and freezing point. Water allows us to live in an environment of fluctuating temperature changes, while keeping our bodies a steady 98.6 degrees.

Water is a universal solvent. This property of water means that various chemicals, minerals and nutrients can be carried throughout our bodies and into the smallest blood vessels.[5] Water is also chemically neutral. Without affecting the makeup of the substances it carries, water enables food, medicines and minerals to be absorbed and used by the body.

Water has a unique surface tension. Water in plants can therefore flow upward against gravity, bringing life-giving water and nutrients to the top of even the tallest trees. Water freezes from the top down and floats, so fish can live in the winter.

Ninety-seven percent of the Earth's water is in the oceans. But on our Earth, there is a system designed which removes salt from the water and then distributes that water throughout the globe. Evaporation takes the ocean waters, leaving the salt, and forms clouds which are easily moved by the wind to disperse water over the land, for vegetation, animals and people. It is a system of purification and supply that sustains life on this planet, a system of recycled and reused water.[6]

The human brain...simultaneously processes an amazing amount of information. Your brain takes in all the colors and objects you see, the temperature around you, the pressure of your feet against the floor, the sounds around you, the dryness of your mouth, even the texture of your keyboard. Your brain holds and processes all your emotions, thoughts and memories. At the same time your brain keeps track of the ongoing functions of your body like your breathing pattern, eyelid movement, hunger and movement of the muscles in your hands.

The human brain processes more than a million messages a second.[7] Your brain weighs the importance of all this data, filtering out the relatively unimportant. This screening function is what allows you to focus and operate effectively in your world. The brain functions differently than other organs. There is an intelligence to it, the ability to reason, to produce feelings, to dream and plan, to take action, and relate to other people.

The eye...can distinguish among seven million colors. It has automatic focusing and handles an astounding 1.5 million messages -- simultaneously.[8] Evolution focuses on mutations and changes from and within existing organisms. Yet evolution alone does not fully explain the initial source of the eye or the brain -- the start of living organisms from nonliving matter.

2. The universe had a start - what caused it?

Scientists are convinced that our universe began with one enormous explosion of energy and light, which we now call the Big Bang. This was the singular start to everything that exists: the beginning of the universe, the start of space, and even the initial start of time itself.

Astrophysicist Robert Jastrow, a self-described agnostic, stated, "The seed of everything that has happened in the Universe was planted in that first instant; every star, every planet and every living creature in the Universe came into being as a result of events that were set in motion in the moment of the cosmic explosion...The Universe flashed into being, and we cannot find out what caused that to happen."[9]

Steven Weinberg, a Nobel laureate in Physics, said at the moment of this explosion, "the universe was about a hundred thousands million degrees Centigrade...and the universe was filled with light."[10]

The universe has not always existed. It had a start...what caused that? Scientists have no explanation for the sudden explosion of light and matter.

3. The universe operates by uniform laws of nature. Why does it?

Much of life may seem uncertain, but look at what we can count on day after day: gravity remains consistent, a hot cup of coffee left on a counter will get cold, the earth rotates in the same 24 hours, and the speed of light doesn't change -- on earth or in galaxies far from us.

How is it that we can identify laws of nature that *never* change? Why is the universe so orderly, so reliable? "The greatest scientists have been struck by how strange this is. There is no logical necessity for a universe that obeys rules, let alone one that abides by the rules of mathematics. This astonishment springs from the recognition that the universe doesn't have to behave this way. It is easy to imagine a universe in which conditions change unpredictably from instant to instant, or even a universe in which things pop in and out of existence."[11]

Richard Feynman, a Nobel Prize winner for quantum electrodynamics, said, "Why nature is mathematical is a mystery...The fact that there are rules at all is a kind of miracle."[12]

4. The DNA code informs, programs a cell's behavior.

All instruction, all teaching, all training comes with intent. Someone who writes an instruction manual does so with purpose. Did you know that in every cell of our bodies there exists a very detailed instruction code, much like a miniature computer program? As you may know, a computer program is made up of ones and zeros, like this: 110010101011000. The way they are arranged tell the computer program what to do. The DNA code in each of our cells is very similar. It's made up of four chemicals that scientists abbreviate as A, T, G, and C. These are arranged in the human cell like this: CGTGTGACTCGCTCCTGAT and so on. There are three billion of these letters in every human cell!!

Well, just like you can program your phone to beep for specific reasons, DNA instructs the cell. DNA is a three-billion-lettered program telling the cell to act in a certain way. It is a full instruction manual.[13]

Why is this so amazing? One has to ask....how did this information program wind up in each human cell? These are not just chemicals. These are chemicals that instruct, that code in a very detailed way exactly how the person's body should develop. Natural, biological causes are completely lacking as an explanation when programmed information is involved. You cannot find instruction, precise information like this, without someone intentionally constructing it.

5. We know God exists because He pursues us. He is constantly initiating and seeking for us to come to Him.

I was an atheist at one time. And like many atheists, the issue of people believing in God bothered me greatly. What is it about atheists that we would spend so much time, attention, and energy refuting something that we don't believe even exists?! What causes us to do that? When I was an atheist, I attributed my intentions as caring for those poor, delusional people...to help them realize their hope was completely ill-founded. To be honest, I also had another motive. As I challenged those who believed in God, I was deeply curious to see if they could convince me otherwise. Part of my quest was to become free from the question of God. If I could conclusively prove to believers that they were wrong, then the issue is off the table, and I would be free to go about my life.

I didn't realize that the reason the topic of God weighed so heavily on my mind, was because God was pressing the issue. I have come to find out that God wants to be known. He created us with the intention that we would know Him. He has surrounded us with evidence of Himself and He keeps the question of His existence squarely before us. It was as if I couldn't escape thinking about the possibility of God. In fact, the day I chose to acknowledge God's existence, my prayer began with, "Ok, you win..." It might be that the underlying reason atheists are bothered by people believing in God is because God is actively pursuing them.

I am not the only one who has experienced this. Malcolm Muggeridge, socialist and philosophical author, wrote, "I had a notion that somehow, besides questing, I was being pursued." C.S. Lewis said he remembered, "...night after night, feeling whenever my mind lifted even for a second from my work, the steady, unrelenting approach of Him whom I so earnestly desired not to meet. I gave in, and admitted that God was God, and knelt and prayed: perhaps, that night, the most dejected and reluctant convert in all of England."

Lewis went on to write a book titled, "Surprised by Joy" as a result of knowing God. I too had no expectations other than rightfully admitting God's existence. Yet over the following several months, I became amazed by his love for me.

6. Unlike any other revelation of God, Jesus Christ is the clearest, most specific picture of God revealing Himself to us.

Why Jesus? Look throughout the major world religions and you'll find that Buddha, Mohammad, Confucius and Moses all identified themselves as teachers or prophets. None of them ever claimed to be equal to God. Surprisingly, Jesus did. That is what sets Jesus apart from all the others. He said God exists and you're looking at Him. Though he talked about His Father in heaven, it was not from the position of separation, but of very close union, unique to all humankind. Jesus said that anyone who had seen Him had seen the Father, anyone who believed in him, believed in the Father.

He said, "I am the light of the world, he who follows Me will not walk in darkness, but will have the light of life."[14] He claimed attributes belonging only to God: to be able to forgive people of their sin, free them from habits of sin, give people a more abundant life and give them eternal life in heaven. Unlike other teachers who focused people on their words, Jesus pointed people to himself. He did not say, "follow my words and you will find truth." He said, "I am the way, the truth, and the life, no one comes to the Father but through Me."[15]

What proof did Jesus give for claiming to be divine?

He did what people can't do. Jesus performed miracles. He healed people...blind, crippled, deaf, even raised a couple of people from the dead. He had power over objects...created food out of thin air, enough to feed crowds of several thousand people. He performed miracles over nature...walked on top of a lake, commanding a raging storm to stop for some friends. People everywhere followed Jesus, because He constantly met their needs, doing the miraculous. He said if you do not want to believe what I'm telling you, you should at least believe in Me based on the miracles you're seeing.[16]

Jesus Christ showed God to be gentle, loving, aware of our self-centeredness and shortcomings, yet deeply wanting a relationship with us. Jesus revealed that although He views us as sinners, worthy of his punishment, His love for us ruled and He came up with a different plan. God himself took on the form of man and accepted the punishment for our sin on our behalf. Sounds ludicrous? Perhaps, but many loving fathers would gladly trade places with their child in a cancer ward if they could. The Bible says that the reason we would love God is because he first loved us.

Jesus died in our place so we could be forgiven. Of all the religions known to humanity, only through Jesus will you see God reaching toward humanity, providing a way for us to have a relationship with Him. Jesus proves a divine heart of love, meeting our needs, drawing us to himself. Because of Jesus' death and resurrection, He offers us a new life today. We can be forgiven, fully accepted by God and genuinely loved by God. He says, "I have loved you with an everlasting love, therefore I have continued my faithfulness to you."[17] This is God, in action.

Does God exist? If you want to know, investigate Jesus Christ. We're told that "God so loved the world that He gave his only Son, that whoever believes in Him should not perish but have eternal life."[18]

God does not force us to believe in him, though He could. Instead, He has provided sufficient proof of His existence for us to willingly respond to Him. The earth's perfect distance from the sun, the unique chemical properties of water, the human brain, DNA, the number of people who attest to knowing God, the gnawing in our hearts and minds to determine if God is there, the willingness for God to be known through Jesus Christ. If you need to know more about Jesus and reasons to believe in Him, please see: Beyond Blind Faith.[45]

If you want to begin a relationship with God now, you can.

This is your decision, no coercion here. But if you want to be forgiven by God and come into a relationship with Him, you can do so right now by asking Him to forgive you and come into your life. Jesus said, "Behold, I stand at the door [of your heart] and knock. He who hears my voice and opens the door, I will come into him [or her]."[19] If you want to do this, but aren't sure how to put it into words, this may help: "Jesus, thank you for dying for my sins. You know my life and that I need to be forgiven. I ask you to forgive me right now and come into my life. I want to know you in a real way. Come into my life now. Thank you that you wanted a relationship with me. Amen."

God views your relationship with him as permanent. Referring to all those who believe in him, Jesus Christ said of us, "I know them, and they follow me; and I give them eternal life, and they shall never perish, and no one shall snatch them out of my hand."[20]

Looking at all these facts, one can conclude that a loving God does exist and can be known in an intimate, personal way.

[45] https://www.everystudent.com/features/faith.html

Footnotes: (1) Romans 1:19-21 (2) Jeremiah 29:13-14 (3) R.E.D. Clark, *Creation* (London: Tyndale Press, 1946), p. 20 (4) The Wonders of God's Creation, Moody Institute of Science (Chicago, IL) (5) Ibid. (6) Ibid. (7) Ibid. (8) Hugh Davson, *Physiology of the Eye,* 5th ed (New York: McGraw Hill, 1991) (9) Robert Jastrow; "Message from Professor Robert Jastrow"; *LeaderU.com;* 2002. (10) Steven Weinberg; *The First Three Minutes: A Modern View of the Origin of the Universe;* (Basic Books, 1988); p 5. (11) Dinesh D'Souza, *What's So Great about Christianity;* (Regnery Publishing, Inc, 2007, chapter 11). (12) Richard Feynman, *The Meaning of It All: Thoughts of a Citizen-Scientist* (New York: BasicBooks, 1998), 43. (13) Francis S. Collins, director of the Human Genome Project, and author of *The Language of God,* (Free Press, New York, NY), 2006 (14) John 8:12 (15) John 14:6 (16) John 14:11 (17) Jeremiah 31:3 (18) John 3:16 (10) Revelation 3:20 (20) John 10:27-29

Used with Permission from EveryStudent
https://www.everystudent.com/features/isthere.html

CAN YOU EXPLAIN THE TRINITY?

The following clearly and briefly explains the Trinity...three gods or one?

You and I live in a three-dimensional world. All physical objects have a certain height, width, and depth. One person can look like someone else, or behave like someone else, or even sound like someone else. But a person cannot actually be the same as another person. They are distinct individuals.

God, however, lives without the limitations of a three-dimensional universe. He is spirit. And He is infinitely more complex than we are. That is why Jesus the Son can be different from the Father. And, yet the same. The Bible clearly speaks of: God the Son, God the Father, and God the Holy Spirit. But emphasizes that there is only ONE God.

If we were to use math, it would not be, $1+1+1=3$. It would be $1 \times 1 \times 1 = 1$. God is a triune God. Thus the term: "Tri" meaning three, and "Unity" meaning one, Tri+Unity = Trinity. It is a way of acknowledging what the Bible reveals to us about God, that God is yet three "Persons" who have the same essence of deity.

Some have tried to give human illustrations for the Trinity, such as H_2O being water, ice and steam (all different forms, but all are H_2O). Another illustration would be the sun. From it we receive light, heat and radiation. Three distinct aspects, but only one sun.

No illustration is going to be perfect.

But from the very beginning we see God as a Trinity. In the book of Genesis, the first book in the Bible, God says, "Let *us* make man in *our* image...male and female *he* created them."[1] You see here a mixture of plural and singular pronouns.

When Moses asked God for His name, God replied, "I am" - eternally existing. Jesus used the same phrase numerous times.
"I am the light of the world..."
"I am the bread of life..."
"I am the way, the truth and the life. No one comes to the Father except through me."

Abraham is someone mentioned in Genesis, thousands of years before Jesus came to earth. Yet, Jesus said of himself, "Before Abraham was born, I am." The Jews understood fully what Jesus was saying because they picked up stones to kill Him for "blasphemy" - claiming to be God.[2] Jesus has always existed.

This came up time and time again. Jesus was so clear about his unique relationship with the Father. This is why, "the Jewish leaders tried all the harder to find a way to kill Him. For He not only broke the Sabbath, He called God his Father, thereby making himself equal with God."[3] For all of eternity, the Father, Son and Holy Spirit have always been in relationship and communication with each other, yet not as three gods…as one God.

This answers the question:

If Jesus is God, who was He praying to?

On earth, Jesus continued to talk to the Father, and the Father and Spirit continued to communicate with Him. Though not a complete list, here is some other Scripture that shows God is one, in Trinity:

- "Hear, O Israel! The LORD is our God, the LORD is one!"[4]

- "I am the LORD, and there is no other; Besides Me there is no God."[5]

- There is no God but one.[6]

- And after being baptized, Jesus went up immediately from the water; and behold, the heavens were opened, and he saw the Spirit of God descending as a dove, and coming upon Him, and behold, a voice out of the heavens, saying, "This is My beloved Son, in whom I am well-pleased."[7]

- "Go therefore and make disciples of all the nations, baptizing them in the name of the Father and the Son and the Holy Spirit."[8]

- Jesus said: "I and the Father are one."[9]
- "He who has seen Me has seen the Father."[10]

- "He who beholds Me beholds the One who sent Me."[11]

- If anyone does not have the Spirit of Christ, he does not belong to Him.[12]

- "Joseph, son of David, do not be afraid to take Mary as your wife; for that which has been conceived in her is of the Holy Spirit."[13]

- And the angel answered and said to her [Mary], "The Holy Spirit will come upon you, and the power of the Most High will overshadow you; and for that reason the holy offspring shall be called the Son of God."[14]

- [Jesus speaking to His disciples] "And I will ask the Father, and He will give you another Helper, that He may be with you forever; the Spirit of truth, whom the world cannot receive, because it does not behold Him or know Him, but you know Him because He abides with you, and will be in you." ... "If anyone loves Me, he will keep My word; and My Father will love him, and We will come to him, and make Our abode with him."[15]

Footnotes: (1) Genesis 1:26,27 (2) John 8:56-59 (3) John 5:16-18 (4) Deut. 6:4 (5) Isa. 45:5 (6) 1Cor. 8:4 (7) Matt. 3:16-17 (8) Matt. 28:19 (9) John 10:30 (10) John 14:9 (11) John 12:45 (12) Rom. 8:9 (13) Matt. 1:20 (14) Luke 1:35 (15) John 14:16-17, 23

Used with Permission from EveryStudent

https://www.everystudent.com/forum/trinity.html

IS IT NOT BLASPHEMY TO SUGGEST THAT GOD WOULD HAVE A SON?

God is spirit. And Jesus is only God's Son in a spiritual sense, not in a physical way. If someone says, "You are the Son of the Cedars" it means that person is from Lebanon. Or, if from Egypt, "You are the Son of the Nile." To say that Jesus is the Son of God, means that Jesus is from God. It is like a title. When the angel appeared to Mary, the angel said, "the holy One to be born will be *called* the Son of God." A title. Christians do not believe that God had any sexual relationship with any woman.

Isaiah said, "For a child is born to us, a son is given to us. The government will rest on his shoulders. *And he will be called:* Wonderful Counselor, Mighty God, Everlasting Father, Prince of Peace."[9]

He is God, who became a man, through Mary. He is God and Son at the same time, born of the virgin Mary. Why do you think God allowed Jesus to be born from a virgin Mary? To be born of a woman, and not from a man & woman, means He did not take on the sinful nature of Adam and Eve. When Adam and Eve fell into sin, they passed on the sinful nature from one generation to another, through their own children, down to us.

We are all born as sinners. We're all born with a tendency toward doing things our way, instead of God's way. We all sin. That's why the prophet David cried out, "With sin, my mother conceived me." We all were born with sin. We live as sinful people and we all need a redeemer.

But for Jesus to redeem us, He needed to have a different nature. He needed to be from the spirit of God, the Holy Spirit, no sinfulness at all. Isaiah said, "No deceit was found in Him." No sin in Him.

In Scripture, God took on the form of a burning bush when revealing Himself to Moses. He took on the voice of heaven when speaking to Abraham. Who is to say that God is not allowed to take on the form of man in order to reveal himself to us?

Footnotes: (9) Isaiah 9:6

Used with Permission from EveryStudent
https://www.everystudent.com/wires/jesusislam.html#3

"IS JESUS GOD'S SON? HOW COULD ALLAH, BEING ONE, HAVE A SON?"

Answer: Muslims ask, "How could Allah, being one, have a Son?" Misunderstanding the Trinity, they sometimes charge Christians with worshiping three gods. However, Christians believe that only one true God exists.

Jesus Himself upheld monotheism. When asked for the greatest command, Jesus responded, "... The Lord our God, the Lord is one. And you shall love the Lord your God with all your heart and with all your soul and with all your mind and with all your strength" (Mark 12:29-30).

Jesus taught that God is one, and Jesus taught that He was one with God (John 10:30). In response, the Jews picked up stones to stone Jesus because they thought He was guilty of blasphemy. Similarly, Muslims would say a man claiming to be God would be guilty of "shirk." However, Jesus is not a mere man claiming to be God. He is the Son of God in human flesh (John 10:36-38).

The title "Son of God" does not mean Jesus was literally born from God. The Bible does not teach a physical relationship between God and Mary, as Muslims sometimes charge. At the birth of Jesus, the angel told the virgin Mary:

"... 'Do not be afraid, Mary, for you have found favor with God. And behold, you will conceive in your womb and bear a son, and you shall call his name Jesus. He will be great and will be called the Son of the Most High. ... of his kingdom there will be no end.' And Mary said to the angel, 'How will this be, since I am a virgin?' And the angel answered her, 'The Holy Spirit will come upon you, and the power of the Most High will overshadow you; therefore the child to be born will be called holy—the Son of God'" (Luke 1:30-35).

Pastor John MacArthur explains these verses: "Since a son bears his father's qualities, calling a person someone else's 'son' was a way of signifying equality. Here the angel was telling Mary that her Son would be equal to the Most High God" (*The MacArthur Study Bible*).

Man's testimony that Jesus is God's Son

When people witnessed Jesus' miracles, teaching, death, resurrection, and ascension to heaven, many believed Jesus is the Son of God.

• Followers of Jesus testified after He calmed a storm: "And when they got into the boat, the wind ceased. And those in the boat worshiped Him, saying, 'Truly you are the Son of God'" (Matthew 14:32-33).

266

• Peter testified: "Now when Jesus came into the district of Caesarea Philippi, He asked His disciples, 'Who do people say that the Son of Man is?' And they said, 'Some say John the Baptist, others say Elijah, and others Jeremiah or one of the prophets.' He said to them, 'But who do you say that I am?' Simon Peter replied, 'You are the Christ, the Son of the living God.' And Jesus answered him, 'Blessed are you, Simon Bar-Jonah! For flesh and blood has not revealed this to you, but my Father who is in heaven'" (Matthew 16:13-17).

• A woman, whose brother Jesus raised to life, testified: "Jesus said to her, 'I am the resurrection and the life. Whoever believes in Me, though he die, yet shall he live, and everyone who lives and believes in Me shall never die. Do you believe this?' She said to him, 'Yes, Lord; I believe that you are the Christ, the Son of God, who is coming into the world'" (John 11:25-27).

• Even the demons know Jesus is the Son of God: "Whenever the evil spirits saw him, they fell down before him and cried out, 'You are the Son of God'" (Mark 3:11).

• A military officer and soldiers who were guarding Jesus at His death on the cross testified: "When the centurion and those who were with him, keeping watch over Jesus, saw the earthquake and what took place, they were filled with awe and said, 'Truly this was the Son of God!'" (Matthew 27:54).

• Thomas testified after Jesus rose from the dead: "Now Thomas, one of the Twelve, called the Twin, was not with them when Jesus came. So the other disciples told him, 'We have seen the Lord.' But he said to them, 'Unless I see in His hands the mark of the nails, and place my finger into the mark of the nails, and place my hand into His side, I will never believe.' Eight days later, His disciples were inside again, and Thomas was with them. Although the doors were locked, Jesus came and stood among them and said, 'Peace be with you.' Then he said to Thomas, 'Put your finger here, and see My hands; and put out your hand, and place it in My side. Do not disbelieve, but believe.' Thomas answered him, 'My Lord and my God!' Jesus said to him, 'Have you believed because you have seen Me? Blessed are those who have not seen and yet have believed.' Now Jesus did many other signs in the presence of the disciples, which are not written in this book; but these are written so that you may believe that Jesus is the Christ, the Son of God, and that by believing you may have life in His name" (John 20:24-31).

Jesus' own testimony that He is God's Son

• "This was why the Jews were seeking all the more to kill [Jesus], because not only was He breaking the Sabbath, but He was even calling God his own Father, making Himself equal with God. So Jesus said to them, 'Truly, truly, I say to you, the Son can do nothing of His own accord, but only what He sees the Father doing. For whatever the Father does, that the Son does likewise. For the Father loves the Son and shows Him all that He himself is doing. And greater works than these will He show him, so that you may marvel. For as the Father raises the dead and gives them life, so also the Son gives life to whom He will. The Father judges no one, but has given all judgment to the Son, that all may honor the Son, just as they honor the Father. Whoever does not honor the Son does not honor the Father who sent Him. Truly, truly, I say to you, whoever hears My word and believes Him who sent Me has eternal life. He does not come into judgment, but has passed from death to life'" (John 5:18-24).

• At Jesus' trial, He testified: ". . . Again the high priest asked Him, 'Are you the Christ, the Son of the Blessed?' And Jesus said, 'I am, and you will see the Son of Man seated at the right hand of Power, and coming with the clouds of heaven'" (Mark 14:61-62).

• "We know also that the Son of God has come and has given us understanding, so that we may know Him who is true. And we are in Him who is true—even in His Son Jesus Christ. He is the true God and eternal life" (1 John 5:20).

God's testimony that Jesus is His Son

• God spoke at Jesus' baptism: "This is my beloved Son in whom I am well pleased" (Matthew 3:17).

• "While He was speaking, a cloud appeared and enveloped them, and they were afraid as they entered the cloud. A voice came from the cloud, saying, 'This is my Son, whom I have chosen; listen to Him'" (Luke 9:34-35).

• "If we receive the testimony of men, the testimony of God is greater, for this is the testimony of God that he has borne concerning his Son. Whoever believes in the Son of God has the testimony in himself. Whoever does not believe God has made him a liar, because he has not believed in the testimony that God has borne concerning his Son. And this is the testimony, that God gave us eternal life, and this life is in his Son. Whoever has the Son has life; whoever does not have the Son of God does not have life. I write these things to you who believe in the name of the Son of God that you may know that you have eternal life" (1 John 5:9-13).

• Previously, God had spoken to man through His prophets, but then He sent His own Son: "In the past God spoke to our forefathers by the prophets at many times and in various ways. But in these last days He has spoken to us by His Son whom He has appointed heir of all things, and through whom He made the universe. The Son is the radiance of God's glory and the exact representation of His being, sustaining all things by His powerful word. After he had provided purification for sins, He sat down at the right hand of the Majesty in heaven" (Hebrews 1:1-3).

Jesus is the "exact representation" of God. Although one with His Father in essence, Jesus is also distinct in Person as God's Son. God has revealed Himself as one God manifest in three Persons: the Father, the Son, and the Holy Spirit.

Even before the world began, Jesus was always with God and was God (John 1:1-2; 17:5). God created all things in the universe through Jesus (John 1:3; Colossians 1:15-20).

Although eternally one with God, Jesus came to earth in the form of man (Philippians 2:5-11). Born to the virgin Mary, Jesus is fully God and fully man at the same time (the incarnation: Matthew 1:22-23; John 1:14; Romans 1:3-4; Colossians 2:9; 1 John 4:1-3; 5:20).

Believe in the Son of God

We must believe God's Word that Jesus is God's Son, even though it's hard to understand. We will die with many hard questions unanswered. But we dare not die without responding to God's promise of judgment and salvation through His Son (John 3:35-36; 5:25-29; Acts 10:38-43; 17:30-31; 1 John 4:14-15).

As the perfect Son of God, Jesus didn't deserve the punishment for sin, death (Romans 6:23). But by dying on the cross and rising from the dead, Jesus paid the penalty of sin and broke the power of sin for those who would be in Him (Romans 8:1-3).

God is calling sinners to turn from their own way to follow the living Lord Jesus in repentance and faith (Luke 24:46-47). We cannot save ourselves. Only those who turn from sin and trust in the Son of God are saved from sin and eternal death.

"God loved the world so much that He gave His only Son that whoever believes in Him should not perish but have everlasting life. For God did not send his Son into the world to condemn the world, but in order that the world might be saved through Him. Whoever believes in Him is not condemned, but whoever does not believe is condemned already, because he has not believed in the name of the only Son of God" (John 3:16-18).

Through reading this article, have you trusted Jesus as Savior from your sin and Leader of your life? If so, please click on the "I have accepted Christ today" button below.

Used with Permission from GotQuestions
https://www.gotquestions.org/God-have-son.html

WHAT DOES THE BIBLE TEACH ABOUT THE TRINITY?

Answer: The most difficult thing about the Christian concept of the Trinity is that there is no way to perfectly and completely understand it. The Trinity is a concept that is impossible for any human being to fully understand, let alone explain. God is infinitely greater than we are; therefore, we should not expect to be able to fully understand Him. The Bible teaches that the Father is God, that Jesus is God, and that the Holy Spirit is God. The Bible also teaches that there is only one God. Though we can understand some facts about the relationship of the different Persons of the Trinity to one another, ultimately, it is incomprehensible to the human mind. However, this does not mean the Trinity is not true or that it is not based on the teachings of the Bible.

The Trinity is one God existing in three Persons. Understand that this is not in any way suggesting three Gods. Keep in mind when studying this subject that the word "Trinity" is not found in Scripture. This is a term that is used to attempt to describe the triune God—three coexistent, co-eternal Persons who are God. Of real importance is that the concept represented by the word "Trinity" does exist in Scripture. The following is what God's Word says about the Trinity:

1) There is one God (Deuteronomy 6:4; 1 Corinthians 8:4; Galatians 3:20; 1 Timothy 2:5).

2) The Trinity consists of three Persons (Genesis 1:1, 26; 3:22; 11:7; Isaiah 6:8, 48:16, 61:1; Matthew 3:16-17, 28:19; 2 Corinthians 13:14). In Genesis 1:1, the Hebrew plural noun "Elohim" is used. In Genesis 1:26, 3:22, 11:7 and Isaiah 6:8, the plural pronoun for "us" is used. The word "Elohim" and the pronoun "us" are plural forms, definitely referring in the Hebrew language to more than two. While this is not an explicit argument for the Trinity, it does denote the aspect of plurality in God. The Hebrew word for "God," "Elohim," definitely allows for the Trinity.

In Isaiah 48:16 and 61:1, the Son is speaking while making reference to the Father and the Holy Spirit. Compare Isaiah 61:1 to Luke 4:14-19 to see that it is the Son speaking. Matthew 3:16-17 describes the event of Jesus' baptism. Seen in this passage is God the Holy Spirit descending on God the Son while God the Father proclaims His pleasure in the Son. Matthew 28:19 and 2 Corinthians 13:14 are examples of three distinct Persons in the Trinity.

3) The members of the Trinity are distinguished one from another in various passages. In the Old Testament, "LORD" is distinguished from "Lord" (Genesis 19:24; Hosea 1:4). The LORD has a Son (Psalm 2:7, 12; Proverbs 30:2-4). The Spirit is distinguished from the "LORD" (Numbers 27:18) and from "God" (Psalm 51:10-12). God the Son is distinguished from God the Father (Psalm 45:6-7; Hebrews 1:8-9). In the New Testament, Jesus speaks to the Father about sending a Helper, the Holy Spirit (John 14:16-17). This shows that Jesus did not consider Himself to be the Father or the Holy Spirit. Consider also all the other times in the Gospels where Jesus speaks to the Father. Was He speaking to Himself? No. He spoke to another Person in the Trinity—the Father.

4) Each member of the Trinity is God. The Father is God (John 6:27; Romans 1:7; 1 Peter 1:2). The Son is God (John 1:1, 14; Romans 9:5; Colossians 2:9; Hebrews 1:8; 1 John 5:20). The Holy Spirit is God (Acts 5:3-4; 1 Corinthians 3:16).

5) There is subordination within the Trinity. Scripture shows that the Holy Spirit is subordinate to the Father and the Son, and the Son is subordinate to the Father. This is an internal relationship and does not deny the deity of any Person of the Trinity. This is simply an area which our finite minds cannot understand concerning the infinite God. Concerning the Son see Luke 22:42, John 5:36, John 20:21, and 1 John 4:14. Concerning the Holy Spirit see John 14:16, 14:26, 15:26, 16:7, and especially John 16:13-14.

6) The individual members of the Trinity have different tasks. The Father is the ultimate source or cause of the universe (1 Corinthians 8:6; Revelation 4:11); divine revelation (Revelation 1:1); salvation (John 3:16-17); and Jesus' human works (John 5:17; 14:10). The Father initiates all of these things.

The Son is the agent through whom the Father does the following works: the creation and maintenance of the universe (1 Corinthians 8:6; John 1:3; Colossians 1:16-17); divine revelation (John 1:1, 16:12-15; Matthew 11:27; Revelation 1:1); and salvation (2 Corinthians 5:19; Matthew 1:21; John 4:42). The Father does all these things through the Son, who functions as His agent.

The Holy Spirit is the means by whom the Father does the following works: creation and maintenance of the universe (Genesis 1:2; Job 26:13; Psalm 104:30); divine revelation (John 16:12-15; Ephesians 3:5; 2 Peter 1:21); salvation (John 3:6; Titus 3:5; 1 Peter 1:2); and Jesus' works (Isaiah 61:1; Acts 10:38). Thus, the Father does all these things by the power of the Holy Spirit.

There have been many attempts to develop illustrations of the Trinity. However, none of the popular illustrations are completely accurate. The egg (or apple) fails in that the shell, white, and yolk are parts of the egg, not the egg in themselves, just as the skin, flesh, and seeds of the apple are parts of it, not the apple itself.

The Father, Son, and Holy Spirit are not parts of God; each of them is God. The water illustration is somewhat better, but it still fails to adequately describe the Trinity. Liquid, vapor, and ice are forms of water. The Father, Son, and Holy Spirit are not forms of God, each of them is God. So, while these illustrations may give us a picture of the Trinity, the picture is not entirely accurate. An infinite God cannot be fully described by a finite illustration.

The doctrine of the Trinity has been a divisive issue throughout the entire history of the Christian church. While the core aspects of the Trinity are clearly presented in God's Word, some of the side issues are not as explicitly clear. The Father is God, the Son is God, and the Holy Spirit is God—but there is only one God. That is the biblical doctrine of the Trinity.

Beyond that, the issues are, to a certain extent, debatable and non-essential. Rather than attempting to fully define the Trinity with our finite human minds, we would be better served by focusing on the fact of God's greatness and His infinitely higher nature. "Oh, the depth of the riches of the wisdom and knowledge of God! How unsearchable his judgments, and his paths beyond tracing out! Who has known the mind of the Lord? Or who has been his counselor?" (Romans 11:33-34).

Recommended Resource: Making Sense of the Trinity: Three Crucial Questions by Millard Erickson and The Forgotten Trinity by James White.

Used with Permission from GotQuestions
https://www.gotquestions.org/Trinity-Bible.html

IS THE NEW WORLD TRANSLATION
A VALID VERSION OF THE BIBLE?

Answer: The *New World Translation* (NWT) is defined by the Jehovah's Witnesses' parent organization (the Watchtower Society) as "a translation of the Holy Scriptures made directly from Hebrew, Aramaic and Greek into modern-day English by a committee of anointed witnesses of Jehovah." The NWT is the anonymous work of the "New World Bible Translation Committee." Jehovah's Witnesses claim that the anonymity is in place so that the credit for the work will go to God. Of course, this has the added benefit of keeping the translators from any accountability for their errors and prevents real scholars from checking their academic credentials.

The New World Translation is unique in one thing — it is the first intentional, systematic effort at producing a complete version of the Bible that is edited and revised for the specific purpose of agreeing with a group's doctrine. The Jehovah's Witnesses and the Watchtower Society realized that their beliefs contradicted Scripture. So, rather than conforming their beliefs to Scripture, they altered Scripture to agree with their beliefs. The "New World Bible Translation Committee" went through the Bible and changed any Scripture that did not agree with Jehovah's Witness theology. This is clearly demonstrated by the fact that, as new editions of the New World Translation were published, additional changes were made to the biblical text. As biblical Christians continued to point out Scriptures that clearly argue for the deity of Christ (for example), the Watchtower Society would publish new editions of the New World Translation with those Scriptures changed. Here are some of the more prominent examples of intentional revisions:

The New World Translation renders the Greek term word *staurós* ("cross") as "torture stake" because Jehovah's Witnesses do not believe that Jesus was crucified on a cross. The New World Translation does not translate the words *sheol*, *hades*, *gehenna*, and *tartarus* as "hell" because Jehovah's Witnesses do not believe in hell. The NWT gives the translation "presence" instead of "coming" for the Greek word *parousia* because Jehovah's Witnesses believe that Christ has already returned in the early 1900s. In Colossians 1:16, the NWT inserts the word "other" despite its being completely absent from the original Greek text. It does this to give the view that "all other things" were created by Christ, instead of what the text says, "all things were created by Christ." This is to go along with their belief that Christ is a created being, which they believe because they deny the Trinity.

The most well-known of all the New World Translation perversions is John 1:1. The original Greek text reads, "the Word was God." The NWT renders it as "the word was a god." This is not a matter of correct translation, but of reading one's preconceived theology into the text, rather than allowing the text to speak for itself. There is no indefinite article in Greek (in English, "a" or "an"), so any use of an indefinite article in English must be added by the translator. This is grammatically acceptable, so long as it does not change the meaning of the text.

There is a good reason why *theos* has no definite article in John 1:1 and why the New World Translation rendering is in error. There are three general rules we need to understand to see why.

1. In Greek, word order does not determine word usage like it does in English. In English, a sentence is structured according to word order: Subject - Verb - Object. Thus, "Harry called the dog" is not equivalent to "the dog called Harry." But in Greek, a word's function is determined by the case ending found attached to the word's root. There are two case endings for the root *theo*: one is -s (*theos*), the other is -n (*theon*). The -s ending normally identifies a noun as being the subject of a sentence, while the -n ending normally identifies a noun as the direct object.

2. When a noun functions as a predicate nominative (in English, a noun that follows a being verb such as "is"), its case ending must match the noun's case that it renames, so that the reader will know which noun it is defining. Therefore, *theo* must take the -s ending because it is renaming *logos*. Therefore, John 1:1 transliterates to "*kai theos en ho logos.*" Is *theos* the subject, or is *logos*? Both have the -s ending. The answer is found in the next rule.

3. In cases where two nouns appear, and both take the same case ending, the author will often add the definite article to the word that is the subject in order to avoid confusion. John put the definite article on *logos* ("the Word") instead of on *theos*. So, *logos* is the subject, and *theos* is the predicate nominative. In English, this results in John 1:1 being read as "and the Word was God" (instead of "and God was the word").

The most revealing evidence of the Watchtower's bias is their inconsistent translation technique. Throughout the Gospel of John, the Greek word *theon* occurs without a definite article. The New World Translation renders none of these as "a god." Just three verses after John 1:1, the New World Translation translates another case of *theos* without the indefinite article as "God." Even more inconsistent, in John 1:18, the NWT translates the same term as both "God" and "god" in the very same sentence.

The Watchtower, therefore, has no hard textual grounds for their translation—only their own theological bias. While New World Translation defenders might succeed in showing that John 1:1 *can* be translated as they have done, they cannot show that it is the *proper* translation. Nor can they explain the fact that the NWT does not translate the same Greek phrases elsewhere in the Gospel of John the same way. It is only the pre-conceived heretical rejection of the deity of Christ that forces the Watchtower Society to inconsistently translate the

Greek text, thus allowing their error to gain some semblance of legitimacy in the minds of those ignorant of the facts.

It is only the Watchtower's pre-conceived heretical beliefs that are behind the dishonest and inconsistent translation that is the New World Translation. The New World Translation is most definitely not a valid version of God's Word.

There are minor differences among all the major English translations of the Bible. No English translation is perfect. However, while other Bible translators make minor mistakes in the rendering of the Hebrew and Greek text into English, the NWT intentionally changes the rendering of the text to conform to Jehovah's Witness theology. The New World Translation is a perversion, not a version, of the Bible.

Recommended Resource: Reasoning from the Scriptures with the Jehovah's Witnesses, Updated and Expanded by Ron Rhodes.

We highly recommend Witnesses for Jesus [46]for more information.

Used with Permission from GotQuestions
https://www.gotquestions.org/New-World-Translation.html

---

[46] http://www.4witness.org/what-we-offer/christians-witnessing-to-jehovahs-witnesses/

"IF GOD KNEW THAT SATAN WOULD REBEL, WHY DID HE CREATE HIM?"

Answer: This is a two-part question. The first part is "Did God know Satan would rebel?" We know from Scripture that God is *omniscient*, which literally means "all-knowing." Job 37:16; Psalm 139:2–4, 147:5; Proverbs 5:21; Isaiah 46:9-10; and 1 John 3:19–20 leave no doubt that God's knowledge is infinite and that He knows everything that has happened in the past, is happening now, and will happen in the future.

Looking at some of the superlatives in these verses—"perfect in knowledge"; "His understanding has no limit"; "He knows everything"—it is clear that God's knowledge is not merely greater than our own, but it is infinitely greater. He knows all things in totality. If God's knowledge is not perfect, then there is a deficiency in His nature. Any deficiency in God's nature means He cannot be God, for God's very essence requires the perfection of all His attributes. Therefore, the answer to the first question is "yes, God knew that Satan would rebel."

Moving on to the second part of the question, "Why did God create Satan knowing ahead of time he was going to rebel?" This question is a little trickier because we are asking a "why" question to which the Bible does not usually provide comprehensive answers. Despite that, we should be able to come to a limited understanding. We have already seen that God is omniscient. So, if God knew that Satan would rebel and fall from heaven, yet He created him anyway, it must mean that the fall of Satan was part of God's sovereign plan from the beginning. No other answer makes sense given what we've seen thus far.

First, we should understand that *knowing* Satan would rebel is not the same thing as *making* Satan rebel. The angel Lucifer had a free will and made his own choices. God did not create Lucifer as the devil; He created him good (Genesis 1:31).

In trying to understand why God created Satan, knowing he would rebel, we should also consider the following facts:

1) Lucifer had a good and perfect purpose before his fall. Lucifer's rebellion does not change God's original intent from something good to something bad.

2) God's sovereignty extends to Satan, even in his fallen condition. God is able to use Satan's evil actions to ultimately bring about God's holy plan (see 1 Timothy 1:20 and 1 Corinthians 5:5).

3) God's plan of salvation was ordained from eternity past (Revelation 13:8); salvation requires something to be saved *from*, and so God allowed Satan's rebellion and the spread of sin.

4) The suffering that Satan brought into the world actually became the means by which Jesus, in His humanity, was made the complete and perfect Savior of mankind: "In bringing many sons and daughters to glory, it was fitting that God, for whom and through whom everything exists, should make the pioneer of their salvation perfect through what he suffered" (Hebrews 2:10).

5) From the very beginning, God's plan in Christ included the destruction of Satan's work (see 1 John 3:8).

Ultimately, we cannot know for sure why God created Satan, knowing he would rebel. It's tempting to assume that things would be "better" if Satan had never been created or to declare that God should have done differently. But such assumptions and declarations are unwise. In fact, to claim we know better than God how to run the universe is to fall into the devil's own sin of promoting himself above the Most High (Isaiah 14:13–14).

Recommended Resource: Basic Theology by Charles Ryrie

Used with Permission from GotQuestions
https://www.gotquestions.org/if-God-knew.html

"WHAT IS SPIRITUALISM?"

Answer: In the last few decades, there has been an increasing fascination with communing with the dead. The hit television shows *Ghost Hunters, Beyond,* and *Crossing Over* provide good examples. Through the stories told by the participants on these and other shows, the world is regaled with tales of contact with the spiritual world, some heartwarming and some horrific. Those who participate in these kinds of practices do not always understand or fully appreciate the considerable spiritual risks they are taking.

Spiritualism is a pseudo-religious system of shared concepts in which a key feature is the belief that a soul survives after the death of the physical body and these disembodied spirits are both willing and able to communicate with living persons. Like Christians, spiritualists believe in a single God—whom they refer to as "infinite Intelligence"—and that God holds each soul accountable for his actions and life choices. Unlike Christians, however, spiritualists do not believe that death marks the final point of judgment for a spirit, but souls have the capacity to learn, grow, and evolve after death to progressively higher planes of knowledge and perfection. They do not believe that Jesus' death paid the penalty for sin and that salvation comes by grace through faith in Christ, but rather souls gradually progress after death through a series of steps toward a state of spiritual perfection. It is, therefore, a works-based route to "salvation" after death.

Spiritualism had its heyday during the 1840s and at the turn of the century in North America and Western Europe. During these periods of wars and upheaval, people sought comfort by contact with their departed loved ones. Historians often point to March 31, 1948, as the birth date of the spiritualism movement, when Margaret and Kate Fox, of Hydesville, New York, first made the astonishing announcement that they had contacted the spirit of a murdered peddler in their home. The peddler communicated with them by knocking on the table or wall. Thereafter, séances flourished among the upper middle class and the wealthy in America. Mediums such as Paschal Beverly Randolph and Cora Scott toured the country giving lectures and demonstrations. During this time, the writings of Franz Mesmer, from whose name the term *mesmerism* is derived, particularly influenced the spiritualist view of the afterlife and contact with the supernatural.

There were many famous devotees of spiritualism, including Mary Todd Lincoln (wife of Abraham Lincoln) and Sir Arthur Conan Doyle, the author of the Sherlock Holmes mysteries. During the late 1880s, investigators began to expose many of the well-known mediums as charlatans, proving that their demonstrations were contrived. Harry Houdini gained early popularity by his campaign to expose fraudulent mediums.

Spiritualism attracted many followers who were unhappy with the established churches and sought reform. Indeed, many of the early Abolitionists and women's rights advocates were spiritualists. Spiritualist meetings provided some of the earliest venues for women to speak publicly and authoritatively in a male-dominated society. Radical Quakers, who were disenchanted with the established churches because of their failure to oppose slavery, used interest in spiritualism as an anti-slavery public forum. Although the movement culminated in necessary societal reforms, it resulted in many people moving to a secular spirituality, focused on personal experiences and unsubstantiated messages from beyond, and deemphasized a personal relationship with Jesus Christ.

Paul referred to religious belief systems that deny the truth of the gospel, the atonement for sins through the death of Jesus Christ on the cross, as "having a form of godliness but denying its power" (2 Timothy 3:1–5). Although many spiritualists attend Sunday services, sing hymns, and worship a single God, spiritualism and Christianity are not compatible belief systems. In addition to their belief in an evolutionary movement of souls through progressively higher celestial planes, spiritualists seek their truth from contact with spirits through séances, Ouija boards, and mediums. Many spiritualists maintain that they have their own personal spirit guides, from whom they receive all kinds of information and direction for their lives. For spiritualists, the Bible is not the primary source of truth and knowledge about the afterlife and God.

The Bible, in fact, contains many stern warnings against spiritualism (Leviticus 19:31; 20:6; Deuteronomy 18:9–13). The first king of Israel, King Saul, broke God's commandment not to engage in spiritualism and ultimately lost his kingdom because of it (1 Samuel 15:23; 1 Chronicles 10:14). When the apostles encountered people who had powers of divination from contact with spirits, they cast these spirits out as demons (Acts 16:16–18). Many scriptural references point out a chief reason that Christians should not seek contact or counsel with spirits, namely, that the spirits contacted are demonic and may give unreliable and deceptive information (1 John 4:1).

It is highly likely that many contacts with the dead through spiritualism are simply faked. Other so-called encounters with departed loved ones through the use of Ouija boards, mediums, and séances are actually encounters with demons who intentionally deliver false information. One common lie that many people receive through supernatural contact is that there is no hell and no final judgment by God. But Hebrews 9:27 expressly states, "It is appointed for man to die once, and after that comes judgment." Death is inevitable, and so is judgment. Sin brings about that judgment, and all persons are guilty (Romans 3:23). The only way for any person to escape judgment is to receive an unmerited pardon from God by acknowledgment of sin, acceptance that Jesus died for that sin, and a willingness to submit his life to Christ before his death (John 3:16; Romans 3:24). The Bible clearly reveals that those who die apart from Christ will suffer an eternity in hell (Matthew 25:41). Believing in false teachings derived from "spirit guides" will lead many persons away from the sound doctrine of the Bible, which is the intent of Satan (1 Peter 5:8; 1 Timothy 4:1).

Those who dabble in spiritualism engage in activities that seem innocuous but actually open the door for demonic contact, harassment and even possession. Many followers of spiritualism have been traumatized and harmed psychologically, if not physically, by contacts with demons that began with séances, Ouija boards, psychic consultations, Reiki healing, and encounters with mediums. For all those who seek the truth, Jesus unequivocally states in John 14:6, "I am the way and the truth and the life. No one comes to the Father except through Me."

Recommended Resource: Wicca's Charm: Understanding the Spiritual Hunger Behind the Rise of Modern Witchcraft by Catherine Sanders

---

Used with Permission from GotQuestions
https://www.gotquestions.org/spiritualism.html

"WHAT IS SPIRITISM?"

Answer: Spiritism, as defined by its founder, Allan Kardec, is "a science dedicated to the relationship between incorporeal beings and human beings." Kardec was a French educator whose real name was Hippolyte Leon Denizard Rivail. Kardec codified the Kardecist Spiritualism Doctrine, the aim of which was to study spirits —their origin, nature, destiny, and relation to the corporeal world. Spiritism became a popular movement and is now represented in 35 countries. Kardec also wrote *The Spirits' Book* in an attempt to show how Spiritism differs from spiritualism.

The main idea of Spiritism is that immortal spirits travel from one body to another over several lifetimes in order to improve themselves morally and intellectually. While this belief sounds similar to reincarnation, it is different in that, according to Spiritism, spirits cannot come back as animals or any lower life form. The migration of the spirit is always forward, and spirits always inhabit human bodies. Spiritists believe that this explains the differences in temperament and intellect in human beings.

Spiritism also claims that disembodied spirits can have benevolent or maleficent effects on the living and that humans can communicate with spirits through séances and mediums. Spiritism came into favor in the 19th century, alongside modernism, and is compatible with that philosophy on several fronts, most notably the belief that man can continually improve by way of rational thought. Author Sir Arthur Conan Doyle and his wife were famous spiritists.

Spiritism is not a religion but rather a philosophy and "way of life," according to spiritists. There are no ministers, and group meetings consist of sharing ideas about spirits, how they may or may not be moving in the world, the results of those movements, etc. Spiritists value scientific research over worship or rule-following, though they affirm moral living and rational intellectual pursuits.

The Bible clearly forbids Spiritism. God's people are to make no attempt to contact spirits. Séances and necromancy are occult activities forbidden by God (Leviticus 19:31; 20:6; Galatians 5:20; 2 Chronicles 33:6). The fact that Spiritism places the occult under a veil of "science" makes no difference. The Bible tells us that the spirit world is off-limits to us, for our own protection.

The spirits with which Spiritism has to do are not human; the Bible says that the spirits of men face judgment after death (Hebrews 9:27), and there is nothing in Scripture to suggest that spirits return to the land of the living for any reason or in any form.

We know that Satan is a deceiver (John 8:44). The rational conclusion from Scripture, is that any contact spiritists have with the "souls of the departed" is actually contact with demons in disguise (Revelation 12:9). Spiritism is not compatible with the Bible and is spiritually dangerous. "Be alert and of sober mind. Your enemy the devil prowls around like a roaring lion looking for someone to devour" (1 Peter 5:8).

Recommended Resource: Wicca's Charm: Understanding the Spiritual Hunger Behind the Rise of Modern Witchcraft by Catherine Sanders

Used with Permission from GotQuestions
https://www.gotquestions.org/Spiritism.html

"WHAT DAY IS THE SABBATH, SATURDAY OR SUNDAY? DO CHRISTIANS HAVE TO OBSERVE THE SABBATH DAY?"

Answer: It is often claimed that "God instituted the Sabbath in Eden" because of the connection between the Sabbath and creation in Exodus 20:11. Although God's rest on the seventh day (Genesis 2:3) did foreshadow a future Sabbath law, there is no biblical record of the Sabbath before the children of Israel left the land of Egypt. Nowhere in Scripture is there any hint that Sabbath-keeping was practiced from Adam to Moses.

The Word of God makes it quite clear that Sabbath observance was a special sign between God and Israel: "The Israelites are to observe the Sabbath, celebrating it for the generations to come as a lasting covenant. It will be a sign between Me and the Israelites forever, for in six days the Lord made the heavens and the earth, and on the seventh day He abstained from work and rested" (Exodus 31:16–17).

In Deuteronomy 5, Moses restates the Ten Commandments to the next generation of Israelites. Here, after commanding Sabbath observance in verses 12–14, Moses gives the reason the Sabbath was given to the nation Israel: "Remember that you were slaves in Egypt and that the Lord your God brought you out of there with a mighty hand and an outstretched arm. Therefore, the Lord your God has commanded you to observe the Sabbath day." (Deuteronomy 5:15).

God's intent for giving the Sabbath to Israel was not that they would remember creation, but that they would remember their Egyptian slavery and the Lord's deliverance. Note the requirements for Sabbath-keeping: A person placed under that Sabbath law could not leave his home on the Sabbath (Exodus 16:29), he could not build a fire (Exodus 35:3), and he could not cause anyone else to work (Deuteronomy 5:14). A person breaking the Sabbath law was to be put to death (Exodus 31:15; Numbers 15:32–35).

An examination of New Testament passages shows us four important points: 1) Whenever Christ appears in His resurrected form and the day is mentioned, it is always the first day of the week (Matthew 28:1, 9, 10; Mark 16:9; Luke 24:1, 13, 15; John 20:19, 26). 2) The only time the Sabbath is mentioned from Acts through Revelation it is for evangelistic purposes to the Jews, and the setting is usually in a synagogue (Acts chapters 13–18). Paul wrote, "to the Jews I became as a Jew, that I might win Jews" (1 Corinthians 9:20). Paul did not go to the synagogue to fellowship with and edify the saints, but to convict and save the lost. 3) Once Paul states "from now on I will go to the Gentiles" (Acts 18:6), the Sabbath is never again mentioned. And 4) instead of suggesting adherence to the Sabbath day, the remainder of the New Testament implies the opposite (including the one exception to point 3 above, found in Colossians 2:16).

Looking more closely at point 4 above will reveal that there is no obligation for the New Testament believer to keep the Sabbath, and will also show that the idea of a Sunday "Christian Sabbath" is also unscriptural. As discussed above, there is one time the Sabbath is mentioned after Paul began to focus on the Gentiles, "Therefore do not let anyone judge you by what you eat or drink, or with regard to a religious festival, a New

Moon celebration or a Sabbath day. These are a shadow of the things that were to come; the reality, however, is found in Christ." (Colossians 2:16–17). The Jewish Sabbath was abolished at the cross where Christ "canceled the written code, with its regulations" (Colossians 2:14).

This idea is repeated more than once in the New Testament: "One man considers one day more sacred than another; another man considers every day alike. Each one should be fully convinced in his own mind. He who regards one day as special, does so to the Lord" (Romans 14:5–6a). "But now that you know God — or rather are known by God — how is it that you are turning back to those weak and miserable principles? Do you wish to be enslaved by them all over again? You are observing special days and months and seasons and years" (Galatians 4:9–10).

But some claim that a mandate by Constantine in A.D. 321 "changed" the Sabbath from Saturday to Sunday. On what day did the early church meet for worship? Scripture never mentions any Sabbath (Saturday) gatherings by believers for fellowship or worship. However, there are clear passages that mention the first day of the week. For instance, Acts 20:7 states that "on the first day of the week we came together to break bread". In 1 Corinthians 16:2 Paul urges the Corinthian believers "on the first day of every week, each one of you should set aside a sum of money in keeping with his income." Since Paul designates this offering as "service" in 2 Corinthians 9:12, this collection must have been linked with the Sunday worship service of the Christian assembly. Historically Sunday, not Saturday, was the normal meeting day for Christians in the church, and its practice dates back to the first century.

The Sabbath was given to Israel, not the church. The Sabbath is still Saturday, not Sunday, and has never been changed. But the Sabbath is part of the Old Testament Law, and Christians are free from the bondage of the Law (Galatians 4:1-26; Romans 6:14). Sabbath keeping is not required of the Christian—be it Saturday or Sunday. The first day of the week, Sunday, the Lord's Day (Revelation 1:10) celebrates the New Creation, with Christ as our resurrected Head. We are not obligated to follow the Mosaic Sabbath—resting, but are now free to follow the risen Christ—serving. The Apostle Paul said that each individual Christian should decide whether to observe a Sabbath rest, "One man considers one day more sacred than another; another man considers every day alike. Each one should be fully convinced in his own mind" (Romans 14:5). We are to worship God every day, not just on Saturday or Sunday.

Recommended Resource: The End of the Law: Mosaic Covenant in Pauline Theology by Jason Meyer

---

Used with Permission from GotQuestions
https://www.gotquestions.org/Saturday-Sunday.html

WHAT DOES THE BIBLE SAY ABOUT IDOLATRY?

A special thanks to Sonia Armour, Cynthia Isaak's mother, who compiled these verses over many years as she lovingly taught hundreds of Bible Studies.

Realize that God repeats His commandment against idolatry:

Immediately following the book of Exodus, in the books of Leviticus and Deuteronomy, God repeated His prohibition of any form of idolatry again and again. See Leviticus 26:1 and Deuteronomy 5:8,9 for examples.

Be aware that God uses the strongest language possible describing it:

God uses the strongest language possible in expressing how He feels. God loves us deeply and calls us to love Him and serve Him, not an empty lie. He describes idolatry as:

→ An abomination.

→ Detestable

→ Prostitution (spiritually speaking)

→ Adultery (spiritually speaking)

→ Betrayal against God.

Examine the Following Key Verses on Idolatry:

1. Idols cannot help you:

"The idols of the nations are silver and gold, made by human hands. They have mouths, but cannot speak, eyes, but cannot see. They have ears, but cannot hear, nor is there breath in their mouths. Those who make them will be like them, and so will all who trust in them." Psalm 135:15-18:

2. God will not share His glory:

"I am the Lord; that is my name! I will not yield my glory to another or my praise to idols." Isaiah 42:8

3. Like a scarecrow in a cucumber patch:

"Like a scarecrow in a cucumber field, their idols cannot speak; they must be carried because they cannot walk. Do not fear them; they can do no harm nor can they do any good." - Jeremiah 10:5

4. **The apostles did NOT allow people to worship them:** They were horrified at the idea and emphasized that they were merely men. Prayer, worship, and veneration are to be given only to God. - *Acts 14:13-18*[47]

5. **God calls idolatry 'exchanging His glory':** *"Professing to be wise, they became fools, and exchanged the glory of the incorruptible God for an image in the form of corruptible man and of birds and four-footed animals and crawling creatures." - Romans 1:22,23*

6. **Demons are behind the idols:** **"***Do I mean then that food sacrificed to an idol is anything, or that an idol is anything? No, but the sacrifices of pagans are offered to demons, not to God, and I do not want you to be participants with demons." I Corinthians 10:19,20*

7. **Jesus is the ONLY Mediator between God and mankind:** Neither "saints" nor the apostles nor Mary are mediators for mankind; only Jesus. *"For there is one God and one mediator between God and mankind, the man Christ Jesus…" I Timothy 2:5*

8. **God includes idolatry in the same list as drunkenness and orgies:** *"For you have spent enough time in the past doing what pagans choose to do—living in debauchery, lust, drunkenness, orgies, carousing and detestable idolatry." - I Peter 4:3*

9. **God includes idolatry in the same list as witchcraft:** *"Blessed are those who wash their robes, so that they may have the right to the tree of life, and may enter by the gates into the city. Outside are the dogs and the sorcerers and the immoral persons and the murderers and the idolaters, and everyone who loves and practices lying." - Revelation 22:14,15*

---

[47] See also Acts 17:29-30; God will not tolerate the worship of idols.

Examine Further What God Says concerning Idolatry:

1. Exodus 20:4-6	37. Isaiah 45:20	73. Ezekiel 20:7,8
2. Leviticus 19:4	38. Isaiah 46:5-7	74. Ezekiel 20:18
3. Leviticus 26:1	39. Isaiah 57:13	75. Ezekiel 20:24
4. Deuteronomy 4:16-19	40. Isaiah 66:3	76. Ezekiel 20:31
5. Deuteronomy 5:8	41. Jeremiah 2:5	77. Ezekiel 20:39
6. Deuteronomy 5:9	42. Jeremiah 3:9	78. Ezekiel 22:3,4
7. Deuteronomy 27:15	43. Jeremiah 4:1,2	79. Ezekiel 23:49
8. Deuteronomy 32:16	44. Jeremiah 7:16-19	80. Ezekiel 36:18
9. Deuteronomy 32:21	45. Jeremiah 7:30	81. Ezekiel 36:25
10. I Samuel 12:21	46. Jeremiah 8:19	82. Hosea 4:12,13
11. II Kings 21:2,3	47. Jeremiah 10:5	83. Hosea 8:4
12. II Kings 21:11	48. Jeremiah 10:8,9	84. Jonah 2:8
13. II Kings 21:20,21	49. Jeremiah 10:14	85. Micah 5:13,14
14. II Kings 22:17	50. Jeremiah 14:22	86. Habakkuk 2:18,19
15. II Kings 23:24,25	51. Jeremiah 16:18	87. Zechariah 10:2
16. II Chronicles 34:3	52. Jeremiah 16:19	88. Matthew 4:10
17. II Chronicles 34:25	53. Jeremiah 17:3	89. Acts 14:13-18
18. II Chronicles 34:33	54. Jeremiah 18:15	90. Acts 17:29,30
19. Psalm 24:3,4	55. Jeremiah 25:6	91. Romans 1:22
20. Psalm 31:6	56. Jeremiah 25:7	92. Romans 1:23
21. Psalm 78:58	57. Jeremiah 44:16-23	93. I Corinthians 6:9-11
22. Psalm 97:7	58. Jeremiah 48:35	94. I Corinthians 8:4-8
23. Psalm 106:28,29	59. Jeremiah 51:17,18	95. I Corinthians 10:7
24. Psalm 106:36	60. Jeremiah 51:52	96. I Corinthians 10:14
25. Psalm 115:4-8	61. Ezekiel 5:8-11	97. I Corinthians 10:19
26. Isaiah 2:8,9	62. Ezekiel 6:4-6	98. I Corinthians 12:2
27. Isaiah 2:17-20	63. Ezekiel 6:9,10	99. II Corinthians 6:16,17
28. Isaiah 10:10,11	64. Ezekiel 6:13	100. I Thessalonians 1:9
29. Isaiah 30:22	65. Ezekiel 7:20	101. I Timothy 2:5
30. Isaiah 31:7	66. Ezekiel 11:18,19	102. I Peter 4:3
31. Isaiah 41:22-24	67. Ezekiel 11:20,21	103. I John 5:21
32. Isaiah 41:29	68. Ezekiel 14:3-6	104. Revelation 19:10
33. Isaiah 42:8	69. Ezekiel 14:7-8	105. Revelation 21:8,9
34. Isaiah 42:17	70. Ezekiel 16:16-18	106. Revelation 22:8,9
35. Isaiah 44:9-20	71. Ezekiel 16:20,21	107. Revelation 22:14,15
36. Isaiah 45:16	72. Ezekiel 16:31	

"IS RELIGIOUS ICONOGRAPHY CONSIDERED IDOLATRY? WHAT IS AN ICON?"

Answer: Broadly speaking, religious iconography is the artistic depiction of religious figures, often using symbolism. In Christianity, iconography features subjects such as Christ, Mary, or the saints. An icon is an image, usually painted on wood, that is to be venerated as a sacred object. Icons can also be engravings, mosaics, or embroideries. Although people who use icons in their worship would deny that they are practicing idolatry, it is difficult to see how "venerating" an object as "sacred" is different from idolatry.

Although Catholics also venerate religious images, iconography is most often associated with the Eastern or Orthodox Church, which teaches that the use of icons during prayer helps the worshiper know God, be united with the holy saints, and develop the fruit of the Spirit. When an Orthodox Christian enters his church, he lights a candle, makes the sign of the cross, and then kisses the icons of Christ, the Theotokos (Mary), and the saints. The church sanctuary will contain many other "Holy Icons," as they're called.

Orthodox Christians are to have icons at home, too, and the place where the icons are kept is where family prayers are offered. Icons are seen as an illustration of the Incarnation of Christ, who left His spiritual abode to dwell in a material world. The devout also believe that an icon is a window into heaven, and their veneration passes straight to heaven, where it is received by the person depicted in the icon. Some claim that icons have facilitated miracles.

John Calvin and the other Protestant Reformers were iconoclasts; that is, they demanded the removal of icons from churches and homes. According to the Reformers, the veneration of icons and other religious artifacts was idolatry, and they were right. Any kissing of, bowing down before, or praying toward an icon is certainly idolatrous. Members of the Orthodox Church insist that they are not worshiping the paint and wood, but they admit that they give veneration, adoration, and reverence to the saints and Mary depicted in the icons. They pray to men and women; they ascribe to the icons a spiritual power that it does not possess.

This is unbiblical.

There is nothing wrong with producing or enjoying religious art, per se. Viewing a painting of a biblical scene in an art gallery and admiring the artist's technique cannot be considered idolatry. Having a picture of Jesus or of angels in one's home may not be idolatry, either. Iconography can be studied as an art form, and icons can be viewed as fascinating examples of historical religious art. But using icons to aid one's worship or viewing them as a "window to heaven" is definitely idolatry.

The Bible strictly forbids idolatry (Leviticus 26:1; Deuteronomy 5:9). God alone deserves to be bowed down to and worshiped. Icons are not intercessors before the throne of grace, and neither are the saints they represent. People in heaven do not have the power to hear our prayers or grant our requests.

Only Jesus Christ and the Holy Spirit can intercede for us before the Father (Romans 8:26–27, 34).

We should stay as far away as we can from anything that could possibly lead to idolatry.

Recommended Resource: Christianity Through the Centuries by Earle Cairns

---

Used with Permission from GotQuestions
https://www.gotquestions.org/religious-iconography.html

"DOES THE BIBLE PROMOTE OR PROHIBIT PRAYING TO ANGELS?"

Answer: While there is no verse which explicitly states, "You shall not pray to angels," it is abundantly clear that we are not to pray to angels. Ultimately, prayer is an act of worship. And, just as angels reject our worship (Revelation 22:8-9), so they would also reject our prayers. Offering our worship or prayer to anyone but God is idolatry.

There are also several practical and theological reasons why praying to angels is wrong. Christ Himself never prayed to anyone but the Father. When asked by His disciples to teach them to pray, He instructed them, "This, then, is how you should pray: 'Our Father in heaven…'" (Matthew 6:9; Luke 11:2). If praying to angels were something we, as His disciples, are to do, this would have been the place for Him to tell us. Clearly, we are to pray only to God.

This is also evident in passages such as Matthew 11:25-26, where Christ's prayer introduction begins with "I praise thee, Father, Lord of heaven and earth...." Jesus not only begins His prayers by addressing the Father, but the content of His prayers usually requests assistance that could only be granted by someone with omnipotent, omniscient, and omnipresent powers.

Praying to angels would be ineffective because they are created beings and do not possess these powers.

The case against praying to angels can also be made by reviewing John 17:1-26 where Jesus prays on behalf of His followers, requesting multiple blessings on them from God the Father, including sanctification, glorification, and preservation of the saints. These three blessings can only come from the source that presently holds them, and again, angels simply do not have this power. Angels cannot sanctify us, they cannot glorify us, and they cannot guarantee our inheritance in Christ (Ephesians 1:13-14).

Second, there is an occasion in John 14:13 when Christ Himself tells believers that whatever we ask in His name, He will accomplish because He pleads directly with the Father. Offering a prayer up to angels would fall short of an effective and biblically guided prayer.

A second occasion in which Christ mentions that prayers must be offered up in His name alone occurs in John 16:26. This verse conveys the message that, after Christ's ascension to heaven, He acts as an intercessor to the

Father for all believers. Neither angels nor any other created being is ever depicted as an intercessor with the Father. Only the Son and the Holy Spirit (Romans 8:26) can intercede before the Father's throne.

Last, 1 Thessalonians 5:17 tells the believer to pray without ceasing. This would only be possible if a believer has access to a God who is always present and available to listen to the pleas of every person at one time. Angels do not have this ability—they are not omnipresent or omnipotent—and as such are not qualified to receive our prayers.

Prayer to the Father through Christ is the only necessary and effective means by which we can communicate with the Father. No, praying to angels is absolutely not a biblical concept.

Recommended Resource: Unseen Realities: Heaven, Hell, Angels, and Demons by R.C. Sproul.

Used with Permission from GotQuestions
https://www.gotquestions.org/praying-to-angels.html

"IS WORSHIP OF SAINTS / MARY BIBLICAL?"

Answer: The Bible is absolutely clear that we are to worship God alone. The only instances of anyone other than God receiving worship in the Bible are false gods, which are Satan and his demons. All followers of the Lord God refuse worship. Peter and the apostles refused to be worshipped (Acts 10:25–26; 14:13–14). The holy angels refuse to be worshipped (Revelation 19:10; 22:9). The response is always the same, "Worship God!"

Roman Catholics attempt to "bypass" these clear Scriptural principles by claiming they do not "worship" Mary or saints, but rather that they only "venerate" Mary and the saints. Using a different word does not change the essence of what is being done. A definition of "venerate" is "to regard with respect or reverence". Nowhere in the Bible are we told to revere anyone but God alone. There is nothing wrong with respecting those faithful Christians who have gone before us (see Hebrews chapter 11). There is nothing wrong with honoring Mary as the earthly mother of Jesus. The Bible describes Mary as "highly favored" by God (Luke 1:28). At the same time, there is no instruction in the Bible to revere those who have gone to heaven. We are to follow their example, yes, but worship, revere, or venerate, no!

When forced to admit that they do, in fact, worship Mary, Catholics will claim that they worship God through her, by praising the wonderful creation that God has made. Mary, in their minds, is the most beautiful and wonderful creation of God, and by praising her, they are praising her Creator. For Catholics, this is analogous to directing praise to an artist by praising his sculpture or painting. The problem with this is that God explicitly commands against worshipping Him through created things. We are not to bow down and worship the form of anything in heaven above or earth below (Exodus 20:4–5). Romans 1:25 could not be more clear: "They exchanged the truth of God for a lie, and worshiped and served created things rather than the Creator—who is forever praised. Amen." Yes, God has created wonderful and amazing things. Yes, Mary was a godly woman who is worthy of our respect. No, we absolutely are not to worship God "vicariously" by praising things (or people) He has created. Doing so is blatant idolatry.

The major way Catholics "venerate" Mary and the saints is by praying to them. But prayer to anyone other than God alone is anti-biblical. Whether Mary and/or the saints are prayed to, or whether they are petitioned for their prayers—neither practice is biblical. Prayer is an act of worship. When we pray to God, we are admitting that we need His help. Directing our prayers to anyone other than God is robbing God of the glory that is His alone.

Another way Catholics "venerate" Mary and the saints is by creating statues and images of them. Many Catholics use images of Mary and/or the saints as "good luck charms". Any cursory reading of the Bible will reveal this practice as blatant idolatry (Exodus 20:4–6; 1 Corinthians 12:1–2; 1 John 5:21). Rubbing rosary beads is idolatry. Lighting candles before a statue or portrayal of a saint is idolatry. Burying a Joseph statue in hopes of selling your home (and countless other Catholic practices) is idolatry.

The terminology is not the issue. Whether the practice is described as "worship" or "veneration" or any other term, the problem is the same. Any time we ascribe something that belongs to God to someone else, it is idolatry. The Bible nowhere instructs us to revere, pray to, rely on, or "idolize" anyone other than God. We are to worship God alone. Glory, praise, and honor belong to God alone. Only God is worthy to "receive glory and honor and power" (Revelation 4:11). God alone is worthy to receive our worship, adoration, and praise (Nehemiah 9:6; Revelation 15:4).

Recommended Resource: The Gospel According to Rome: Comparing Catholic Tradition and The Word of God by James McCarthy

---

Used with Permission from GotQuestions
https://www.gotquestions.org/worship-saints-Mary.html

"WHAT DOES THE BIBLE SAY ABOUT SEX BEFORE MARRIAGE?"

Answer: There is no Hebrew or Greek word used in the Bible that precisely refers to sex before marriage. The Bible undeniably condemns adultery and sexual immorality, but is sex before marriage considered sexually immoral? According to 1 Corinthians 7:2, "yes" is the clear answer: "But since there is so much immorality, each man should have his own wife, and each woman her own husband." In this verse, Paul states that marriage is the "cure" for sexual immorality. First Corinthians 7:2 is essentially saying that, because people cannot control themselves and so many are having immoral sex outside of marriage, people should get married. Then they can fulfill their passions in a moral way.

Since 1 Corinthians 7:2 clearly includes sex before marriage in the definition of sexual immorality, all of the Bible verses that condemn sexual immorality as being sinful also condemn sex before marriage as sinful. Sex before marriage is included in the biblical definition of sexual immorality. There are numerous Scriptures that declare sex before marriage to be a sin (Acts 15:20; 1 Corinthians 5:1; 6:13, 18; 10:8; 2 Corinthians 12:21; Galatians 5:19; Ephesians 5:3; Colossians 3:5; 1 Thessalonians 4:3; Jude 7). The Bible promotes complete abstinence before marriage. Sex between a husband and his wife is the only form of sexual relations of which God approves (Hebrews 13:4).

Far too often we focus on the "recreation" aspect of sex without recognizing that there is another aspect—procreation. Sex within marriage is pleasurable, and God designed it that way. God wants men and women to enjoy sexual activity within the confines of marriage. Song of Solomon and several other Bible passages (such as Proverbs 5:19) clearly describe the pleasure of sex.

However, the couple must understand that God's intent for sex includes producing children. Thus, for a couple to engage in sex before marriage is doubly wrong—they are enjoying pleasures not intended for them, and they are taking a chance of creating a human life outside of the family structure God intended for every child.

While practicality does not determine right from wrong, if the Bible's message on sex before marriage were obeyed, there would be far fewer sexually transmitted diseases, far fewer abortions, far fewer unwed mothers and unwanted pregnancies, and far fewer children growing up without both parents in their lives.

Abstinence is God's only policy when it comes to sex before marriage. Abstinence saves lives, protects babies, gives sexual relations the proper value, and most importantly, honors God.

Recommended Resource: Why True Love Waits by Josh McDowell.

Men - Every Young Man's Battle : Strategies for Victory in the Real World of Sexual Temptation by Stephen Arterburn.

Women - Every Young Woman's Battle: Guarding Your Mind, Heart, and Body in a Sex-Saturated World by Shannon Ethridge

---

Used with Permission from GotQuestions
https://www.gotquestions.org/sex-before-marriage.html

"CAN A PERSON BE BORN GAY?"

Answer: In 1996, *The Advocate*, a gay and lesbian magazine, asked readers what they believed the potential impact would be to the advancement of gay and lesbian rights if a scientific discovery proves a biological basis for homosexuality. About 61 percent of the magazine's readers asserted that such scientific research would advance the cause of gays and lesbians and lead to more positive attitudes toward homosexuality. For example, if one can be born gay, much as one can be born with brown eyes, then a fair society could not possibly condemn him as being unnatural or immoral. To that end, gay activists and the liberal media have actively encouraged the idea that homosexuality is inherited and unchangeable, and researchers have diligently sought scientific evidence to back up that claim. Unfortunately for the pro-homosexuality movement, the research on this subject has failed to establish any scientific evidence that shows a purely genetic basis for homosexuality.

The controversy began with the work of Simon LeVay, M.D. In 1991, LeVay tested the brains of 41 cadavers and noted differences between homosexual versus heterosexual males. The hypothalamus, an area believed to regulate sexual activity, was smaller in homosexual males than in heterosexuals. Dr. LeVay believed the differences proved a biological basis for homosexuality, but he failed to consider a variety of reasons, other than genetic, that the brains were different. First, all 19 of the homosexual cadavers had died of AIDS, a disease known to affect the neurological system. It could be that the disease had shrunk the hypothalamus. Second, scientists who study brain biochemistry know that the way a person thinks affects the way his brain functions; specifically, it affects the neurochemicals released in the brain and the way certain pathways grow and change. Could the structural brain differences have started with the difference in *thoughts* between homosexuals and heterosexuals, rather than with genetics? Third, there is no proof linking hypothalamus size with homosexuality, either as a cause or effect.

In 1993, Dr. Dean Hamer, a pro-gay activist, made the astounding claim in his research that there may be a gene for homosexuality. His team of researchers began a series of gene linkage studies, in which families with several homosexuals underwent genetic analysis to determine if any chromosomal variants could be found in the family and if the variant correlated with those individuals who displayed the homosexuality. Although Hamer's study sample was very small, he found a significant linkage between gays and a marker on the maternal X chromosome, Xq28. Additional studies with larger sample sizes produced conflicting results in the linkage to Xq28. It is important to note that Hamer's experiments have never been validated; in fact, other groups of researchers have discredited Hamer's work as non-replicable or even fraudulent.

Even if there were some genetic commonalities among homosexuals, associated characteristics do not prove a causal link. To illustrate, a genetic study among professional athletes would probably show that a significant percentage of these stars share certain genetic sequences. One might erroneously conclude that the genetic sequences for increased speed, agility and strength prove that engaging in professional sports is a heritable trait.

However, no genetic sequence can account for human choice and the effects of environment. People who have the genetic traits of an athlete may naturally gravitate toward professional sports or be encouraged to play. Although athletes share some common traits, being a professional athlete itself is not heritable. The culture in which an individual matures and the choices he makes decide his career path.

There are many researchers who cite environmental factors as major contributors to homosexual feelings. They strongly believe that negative early childhood experiences in an unloving or non-supportive home environment are a critical part of this process. Common elements seem to include an emotionally withdrawn or physically absent father and an overbearing, fawning or over-protective mother. In many cases, there are reports of physical, sexual or emotional abuse. Disruption of gender identification may contribute to the development toward homosexuality. This process begins between ages two and four. During this phase, children move from their primary connection with the mother to seek out deeper attachments with the parent of the same gender. For males, the relationship between a boy and his father is the primary means of developing a secure gender identity. As a father and son share time together, the father expresses his value and interest in the son and gives to the son a sense of masculinity. The boy begins to develop a sense of his own gender by understanding himself in relation to his father. Conversely, a mother who is distant, abusive, or physically absent or a mother who is viewed by her daughter as being weak (such as when the mother is abused by males) may disrupt her daughter's identification with being feminine.

Peer attachments with same-sex friends also play a role in developing gender identity. Eventually, after years of interaction and bonding with same-sex peers, children enter puberty and begin to pay attention to the opposite sex. When this natural process is disrupted, it feels natural for a child to love and crave the attention of those of the same sex. When children with certain temperaments initially perceive rejection of the same-sex parent, they detach and bond with the other parent. They begin to adopt the patterns and attributes of the opposite sex. However, there is always a longing for a connection with the same-sex parent, love and affirmation from the same gender. These children *believe* that they were born that way, having craved love and attachment with the same-sex parents for as long as they can remember. Homosexual behavior thus begins as an emotional craving, not a sexual craving. It reflects a legitimate need for non-sexual love, an emotional need that ultimately becomes sexualized with the onset of puberty.

Most researchers have concluded that sexual orientation is a complex, multifactorial issue in which biological, social and psychological factors combine to play a role in the ultimate sexual orientation of an individual. According to Julie Harren, Ph.D., the formula for this interplay between factors might be represented by these equations:

--Genes + Brain Wiring + Prenatal Hormonal Environment = Temperament.

--Parents + Peers + Experiences = Environment.

--Temperament + Environment = Homosexual Orientation.

What's missing from these equations are the existence of a soul, the choice of the individual, and the temptation of the devil (see James 1:14).

Although it may be easier, psychologically, for a homosexual to believe that homosexuality is inborn, the accumulated scientific evidence suggests otherwise. Homosexuals may have a genetic predisposition, but human choice is still a factor. A predisposition is not a constraint. Ultimately, sexual orientation is determined outside of the womb. For those who are unhappy living a homosexual lifestyle, this truth offers hope for change. Clinical experience has shown that, with help, some homosexuals can change learned responses and defense mechanisms to early painful experiences.

In 1 Corinthians 6:9-10, the sin of homosexuality is listed right next to theft. Just as there is no genetic excuse for stealing, there is no genetic excuse for homosexuality. Environment, culture, and choice make one a thief, and the same factors make one a homosexual.

Christ died for homosexuals. God loves persons of all sexual orientations, just as He loves all sinners. The Bible says, "God demonstrates his own love for us in this: While we were still sinners, Christ died for us" (Romans 5:8). Jesus Christ "is the atoning sacrifice for our sins, and not only for ours but also for the sins of the whole world" (1 John 2:2).

The gospel of Christ "is the power of God for the salvation of everyone who believes" (Romans 1:16). In Christ alone we find the definitive source for healing, restoration, forgiveness, and comfort. He is the way by which we can all experience the affirming, unconditional love, value, and acceptance of our Father in heaven.

Recommended Resource: 101 Frequently Asked Questions About Homosexuality by Mike Haley

---

Used with Permission from GotQuestions
https://www.gotquestions.org/born-gay.html

"IF GOD IS LOVE, WHY DOES HE CONDEMN HOMOSEXUALITY?"

Answer: A common argument for the acceptance of homosexuality and same-sex marriage is that, if God is love, He would not condemn the love of others. The main problem with this is what kind of "love" we're talking about.

First John 4:8 says, "Whoever does not love does not know God, because God is love." The "love" referenced here is the Greek *agape*. This type of love is the conscious act of sacrificing one's own desires, comfort, and even well-being for the sake of another. It is the love that sent Jesus to die on the cross for our sins (Romans 5:8). And the love that led God to send Him (John 3:16). The greatest fulfillment of this love is to sacrifice one's life for another (John 15:13).

The question, then, becomes what constitutes the well-being of another? The world and maybe even our own sensitivities might say that to allow another to live in a homosexual relationship is to see to their well-being. The Bible says otherwise. Romans 1:26 says it is disgraceful and dishonoring. First Corinthians 6:9 says it will keep a person from the kingdom of God. First Corinthians 6:18 says that homosexual behavior is a sin against one's own body.

If this is true and homosexual behavior is dishonoring, a separation from God's blessing, and self-harm, then the loving thing to do is to stay away from it. To encourage others to indulge in sin is to encourage them to reject God's blessings on their lives. It is the opposite of love.

That being said, those with homosexual attractions are in desperate need of love. Even if they agree with the Bible that homosexuality is a sin and resolve not to seek fulfillment of their sexual desires, they must still find love in other relationships—the self-sacrificing love of *agape* and the friendly companionship of *phileo*. When our emotional and social needs for love are met, we are less likely to seek fulfillment in unbiblical ways. It's no different for single heterosexuals than for those with homosexual attraction.

Can someone with same-sex sexual attraction be healed and become heterosexual in thought, desire, and deed? It is possible, but it is not certain. Being saved and forgiven does not rid one of temptation. For the believer, as long as same-sex attractions are present, abstinence is crucial—as it is for anyone not in a heterosexual marriage. Believers should not condone sexual relationships outside of a heterosexual marriage, even as they show *agape* and *phileo* love.

It is a lie that all humans need sexual fulfillment (Matthew 19:12). It is a lie that sex equates to love. The God who created us insists that sex is an expression of love between a man and woman who are married to each other. Outside of that context, sex is harmful and very much *unloving*. If we love others, we will not encourage them to sin, bringing harm to themselves. Instead, we will follow the greatest commandment and provide for them the real love they need from us.

Recommended Resource: 101 Frequently Asked Questions About Homosexuality by Mike Haley

Used with Permission from GotQuestions
https://www.gotquestions.org/God-love-and-homosexuality.html

GAY, LESBIAN, GOD'S LOVE

If you are LGBTQ, how you can be sure that God and His love welcomes you. See this...

By Marilyn Adamson

Life often demands certain qualifications. To get a driver's license, you have to pass a test. To land a certain job, you must show that you have the credentials deserving of that job.

If "A," then "B." Prove you are worthy. Prove you have qualified. Prove you are "acceptable".

At what point can you know that God fully accepts you?

Unlike anything else you have encountered, a relationship with God does not begin with you filling in the blank, "Accept me because..." It starts with God saying, "I accept you." "I welcome you". Whether you are gay, lesbian, bisexual, transgendered or have questions, God is not our enemy. If you have not already begun one, God wants a relationship with you. He offers this to anyone and everyone.

In Scripture, you'll see only one group that consistently angered Jesus...the religious self-righteous. Jesus seemed comfortable around everyone else, including prostitutes and criminals. However, the religious elite irritated and saddened Jesus. He saw them as judgmental, arrogant, unloving, and hypocritical.

You might see those words and immediately think of religious people who have been hurtful, rude or judgmental toward you. Does that represent Jesus' heart? No. Jesus said to love your neighbor as yourself. How would hurtful comments fit into that? Not very well.

This is Jesus' heart revealed. He said, "Come to me, all of you who are weary and carry heavy burdens, and I will give you rest. Take my yoke upon you. Let me teach you, because I am humble and gentle at heart, and you will find rest for your souls."[1]

Have you ever had a chance to seriously consider Jesus?

Unlike any other person who has ever lived, Jesus can explain life to you...how to experience life, more abundantly. He is the Creator of all that exists, yet became a man, so that we could know Him, know God.

John, one of Jesus' friends, made this comment about Jesus, "For from His fullness we have all received grace upon grace. For the Law was given through Moses; grace and truth came through Jesus Christ."[2] "Grace" isn't a word we use much. It means God's kindness given to us, without our earning it. Jesus offers us both His kindness and truth, to guide us through this often-confusing life.

I used to wonder what it takes to be accepted by God. Perhaps you'll be as amazed as I was. Here it is: "For God so loved the world, that He gave His only Son, that whoever believes in Him should not perish but have eternal life. For God did not send his Son into the world to condemn the world, but in order that the world might be saved through Him. Whoever believes in Him is not condemned, but whoever does not believe is condemned already, because he has not believed in the name of the only Son of God."[3]

Did you catch it? "Whoever believes in Him." Whoever believes in Him has eternal life. Whoever believes in Him is saved through Him. Whoever believes in Him is not condemned.

This is what He asks of us...to believe in Him.

John said of Jesus, "He came to his own, and his own people did not receive Him. But to all who did receive Him, who believed in His name, He gave the right to become children of God..."[4]

He was not just a prophet or teacher or religious leader. Jesus said that to know Him was to know God. To believe in Him was to believe in God. This is what led to His crucifixion. They charged Him with blasphemy. The people said that Jesus was "calling God His own Father, making Himself equal with God."[5]

He offered proof. Jesus had already done what no human could do, instantly healing those who were blind, couldn't walk, or who struggled with diseases.

Yet Jesus went far beyond that. He said on numerous occasions, that He would be arrested, beaten, and crucified...and three days later rise from the dead. That's pretty solid proof. No reincarnation later, no mystical "you'll see me in your dreams." No. Three days after being buried, He would rise from the dead.

The Romans knew about this so they posted an entire guard of soldiers at Jesus' tomb. However, three days after being tortured and killed on a cross, Jesus physically rose from the tomb. His body was gone, and only the grave clothes that He had been buried in were left. Jesus physically showed up numerous times over the next 40 days. This is what started the Christian faith. He proved that He was all that He claimed to be...God in the flesh, equal with God the Father.

Jesus was clear about it: "The Father judges no one, but has given all judgment to the Son, that all may honor the Son, just as they honor the Father. Whoever does not honor the Son does not honor the Father who sent Him. Truly, truly, I say to you, whoever hears my word and believes Him who sent Me has eternal life. He does not come into judgment, but has passed from death to life."[6]

You might wonder, "Okay. Eternal life is great. But what about now, in this life?"

You can go through this life knowing you are loved by God. Everyone hungers to be loved. Human love is important. Yet every person who loves you, loves you imperfectly, because people are imperfect.

But God is able to love you perfectly. He loves us because it is his nature to love, and it never changes, never stops.

We all mess up. We all fail to live up to our own standards, let alone God's standards. But God doesn't accept us based on our performance. He accepts us if we will simply believe in Him, come to Him, invite Him to be God in our lives.

This is how Jesus describes having a relationship with Him:
"As the Father has loved Me, so have I loved you. Abide in my love. If you keep My commandments, you will abide in My love, just as I have kept my Father's commandments and abide in His love. These things I have spoken to you, that my joy may be in you, and that your joy may be full. This is my commandment, that you love one another as I have loved you."[7]

What happens if you take him up on it? What happens if you begin a relationship with God?

Any significant relationship you have had in your life has had an effect on you, either positively or negatively. Right? This is true for everyone. The more important the relationship, the greater impact it has.

So, it makes sense that knowing God is going to be a significant relationship. He will lead your life according to His love and His desires for your life. You still make decisions. You maintain your free will. He does not take over your life, forcing you to act as He wants. Yet, I found myself deeply impressed by His wisdom, His kindness, and the way God views people and life.

God is not going to take His cues from what society dictates. God, who created the universe, doesn't really need society to guide Him, does He? I like that. I find that freeing.

Here's what God did in my life, when I began a relationship with Him. I had been an atheist. Believing in God, reading the Bible about Him, was a major shift in my life. It was monumental, actually. A couple of months after asking Jesus into my life, my closest friend asked me, "Have you noticed a change in your life?" And I said, "What do you mean?" She said, "Lately I can share things with you and you don't make jokes. You seem to be really listening to me." I was kind of embarrassed. I mean, here's my closest friend telling me that I was finally acting like a decent human being and listening to her!
(She was so amazed by what she was noticing in my life, that she decided to ask Jesus into her life also.)

Here's what I think was happening in my life.

When I began a relationship with God, I became very aware of His love for me. It really surprised me. Things I would read in the Bible were like personal messages from God to me about how much He loved me. (I grew up thinking God was pretty mad at us, for not measuring up.) So this was amazing to me - that God loves us.

And I guess my emotional need for love was met by God on such a deep level, that I became more of an emotionally secure person. I started thinking more, caring more about other people, than about myself. And evidently I became a better listener and more caring. I also found the racial bigotry I was raised in subsiding.

Jesus promises us that as we let Him teach us and guide us, He says, "you will know the truth, and the truth will set you free."[8]

If you begin a relationship with Jesus, you might see changes in your attitudes, or hopefulness, or how you view others, or how you spend your time. Only God knows. But as you get to know Him, He will impact your life. Ask anyone who follows Jesus, and they'll tell you how knowing Him has affected their life.

He tends to give us greater desire to choose His ways. How He does this is unexpected. It isn't like He gives you a new set of commands that you must now follow. This isn't self-effort or you performing for God. And it isn't religious dedication. It is a relationship, an intimate friendship with God. It is God personally leading you and teaching you about Himself, about life. He enters our lives when we invite Him in. He affects our lives, from the inside out, at a heart level.

Jesus offers you more of life. You know how relationships, jobs, sports, entertainment...all of it has great moments, yet the fulfillment is often fleeting. The satisfaction of it does not keep us full. And nothing on earth ever will.

We have a constant hunger for something that lasts, that's reliable. Jesus said, "I am the bread of life; whoever comes to Me shall not hunger, and whoever believes in Me shall never thirst."[9] He finishes His statement with, "...whoever comes to Me I will never cast out."[9] I searched for years for a philosophy of life that would always work, in any situation. When I came to know God, my search ended. I found him to be trustworthy.

Your relationship with Him is going to look different than anyone else's relationship with Him. You are an individual with unique experiences, thoughts, interests, dreams, needs. Read the Gospels and you'll see Jesus relating to individuals...as individuals.

I'm concerned at this point that I'm showing you only the upside of knowing God.

A relationship with God is no guarantee that you will be shielded from really hard things in life. You might go through financial stress, serious illness, accidents, earthquakes, relationship heartaches, etc. There is no question that there is suffering in this life. You can go through it alone. Or, you can be certain of God's love, His presence and intimacy, in the midst of it. Here's another caution. He might lead you into some really challenging careers, at personal sacrifice, in order to care for others.

Most of Jesus' disciples (and many of Jesus' followers today) have gone through tremendous suffering. For example, Paul was frequently arrested, beaten with rods and whipped, countless times. Once he was nearly stoned to death by an angry mob. He was shipwrecked several times, many days without food, and fleeing for his life, often.

Clearly, Jesus' followers didn't live easy lives. Yet Paul, and other believers, remained unshakably convinced of God's love for them.

Paul writes, "No, in all these things we are more than conquerors through Him who loved us. For I am sure that neither death nor life, nor angels nor rulers, nor things present nor things to come, nor powers, nor height nor depth, nor anything else in all creation, will be able to separate us from the love of God in Christ Jesus our Lord."[10]

You don't plan your course. If you are gay, lesbian, bisexual, transgender, or questioning your sexuality...if you will let Him, Jesus will guide your life. And it's greater than what you could imagine. Jesus said, "I am the light of the world. Whoever follows Me will not walk in darkness, but will have the light of life."[11]

Here's how you can begin a relationship with God, right now.

Whatever you've done in your life, Jesus offers you His complete forgiveness. Our sin wasn't merely overlooked. It was paid for, by Jesus on the cross, sacrificing Himself in our place.

Have you ever had someone sacrifice for you? This is what Jesus did to the ultimate degree. He loves you that much. He offers to enter your heart and establish a relationship with you.

Would you like to know God? I would encourage you to let Him into your life, if you haven't already. He says that THIS is the relationship that satisfies us. We never were meant to go through this life without Him.

You can talk to Him using whatever words you want. If you need help, here's what you might say:
"Jesus, I believe in you. Thank you for dying for me and offering me a relationship with you. I want you to be God in my life, I want to know you, experience your love, and right now, I ask you to lead my life."

Footnotes: (1) Matt 11:28-29 (2) John 1:16,17 (3) John 3:16-18 (4) John 1:11,12 (5) John 5:18 (6) John 5:22-24 (7) John 15:9-12 (8) John 8:32 (9) John 6:35,37 (10) Romans 8:37-39 (11) John 8:12

_____

Used with Permission from EveryStudent
https://www.everystudent.com/wires/gay-lesbian.html

"WHAT DOES THE BIBLE SAY ABOUT REINCARNATION?"

Answer: The concept of reincarnation is completely without foundation in the Bible, which clearly tells us that we die once and then face judgment (Hebrews 9:27). The Bible never mentions people having a second chance at life or coming back as different people or animals. Jesus told the criminal on the cross, "Today you will be with Me in paradise" (Luke 23:43), not "You will have another chance to live a life on this earth." Matthew 25:46 specifically tells us that believers go on to eternal life while unbelievers go on to eternal punishment. Reincarnation has been a popular belief for thousands of years, but it has never been accepted by Christians or followers of Judaism because it is contradictory to Scripture.

The one passage that some point to as evidence for reincarnation is Matthew 17:10-12 which links John the Baptist with Elijah. However, the passage does not say that John the Baptist was Elijah reincarnated but that he would have fulfilled the prophecy of Elijah's coming if the people had believed his words and thereby believed in Jesus as the Messiah (Matthew 17:12). The people specifically asked John the Baptist if he was Elijah, and he said, "No, I am not" (John 1:21).

Belief in reincarnation is an ancient phenomenon and is a central tenet within the majority of Indian religious traditions, such as Hinduism, Sikhism, and Jainism. Many modern pagans also believe in reincarnation as do some New Age movements, along with followers of spiritism. For the Christian, however, there can be no doubt: reincarnation is unbiblical and must be rejected as false.

Recommended Resource: I'm Back Again???: A Christian Analysis of Reincarnation in Contemporary American Society by Mark Tabata

---

Used with Permission from GotQuestions
https://www.gotquestions.org/reincarnation.html

"WHAT DOES THE BIBLE SAY ABOUT THE VIRGIN MARY?"

Answer: Mary the mother of Jesus was described by God as "highly favored" (Luke 1:28). The phrase "highly favored" comes from a single Greek word, which essentially means "much grace". Mary received God's grace.

Grace is "unmerited favor", meaning something we receive despite the fact that we do not deserve it. Mary needed grace from God just as the rest of us do. Mary herself understood this fact, as she declared in Luke 1:47, "...and my spirit rejoices in God my Savior..."

Mary recognized that she needed the Savior. The Bible never says that Mary was anyone but an ordinary human whom God chose to use in an extraordinary way. Yes, Mary was a righteous woman and favored (graced) by God (Luke 1:27-28). At the same time, Mary was a sinful human being who needed Jesus Christ as her Savior, just like everyone else (Ecclesiastes 7:20; Romans 3:23; 6:23; 1 John 1:8).

Mary did not have an "immaculate conception". The Bible doesn't suggest Mary's birth was anything but a normal human birth. Mary was a virgin when she gave birth to Jesus (Luke 1:34-38), but the idea of the perpetual virginity of Mary is unbiblical. Matthew 1:25, speaking of Joseph, declares, "But he had no union with her until she gave birth to a son. And he gave Him the name Jesus."

The word "until" clearly indicates that Joseph and Mary did have sexual union after Jesus was born. Joseph and Mary had several children together after Jesus was born. Jesus had four half-brothers: James, Joseph, Simon, and Judas (Matthew 13:55). Jesus also had half-sisters, although they are not named or numbered (Matthew 13:55-56). God blessed and graced Mary by giving her several children, which in that culture was the clearest indication of God's blessing on a woman.

One time when Jesus was speaking, a woman in the crowd proclaimed, "Blessed is the womb that bore You and the breasts at which You nursed" (Luke 11:27). There was never a better opportunity for Jesus to declare that Mary was indeed worthy of praise and adoration. What was Jesus' response? "On the contrary, blessed are those who hear the word of God and observe it" (Luke 11:28). To Jesus, obedience to God's Word was more important than being the woman who gave birth to the Savior.

Nowhere in Scripture does Jesus, or anyone else, direct any praise, glory, or adoration towards Mary. Elizabeth, Mary's relative, praised Mary in Luke 1:42-44, but her praise is based on the blessing of giving birth to the Messiah. It was not based on any inherent glory in Mary.

Mary was present at the cross when Jesus died (John 19:25). Mary was also with the apostles on the day of Pentecost (Acts 1:14). However, Mary is never mentioned again after Acts chapter 1. The apostles did not give Mary a prominent role. Mary's death is not recorded in the Bible. Nothing is said about Mary ascending to heaven or having an exalted role there. As the earthly mother of Jesus, Mary should be respected, but she is not worthy of our worship or adoration.

The Bible nowhere indicates that Mary can hear our prayers or that she can mediate for us with God. Jesus is our only advocate and mediator in heaven (1 Timothy 2:5). If offered worship, adoration, or prayers, Mary would say the same as the angels: "Worship God!" (see Revelation 19:10; 22:9.) Mary herself sets the example for us, directing her worship, adoration, and praise to God alone: "My soul glorifies the Lord and my spirit rejoices in God my Savior, for He has been mindful of the humble state of His servant. From now on all generations will call me blessed, for the Mighty One has done great things for me — holy is His name" (Luke 1:46-49).

Recommended Resource: The Gospel According to Rome: Comparing Catholic Tradition and The Word of God by James McCarthy

---

Used with Permission from GotQuestions
https://www.gotquestions.org/virgin-Mary.html

"IS THE PERPETUAL VIRGINITY OF MARY BIBLICAL?"

Answer: It is the official position of the Roman Catholic Church that Jesus' mother Mary remained a virgin for her entire life. Is this concept biblical? Before we look at specific Scriptures, it is important to understand why the Roman Catholic Church believes in the perpetual virginity of Mary. The Roman Catholic Church views Mary as "the Mother of God" and "Queen of Heaven". Catholics believe Mary to have an exalted place in Heaven, with the closest access to Jesus and God the Father. Such a concept is nowhere taught in Scripture. Further, even if Mary did occupy such an exalted position, her having sexual intercourse would not have prevented her from gaining such a position. Sex in marriage is not sinful. Mary would have in no way defiled herself by having sexual relations with Joseph her husband. The entire concept of the perpetual virginity of Mary is based on an unbiblical teaching, Mary as Queen of Heaven, and on an unbiblical understanding of sex.

So, what does the Bible say about the perpetual virginity of Mary? Using the New American Bible, which is a Catholic translation, we can see that the perpetual virginity of Mary is not taught in the Bible. Matthew 1:25 NAB tells us, "He had no relations with her until she bore a son, and he named Him Jesus." He, Joseph, did not have sexual relations with her, Mary, UNTIL after she bore a son, Jesus. The meaning of this Scripture is abundantly clear. Joseph and Mary did not have sexual relations until after Jesus was born. Matthew 13:55-56 NAB declares, "Is He not the carpenter's son? Is not His mother named Mary and His brothers James, Joseph, Simon, and Judas? Are not His sisters all with us?" Catholics claim, correctly, that the Greek terms for "brothers" and "sisters" in these verses could also refer to male and female relatives, not necessarily literal brothers and sisters. However, the intended meaning is clear, they thought Jesus to be Joseph's son, the son of Mary, and the brother of James, Joseph, Simon, and Judas, and the brother of the unnamed and unnumbered sisters. Father, mother, brother, sister. It is straining the meaning of the text to interpret "brothers" and "sisters" as "cousins" or "relatives" with the mentioning of Jesus' mother and father.

Matthew 12:46 NAB tells us, "While He was still speaking to the crowds, His mother and His brothers appeared outside, wishing to speak with Him." See also Mark 3:31-34; Luke 8:19-21; John 2:12; and Acts 1:14. All mention Jesus' mother with His brothers. If they were His cousins, or the sons of Joseph from a previous marriage, why were they mentioned with Mary so often? The idea of the perpetual virginity of Mary cannot be drawn from Scripture. It must be forced on Scripture, in contradiction to what the Scriptures clearly state.

Recommended Resource: The Gospel According to Rome: Comparing Catholic Tradition and The Word of God by James McCarthy

---

Used with Permission from GotQuestions
https://www.gotquestions.org/perpetual-virginity-Mary.html

"IS MARY THE MOTHER OF GOD (THEOTOKOS)?"

Answer: The phrase "mother of God" originated with and continues to be used in the Roman Catholic Church. One of the topics at the Council of Ephesus in A.D. 431 was the use of the Greek term *Theotókos*, or "God-bearer", in reference to Mary. That council officially proclaimed Mary as the "mother of God", and the doctrine was later included in the Catholic catechism. The idea behind calling Mary the "mother of God" is that, since Jesus is God and Mary is the mother of Jesus, she is the mother of God.

The major problem with this logic is that the term "God" implies the totality of Yahweh, and we know that Yahweh has no beginning and no end (Psalm 90:2). First Timothy 6:15-16 says that God is immortal. Being immortal, God never was "born" and never had a "mother." The second Person of the Trinity, Jesus, did have a beginning to His *earthly* ministry when He was conceived in Mary's womb and was born, but from eternity past He had always been the Son of God.

Philippians 2:6–7 gives us a bit more insight on what transpired when Jesus left heaven to become man. The New Living Translation says, "Though He was God, He did not think of equality with God as something to cling to. Instead, He gave up His divine privileges; He took the humble position of a slave and was born as a human being." Jesus was already one with the Father, but He set aside His rights as Divinity and took the form of a baby (John 1:1). He went on to live the normal life of a Jewish boy, obeying His earthly parents (Luke 2:51).

A mother by definition precedes her child and at some point is more powerful than her child. So, to call Mary the "mother of God" gives the misleading implication that Mary preceded and at one time was more powerful than the Lord God Almighty. Although Catholic doctrine tries to deny this implication, it is inescapable.

It is biblical to say that Mary was the mother of the Lord Jesus Christ during His incarnation on the earth. However, Catholics believe it is not enough to say that Mary was the mother of Jesus. Pope John Paul II, in a speech in 1996, encouraged people "not only to invoke the Blessed Virgin as the Mother of Jesus, but also to recognize her as Mother of God" (*L'Osservatore Romano*, 4 December 1996, p. 11). This is not biblical. The Lord God Almighty has no mother, since He has no beginning and no end (Genesis 1:1; Revelation 4:8).

Recommended Resource: The Gospel According to Rome: Comparing Catholic Tradition and The Word of God by James McCarthy

---

Used with Permission from GotQuestions
https://www.gotquestions.org/Mary-mother-God-theotokos.html

"IS MARY THE CO-REDEMPTRIX / MEDIATRIX?"

Answer: Some Catholics view Mary as a co-redemptrix or a mediatrix who plays a key role in the salvation of mankind. (The suffix *-trix* is a feminine word ending in Latin, so a redemptrix is a female redeemer, and a mediatrix is a female mediator.) Within Catholicism, there is a drive to define a new Marian dogma in which Catholics, as a matter of faith, would be obliged to accept these three doctrines: (1) Mary participates in redemption with Jesus Christ, (2) grace is granted by Jesus only through the intercession of Mary, and (3) all prayers from the faithful must flow through Mary, who brings them to the attention of her Son. This movement would, in practice, redefine the Trinity as a kind of Quartet.

The belief in Mary as a co-redemptrix would be in addition to current Catholic teaching on Mary, which states that Mary was a virgin perpetually, that she never had intercourse with her husband, Joseph; that she never had children other than Jesus; and that she was sinless and ascended into heaven. These teachings are more than unscriptural; Scripture directly refutes them.

The idea that Mary is a co-redemptrix or mediatrix contradicts 1 Timothy 2:5, which says, "For there is one God and one mediator between God and mankind, the man Christ Jesus." Jesus is the Mediator. There is no mediator between man and Jesus. Jesus Himself dwells in believers; thus, none is required (Colossians 1:27).

Jesus is the perfect and sole Mediator between man and God because He is the sinless Son of God. Mary was not sinless. There is no Scripture whatsoever to back the claim of Mary's sinlessness or of her assumption into heaven. This dogma was accepted as a result of papal proclamation. In the biblical narratives, Mary is pictured as a humble and submissive young woman, faithful to God, grasping the implications of what is about to happen to her, and uttering praises and doxologies (Luke 1:46–55). In fact, in her *Magnificat*, Mary says, "My spirit rejoices in God my Savior" (verse 47). The clear implication of Mary's calling God her "Savior" is that she recognized her need of salvation. Just like the rest of us, Mary needed a Savior, a Redeemer.

Jesus Himself indicated that Mary holds no special place relative to redemption or mediation. In Matthew 12:47–50, Mary and her other sons were trying to see Jesus while He was teaching. "Someone told Him, 'Your mother and brothers are standing outside, wanting to speak to you.' He replied to him, 'Who is my mother, and who are my brothers?' Pointing to His disciples, He said, 'Here are my mother and my brothers. For whoever does the will of my Father in heaven is my brother and sister and mother.'"

Later, at the foot of the cross, Mary is a grief-stricken mother. She did not suffer for mankind as a whole; she clearly suffered her own pain and mourning. She is one of the people receiving salvation from Jesus, not a contributor to His work. She is anguished and must be cared for by the apostle John.

After Jesus' death and resurrection, Mary was part of the community of believers continuing in prayer and supplication prior to Pentecost (Acts 1:14). Mary is "most blessed among women" (Luke 1:42) because she was the mother of the Messiah. But she is not divine and cannot be seen as part of the Trinity.

She did not redeem us from sin and cannot be made part of the redemptive process.

Recommended Resource: The Gospel According to Rome: Comparing Catholic Tradition and The Word of God by James McCarthy

---

Used with Permission from GotQuestions
https://www.gotquestions.org/Mary-redemptrix-mediatrix.html

"WHAT IS MARIOLATRY?"

Answer: *Mariolatry* is defined as "excessive veneration or worship of Mary, the mother of Jesus." The word literally means "Mary-worship". Protestants often accuse Catholics of Mariolatry, and Catholics deny the charge, insisting that they venerate Mary but stop short of giving her divine worship. The official teaching of the Roman Catholic Church is that God alone deserves "adoration", also called *latria*; however, saints are worthy of a lesser honor called "veneration" or *dulia*. Catholic doctrine goes on to say that God has exalted the Virgin Mary above all other saints, and she should thus receive the highest form of *dulia*, called *hyperdulia*. But, Catholics are careful to say, *hyperdulia* is inferior to *latria*. Catholics claim that, since they do not give Mary the adoration that only the Creator can receive, they are not guilty of Mariolatry. The Eastern Orthodox Church also venerates Mary as the foremost saint, calling her the "Most Holy Virgin Mary", singing hymns to her, praying to her, and kissing her icon.

As a form of idolatry, Mariolatry is sinful. The Bible lists idolatry with other sins such as sorcery, jealousy, divination, sexual immorality, and enmity—these are works of the flesh (Galatians 5:20). An idol is anything that replaces the one, true God or that is given equal honor. Idolatry was expressly forbidden in the Ten Commandments (Exodus 20:3–4). The Israelites were warned that "the Lord your God is a consuming fire, a jealous God" (Deuteronomy 4:24).

Mariolatry holds Jesus' mother up as an object of trust, veneration, and deification. There are biblical warnings against worshiping anyone other than God. Mary was a natural woman. She has no power to connect us to God, heal us, or hear our prayers. Do the Catholic and Orthodox Churches promote Mariology? They deny they do; however, the difference between "adoration" and "highest veneration" is difficult to see. Elevating Mary with titles such as Mediatrix, Co-redemptrix, Cause of Our Salvation, Most Holy Mother of God, Our Immaculate Lady, and Queen of Heaven cannot help but foster Mariolatry. Singing hymns to Mary, praying to her, kissing her picture, parading her image through the streets, and bowing down before her statue reflect a degree of reverence that certainly imitates idolatry and might as well be called Mariolatry.

Recommended Resource: The Gospel According to Rome: Comparing Catholic Tradition and The Word of God by James McCarthy

---

Used with Permission from GotQuestions
https://www.gotquestions.org/Mariolatry.html

"WHAT IS THE HAIL MARY THAT CATHOLICS SAY SO OFTEN?"

Answer: The "Hail Mary," *Ave Maria* in Latin, is a Roman Catholic prayer to the Virgin Mary that consists of salutations and a plea for her intercession. Also, the term "Hail Mary pass" was used by the press to describe a pass by Dallas Cowboys quarterback Roger Staubach in a 1975 divisional playoff game and has come to be synonymous in football with a long pass that has little chance of success. The text of the Hail Mary prayer incorporates two Bible passages: "Hail Mary; full of grace, the Lord is with thee". (Luke 1:28) and "Blessed art thou amongst women and blessed is the fruit of thy womb" (Luke 1:42). The first passage is the angel Gabriel's greeting to Mary when he came to inform her that she had been chosen to bear the Messiah. The second is her cousin Elizabeth's greeting to Mary when Mary came to visit her cousin, who was also pregnant at the time with John the Baptist. The third part of the Hail Mary prayer is not from the Bible and is, in fact, in direct contradiction to Scriptural truth: "Holy Mary, Mother of God, pray for us sinners, now and at the hour of our death. Amen."

This last part of the Hail Mary prayer has three unbiblical parts to it. First, Mary is not and never was "holy". Mary was a human being who was born, as all humans are, with a sin nature and who recognized that she needed a Savior. In fact, the very passage used in the Hail Mary, known as Mary's Magnificat (Luke 1:46-55), contains the declaration "my spirit rejoices in God my Savior", a clear indication that she understood her need for a Savior from sin. The Bible never says that Mary was anyone but an ordinary human whom God chose to use in an extraordinary way. Yes, Mary was a righteous woman and favored (graced) by God (Luke 1:27-28). At the same time, Mary was a sinful human being who needed Jesus Christ as her Savior, just like everyone else (Ecclesiastes 7:20; Romans 3:23; 6:23; 1 John 1:8).

The second unbiblical part of the Hail Mary is addressing Mary as the "Mother of God". Mary was the human mother of the human Jesus Christ, who was indeed God incarnate. But she was not the mother of God, neither is she the "queen of heaven", another title given to her by the Catholic Church which has no basis in Scripture. God doesn't have a mother, nor does He have a queen. He is an eternal, infinite Being, uncreated and unborn, self-sufficient and self-sustaining.

The third unbiblical statement in the Hail Mary is the plea for her to "pray for us sinners". Here, we see the unbiblical practice of praying to Mary to intercede with God for us. First, we do not need another intercessor with God. Christ is the only intercessor we need. Through Jesus and Him alone, we have direct access to the Father. Christ alone mediates and intercedes between God and man. "For there is one God and one mediator between God and men, the man Christ Jesus" (1 Timothy 2:5). Prayer to anyone other than God alone is anti-biblical. Praying to Mary or petitioning her to pray for us is against the Scriptures. Prayer is an act of worship. When we pray to God, we are admitting that we need His help. Directing our prayers to anyone other than God is robbing God of the glory that is His alone, something God hates and will not tolerate (Isaiah 42:8).

While Mary was certainly a godly young woman greatly blessed in that she was chosen to bear the Savior of the world, she was not in any way divine, nor was she sinless, nor is she to be worshipped, revered, venerated, or prayed to.

Recommended Resource: The Gospel According to Rome: Comparing Catholic Tradition and The Word of God by James McCarthy

---

Used with Permission from GotQuestions
https://www.gotquestions.org/Hail-Mary.htm

"IS JESUS GOD IN THE FLESH? WHY IS IT IMPORTANT THAT JESUS IS GOD IN THE FLESH?"

Answer: Since Jesus' conception by the Holy Spirit in the womb of the virgin Mary (Luke 1:26-38), the real identity of Jesus Christ has always been questioned by skeptics. It began with Mary's fiancé, Joseph, who was afraid to marry her when she revealed that she was pregnant (Matthew 1:18-24). He took her as his wife only after the angel confirmed to him that the child she carried was the Son of God.

Hundreds of years before the birth of Christ, the prophet Isaiah foretold the coming of God's Son: "For to us a child is born, to us a son is given, and the government will be on his shoulders. And he will be called Wonderful Counselor, Mighty God, Everlasting Father, Prince of Peace" (Isaiah 9:6). When the angel spoke to Joseph and announced the impending birth of Jesus, he alluded to Isaiah's prophecy: "The virgin will conceive and give birth to a son, and they will call Him Immanuel (which means 'God with us')" (Matthew 1:23). This did not mean they were to name the baby Immanuel; it meant that "God with us" was the baby's identity. Jesus was God coming in the flesh to dwell with man.

Jesus Himself understood the speculation about His identity. He asked His disciples, "Who do people say that I am?" (Matthew 16:13; Mark 8:27). The answers varied, as they do today. Then Jesus asked a more pressing question: "Who do you say that I am?" (Matthew 16:15). Peter gave the right answer: "You are the Christ, the Son of the living God" (Matthew 16:16). Jesus affirmed the truth of Peter's answer and promised that, upon that truth, He would build His church (Matthew 16:18).

The true nature and identity of Jesus Christ has eternal significance. Every person must answer the question Jesus asked His disciples: "Who do you say that I am?"

He gave us the correct answer in many ways. In John 14:9-10, Jesus said, "Anyone who has seen Me has seen the Father. How can you say, 'Show us the Father'? Don't you believe that I am in the Father, and that the Father is in Me? The words I say to you I do not speak on my own authority. Rather, it is the Father, living in Me, who is doing His work."

The Bible is clear about the divine nature of the Lord Jesus Christ (see John 1:1-14). Philippians 2:6-7 says that, although Jesus was "in very nature God, He did not consider equality with God something to be used to His own advantage; rather, He made Himself nothing by taking the very nature of a servant, being made in human likeness." Colossians 2:9 says, "In Christ, all the fullness of the Deity lives in bodily form."

Jesus is fully God and fully man, and the fact of His incarnation is of utmost importance. He lived a human life but did not possess a sin nature as we do. He was tempted but never sinned (Hebrews 2:14-18; 4:15). Sin entered the world through Adam, and Adam's sinful nature has been transferred to every baby born into the world (Romans 5:12)—except for Jesus. Because Jesus did not have a human father, He did not inherit a sin nature. He possessed the divine nature from His Heavenly Father.

Jesus had to meet all the requirements of a holy God before He could be an acceptable sacrifice for our sin (John 8:29; Hebrews 9:14). He had to fulfill over three hundred prophecies about the Messiah that God, through the prophets, had foretold (Matthew 4:13-14; Luke 22:37; Isaiah 53; Micah 5:2).

Since the fall of man (Genesis 3:21-23), the only way to be made right with God has been the blood of an innocent sacrifice (Leviticus 9:2; Numbers 28:19; Deuteronomy 15:21; Hebrews 9:22). Jesus was the final, perfect sacrifice that satisfied forever God's wrath against sin (Hebrews 10:14). His divine nature made Him fit for the work of Redeemer; His human body allowed Him to shed the blood necessary to redeem. No human being with a sin nature could pay such a debt. No one else could meet the requirements to become the sacrifice for the sins of the whole world (Matthew 26:28; 1 John 2:2). If Jesus were merely a good man as some claim, then He had a sin nature and was not perfect. In that case, His death and resurrection would have no power to save anyone.

Because Jesus was God in the flesh, He alone could pay the debt we owed to God. His victory over death and the grave won the victory for everyone who puts their trust in Him (John 1:12; 1 Corinthians 15:3-4, 17).

Recommended Resource: The Moody Handbook of Theology by Paul Enns

---

Used with Permission from GotQuestions
https://www.gotquestions.org/God-in-the-flesh.html

"HOW CAN JESUS BE GOD, WHEN NUMBERS 23:19 SAYS GOD IS NOT A MAN OR SON OF MAN?"

Answer: Some claim that the Old Testament proves that Jesus cannot be God because of Numbers 23:19a, which says, "God is not a man, that He should lie; neither the son of man, that He should repent" (KJV). The reasoning is that, if God is not a man, then the Christian claim that Jesus, a man, is God is false. Just as troublesome is the fact that Jesus repeatedly calls Himself the "Son of Man" in the gospels (e.g., Mark 14:21).

The Old Testament does indeed teach that God is not a human being, not only in Numbers 23:19 but also in 1 Samuel 15:29 and Hosea 11:9. However, the New Testament shows us that Jesus made claims to be God—and at the same time He calls Himself the "Son of Man," a title that proclaims His humanity. With all this being true, how can we prove that Jesus is God?

Jesus claimed to be both the Son of God and the Son of Man. There are no tricks here. He said that He is God, and He said that He is (at the same time) human. No one had ever said such a thing before. It was strange then, and it is strange now—strange enough for a new term, the *hypostatic union*. No one will ever fully understand the union of Christ's divine and human natures, no matter how much we talk about it, define it, or typify it. Therefore, "proof" cannot be obtained. We either believe Jesus, or we do not.

It is critical to understand at this point that the Bible is true in detail and *in toto*—both the Old and New Testaments. So, when Jesus began teaching new things, the old things did not become untrue; they became unveiled. Remember what He said about the Law: "Do not think that I have come to abolish the Law or the Prophets; I have not come to abolish them but to fulfill them" (Matthew 5:17). All of Jesus' new revelations work exactly the same way. The old knowledge was shadowy, and, as the Light of the world, Jesus dispelled the shadows (see Colossians 2:16–17). This process is not destructive of the old knowledge—it is instructive, as Philip's encounter with the Ethiopian shows (Acts 8:30–35).

We must also consider what the Old Testament is really saying about God when it says He is not a human being. The point being made in Numbers 23:19, 1 Samuel 15:29, and Hosea 11:9 is that God does not lie. He is not fickle. His emotions do not change His eternal purposes. This is unlike fallen humanity, who cannot see the big picture, who often breaks promises, and whose feelings often cloud discernment. In other words, the statements that God is not a man are contrasting one aspect of God's nature with a corresponding part of man's. Saying, "God is not a man", has nothing to do with whether or not God can ever exist in the flesh.

The Old Testament references to God being unlike man do not apply to Jesus' particular type of humanity. All they are telling us is that God is not a man as we think of men. It's a contrast, not a restriction. There is nothing that logically prevents God from becoming a man in a whole new way—in fact, redemption *requires* this, and redemption was God's plan from before the foundation of the world (Revelation 13:8). Thus, it can be said that God knew He would become a man before Numbers 23:19 was even penned!

If we consider the Old Testament in isolation (which is the Jewish perspective), we shall not likely "prove" that Jesus Christ was man, God, Messiah, and Savior—although the indicators are all there (see Isaiah 53, for example). Christians see the foreshadowing of the God-man in the Old Testament because the New Testament revelation helps interpret the Old Testament references (e.g., Matthew 2:15; cf. Hosea 11:1). This brings up an important fact regarding biblical interpretation: God reveals His truth progressively, over time. He has unfolded His purposes sequentially and as needed over the millennia.

For example, Adam and Eve in their innocence had no need to know about redemption, but *after* they sinned, then the time was appropriate, and God laid it out for them in Genesis 3:15. That bit of revelation was given at a point in time, but its full meaning did not become clear until after Christ came in the flesh—and as the authors of the New Testament were writing under inspiration. We understand *now* that Genesis 3:15 points directly to Jesus' atoning death—and this revelation is necessary for us today. But that information was not necessary for Adam and Eve. Their pre-fall ignorance, couched as it was in innocence, was appropriate for them.

In like manner, God revealed His will progressively to His people in the Old Testament Scriptures, and those people were responsible to behave in obedience according to where they were on revelation's timeline. Today, Christians are responsible for all of God's Word, because we live in a time when it is complete. Additionally, believers have the indwelling Holy Spirit, so there are no excuses for not acknowledging Jesus Christ as God.

Since revelation is progressive, a person's response to God depends on where he is on the timeline. An Old Testament Jew would have no concept of the God-man, although clues (such as Psalm 110:1) were present. But John the Baptist's prophecies, followed by Jesus' miracles, were further revelation. In fact, Jesus' miracles were signs to prove who He is: "Jesus performed many other signs in the presence of His disciples, which are not recorded in this book. But these are written that you may believe that Jesus is the Messiah, the Son of God" (John 20:30–31). People today still need to respond in faith to Jesus' miracles. Those who do not are spiritually blind.

To summarize, God's statement that He is not a man and Jesus' statement that He is the Son of God coexist as true; they are not in conflict. Revelation is progressive, and Old Testament concepts are more fully developed in the New Testament. Finally, God always had it in mind that the Son would become flesh and dwell among men, so God never "changed His mind" about becoming a man.

Recommended Resource: Jesus: The Greatest Life of All by Charles Swindoll

---

Used with Permission from GotQuestions
https://www.gotquestions.org/God-is-not-a-man.html

CONNECTING WITH THE DIVINE

The major world religions and their beliefs about God. Hinduism, Buddhism, Islam, Christianity, and New Age...

By Marilyn Adamson[48]

We all want to make it through life with success, some sense that we did it right. So what about the major world religions? Is there anything in them that might give our lives greater depth and direction?

The following looks at the major world religions... Hinduism, New Age, Buddhism, Islam, and Christianity.* There is a brief description of each, their view of God, and what a person can gain from that religion. The ending explains how Jesus' teaching differs from the major religions.

*Each of these religions has sects with differing beliefs. The description given here focuses on the core beliefs of each religion. Other major religions, such as Judaism, could be discussed, but for brevity, we have chosen these.

Hinduism and its beliefs

Most Hindus worship one Being of ultimate oneness (Brahman) through infinite representations of gods and goddesses. These various deities become incarnate within idols, temples, gurus, rivers, animals, etc.

Hindus believe their position in this present life was determined by their actions in a previous life. Hinduism therefore provides a possible explanation for suffering and evil in this life. If a person's behavior before was evil, they might justifiably experience tremendous hardships in this life. Pain, disease, poverty or a disaster like a flood is deserved by that person because of their own evil actions, usually from a previous lifetime.
A Hindu's goal is to become free from the law of karma...to be free from continuous reincarnations. Only the soul matters which will one day be free of the cycle of rebirths and be at rest.

Hinduism gives a person freedom to choose how to work toward spiritual perfection. There are three possible ways to end this cycle of karma: 1. Be lovingly devoted to any of the Hindu deities; 2. Grow in knowledge through meditation of Brahman (oneness)...to realize that circumstances in life are not real, that selfhood is an illusion and only Brahman is real; 3. Be dedicated to various religious ceremonies and rites.

---

[48] To read about the author go to: https://www.everystudent.com/menus/marilyn.html

New Age and its beliefs

New Age promotes the development of the person's own power or divinity. When referring to deity, a follower of New Age is not talking about a transcendent, personal God who created the universe, but is referring to a higher consciousness within themselves. A person in New Age would see themselves as deity, the cosmos, the universe. In fact, everything that the person sees, hears, feels or imagines is to be considered divine.

Highly eclectic, New Age presents itself as a collection of ancient spiritual traditions. It acknowledges many gods and goddesses, as in Hinduism. The Earth is viewed as the source of all spirituality, and has its own intelligence, emotions and deity. But superseding all is self. Self is the originator, controller and power over all. There is no reality outside of what the person determines.

New Age teaches a wide array of eastern mysticism and spiritual, metaphysical and psychic techniques, such as breathing exercises, chanting, drumming, meditating...to develop an altered consciousness and one's own divinity.

Anything negative a person experiences (failures, sadness, anger, selfishness, hurt) is considered an illusion. Believing themselves to be completely sovereign over their life, nothing about their life is wrong, negative or painful. Eventually a person develops spiritually to the degree that there is no objective, external reality. A person, becoming a god, creates his own reality.

Buddhism and its beliefs

Buddhists do not worship any gods or God. People outside of Buddhism often think that Buddhists worship the Buddha. However, the Buddha (Siddhartha Gautama) never claimed to be divine, but rather he is viewed by Buddhists as having attained what they are also striving to attain, which is spiritual enlightenment and, with it, freedom from the continuous cycle of life and death. Most Buddhists believe a person has countless rebirths, which inevitably include suffering. A Buddhist seeks to end these rebirths. Buddhists believe it is a person's cravings, aversion and delusion that cause these rebirths. Therefore, the goal of a Buddhist is to purify one's heart and to let go of all yearnings toward sensual desires and the attachment to oneself.

Buddhists follow a list of religious principles and very dedicated meditation. When a Buddhist meditates it is not the same as praying or focusing on a god, it is more of a self-discipline. Through practiced meditation a person may reach Nirvana -- "the blowing out" of the flame of desire.
Buddhism provides something that is true of most major religions: disciplines, values and directives that a person may want to live by.

Islam and its beliefs

Muslims believe there is the one almighty God, named Allah, who is infinitely superior to and transcendent from humankind. Allah is viewed as the creator of the universe and the source of all good and all evil. Everything that happens is Allah's will. He is a powerful and strict judge, who will be merciful toward followers depending on the sufficiency of their life's good works and religious devotion. A follower's relationship with Allah is as a servant to Allah.

Though a Muslim honors several prophets, Muhammad is considered the last prophet and his words and lifestyle are that person's authority. To be a Muslim, one has to follow five religious duties: 1. Repeat a creed about Allah and Muhammad; 2. Recite certain prayers in Arabic five times a day; 3. Give to the needy; 4. One month each year, fast from food, drink, sex and smoking from sunrise to sunset; 5. Pilgrimage once in one's lifetime to worship at a shrine in Mecca. At death -- based on one's faithfulness to these duties -- a Muslim hopes to enter Paradise. If not, they will be eternally punished in hell.

For many people, Islam matches their expectations about religion and deity. Islam teaches that there is one supreme deity, who is worshiped through good deeds and disciplined religious rituals. After death a person is rewarded or punished according to their religious devotion. Muslims believe that giving up one's life for Allah is a sure way of entering Paradise.

Christianity and its beliefs

Christians believe in a loving God who has revealed Himself and can be known in a personal way, in this life. With Jesus Christ, the person's focus is not on religious rituals or performing good works, but on enjoying a relationship with God and growing to know Him better.

Faith in Jesus Christ Himself, not just in His teachings, is how the Christian experiences joy and a meaningful life. In His life on Earth, Jesus did not identify Himself as a prophet pointing to God, or as a teacher of enlightenment. Rather, Jesus claimed to be God in human form. He performed miracles, forgave people of their sin and said that anyone who believed in Him would have eternal life. He made statements like, "I am the light of the world; he who follows Me will not walk in darkness, but will have the light of life."[1]

Christians regard the Bible as God's written message to humankind. In addition to being an historical record of Jesus' life and miracles, the Bible reveals his personality, his love and truth, and how one can have a relationship with him. Whatever circumstances a Christian is dealing with in their life, the Bible teaches that they can confidently turn to a wise and powerful God who genuinely loves them. They believe that he answers prayer and that life takes on meaning as they live to honor him.

How distinct are these major religions?

In looking at these major belief systems and their views of God, we find tremendous diversity:

- Hindus acknowledge multitudes of gods and goddesses.
- Buddhists say there is no deity.
- New Age followers believe they are God.
- Muslims believe in a powerful but unknowable God.
- Christians believe in a God who is loving and approachable.

Are all religions worshiping the same God? Let's consider that. New Age teaches that everyone should come to center on a cosmic consciousness, but it would require Islam to give up their one God, Hinduism to give up their numerous gods, and Buddhism to establish that there is a God.

The world's major religions (Hinduism, New Age, Buddhism, Islam, following Jesus Christ) are each quite unique. And of these, one affirms that there is a personal, loving God who can be known now, in this life. Jesus Christ spoke of a God who welcomes us into a relationship with Him and comes along side us as a comforter, counselor and powerful God who loves us.

In Hinduism a person is on their own trying to gain release from karma. In New Age a person is working at their own divinity. In Buddhism it is an individual quest at being free from desire. And in Islam, the individual follows religious laws for the sake of paradise after death. In Jesus' teaching, you see a personal relationship with a personal God -- a relationship that carries over into the next life.

Can a person connect with God in this life?

The answer is yes. Not only can you connect with God, you also can know that you are fully accepted and loved by Him.

Many world religions place an individual on their own, striving for spiritual perfection. Buddha, for example, never claimed sinlessness. Muhammad also admitted that he was in need of forgiveness. "No matter how wise, no matter how gifted, no matter how influential other prophets, gurus, and teachers might be, they had the presence of mind to know that they were imperfect just like the rest of us."[2]

Jesus Christ, however, never alluded to any personal sin. Instead, Jesus forgave people of their sin and He wants to forgive us of our sin also. We all are aware of our faults, the areas of our lives that may cause others to think less of us, areas that we ourselves wish were not there...maybe it's an addiction, a bad temper, impurity, hateful remarks. God loves us but hates sin, and He has said that the consequence for sin is separation from knowing Him. But He provided a way for us to be forgiven and know Him. Jesus, the Son of God, God in human form, took all of our sin on Himself, suffered on a cross, and willingly died in our place. The Bible says, "By this we know love, that He laid down his life for us."[3]

God is offering us complete forgiveness because of Jesus' death for us. This means forgiveness for all our sins...past, present and future. Jesus paid for them all. God, who created the universe, loves us and wants to be in a relationship with us. "This is how God showed His love among us: He sent his one and only Son into the world that we might live through Him."[4]

Christ offers us real freedom from our sin and guilt. He does not leave a person's failures on their shoulders, with a dim hope of becoming a better person tomorrow. In Jesus Christ, God reached toward humanity, providing a way for us to know Him. "For God so loved the world that He sent His one and only Son, that whoever believes in Him should not perish, but have eternal life."[5]

God wants us to know him.

We were created by God to live in relationship with Him. Jesus said, "He who comes to Me will never go hungry, and he who believes in Me will never be thirsty...and whoever comes to Me I will never drive away."[6] Jesus called people not only to follow His teachings, but to follow Him. He said, "I am the way, and the truth and the life."[7] In claiming to be the truth, Christ goes beyond mere prophets and teachers who simply said they were speaking the truth.[8]

Jesus identified himself as equal to God, and even gave proof. Jesus said that He would be crucified on a cross and that three days after His death, He would come back to life. He didn't say He would reincarnate someday into a future life. (Who would know if He actually did it?) He said three days after being buried He would show Himself alive to those who saw His crucifixion. On that third day, Jesus' tomb was found empty and many people testified that they saw Him alive again. He now offers eternal life to us.

Unlike many world religions...

Many religions focus on a person's spiritual efforts. With Jesus Christ it's a two-way interaction between you and God. He welcomes us to go to Him. "The Lord is near to all who call upon Him, to all who call upon Him in truth."[9] You can communicate with God, who will answer your prayer, give you greater peace and joy, provide direction, show you His love, and transform your life. Jesus said, "I came that they might have life, and have it more abundantly."[10] It will not mean that life will become perfect and free of problems. But it means that in the midst of life, you can relate to God who is willing to be involved in your life and faithful in His love.

This is not a commitment to a method of self-improvement like the Eight Fold Path or the Five Pillars, or meditation, or good works or even the Ten Commandments. These seem clear, well-defined, easy-to-follow paths for spirituality. But they become a burdensome striving for perfection, and connection with God is still distant.

Our hope is not in following laws or standards, but in knowing a Savior who fully accepts us because of our faith in Him and His sacrifice for us. We don't earn our place in heaven by religious efforts or good deeds. Heaven is a free gift to us, when we begin a relationship with Jesus Christ. Would you like to be totally forgiven and personally come to know God's love for you?

Beginning a relationship with God.

You can begin a relationship with God right now. It is as simple as sincerely asking Him for His forgiveness of your sin and inviting Him to enter your life. Jesus said, "Behold, I stand at the door [of your heart] and knock. If anyone hears My voice and opens the door, I will come into him."[11] Would like to begin a relationship with the God who created you, who deeply loves you? You can do so right now, if it is your heart's desire: "God, I ask you to forgive me and invite you to enter my heart right now. Thank you Jesus for dying for my sins. Thank you for coming into my life as you said you would."

The Bible tells us that "as many as received Him, to them He gave the right to become children of God."[12] If you sincerely asked God to come into your life, you have begun a personal relationship with Him. It is like you have just met God and He wants to help you grow to know Him better, to know His love for you, to guide you with wisdom in whatever decisions confront you. The book called "John" in the Bible is a good place to learn more about a relationship with God. Perhaps you might want to tell someone else about the decision you have made to ask Jesus into your life.

In the world's religions a person has a relationship with teachings, ideas, paths, rituals. Through Jesus, a person can have a relationship with the loving and powerful God. You can talk with Him and He will guide you in this life now. He doesn't just point you to a path, a philosophy, or a religion. He welcomes you to know Him, to experience joy, and to have confidence in His love in the midst of life's challenges. "See what love the Father has given us, that we should be called children of God."[13]

Footnotes: (1) John 8:12 (2) Erwin W. Lutzer, *Christ Among Other Gods* (Chicago: Moody Press, 1994), p. 63 (3) I John 3:16 (4) I John 4:9 (5) John 3:16 (6) John 6:35 (7) John 14:6 (8) Lutzer, p. 106 (9) Psalms 145:18 (10) John 10:10 (11) Revelation 3:20 (12) John 1:12 (13) I John 3:1

Used with Permission from EveryStudent
https://www.everystudent.com/features/connecting.html

"IS JESUS DEAD?"

Answer: Many world leaders have left their marks on the pages of history. Religious gurus have helped shape culture and thought. But regardless of what they taught, accomplished, or believed, they all have one thing in common—they are all dead. There was a point at which each mystic, emperor, and philosopher came into being and another point at which they exited this world. We can visit their grave sites or memorials, and beneath the ground their corpses or bone fragments are still there. Every leader, prophet, or king has died or will die, and, once they die, that's it. They face the judgment of God just like every other human being (Hebrews 9:27; 2 Corinthians 5:10)—with one exception. Jesus Christ, the One upon whom the entire world's dating system is based, is not dead.

Because He was not just a mere man, Jesus did not come into existence at a specific point in time. He has always existed as the Son of God (John 1:1–5; 8:58). He chose to leave heaven and enter this world in the form of a human baby (Luke 1:35; Philippians 2:5–8). And, although His mother was human, His Father was God. Jesus Christ was fully God and fully man living this earthly life so that He could become the intermediary between sinful mankind and a holy Creator (1 Timothy 2:5). He suffered as we do, yet He never sinned (Hebrews 4:15). He always did what pleased His Father (John 8:29; 14:31). And when the time came, He offered Himself as the final sacrifice for our sins (John 10:18; 2 Corinthians 5:21).

Jesus was arrested and put on trial because He claimed to be God (John 5:18; 10:33). They crucified Him as it had been prophesied in Psalm 22 and Isaiah 53 (Luke 22:37). As He hung on the cross, Jesus became every sin that humanity has invented (2 Corinthians 5:21; 1 John 2:2). He paid in full the price we owe God so that we could be considered righteous and forgiven. When He cried out, "It is finished!" (John 19:30), He was not referring to His earthly life, because He had already told His followers that God would raise Him from the dead in three days (Mark 9:31; 10:33–34). He meant that the plan to redeem fallen man, which He and the Father had known from the beginning, had now been completed (1 Peter 1:18–20; Acts 2:23; Ephesians 1:4). Jesus really did die physically and stayed dead for the better part of three days.

Jesus was buried in a borrowed tomb, because He would not be needing it for long (Matthew 27:59–60). The tomb was secured by Roman officials with a seal and a heavy boulder, making it nearly impossible to open. Then guards were assigned to keep watch for fear the disciples would try to steal the body and pretend He had risen as He had promised (Matthew 27:62–66). Everyone was familiar with Jesus' prediction, even though no one understood exactly what it meant (Mark 9:31–32). The guards were an extra precaution requested by the Jewish religious leaders in an effort to silence forever the new teachings Jesus of Nazareth had introduced into their culture. They figured that, once the Leader was dead and gone, the fervor of His followers would die down and things could go back to the way they had been.

Things would have settled down if Jesus had stayed in the tomb. If Jesus had not risen from the dead, He would have been no different from any other zealous reformer. In fact, Paul writes in 1 Corinthians 15:14 that, "if Christ has not been raised, our preaching is useless and so is your faith." Then in verses 17–19 he writes, "And if Christ has not been raised, your faith is futile; you are still in your sins. Then those also who have fallen asleep in Christ are lost. If only for this life we have hope in Christ, we are of all people most to be pitied."

But Jesus did not stay dead. On the third day, just as He had said, He walked out of that tomb (Matthew 28:2–10; Mark 16:4–7; Luke 24:1–8; John 20:1–8, 19). An angel knocked the guards out, kicked the stone out of the way, and sat on it, waiting for Jesus' friends to show up (Matthew 28:2; John 20:1, 11–12). For the next forty days, Jesus appeared to over five hundred people (1 Corinthians 15:3–7), demonstrating that He was indeed fully, physically alive (Luke 24:36–42). He then ascended back into heaven in the sight of His disciples (Luke 24:51; Acts 1:9–11).

Jesus is very much alive and is now seated at the right hand of the Father (Hebrews 1:3). He "ever lives" to make intercession for His people (Hebrews 7:25) and has promised that He will come again (John 14:3; Revelation 22:2). He endured separation from God (Matthew 27:46) so that we don't have to and conquered death so that we can, too (1 Corinthians 15:55). He has set Himself apart from every other religious leader because there is no grave with His name on it. There is no tomb with a body in it. Only the Son of God could die for the sins of the world and then rise from the dead. Because of His resurrection, all who place their trust in Him can have hope of a similar resurrection. Jesus is not dead, and because He lives, we can live in eternity with Him (John 3:16–18; 14:19).

Recommended Resource: The Case for the Resurrection of Jesus by Gary Habermas

---

Used with Permission from GotQuestions
https://www.gotquestions.org/is-Jesus-dead.html

"WHAT IS THE SWOON THEORY? DID JESUS SURVIVE THE CRUCIFIXION?"

Answer: The Swoon Theory is the belief that Jesus didn't really die at His crucifixion, but was merely unconscious when He was laid in the tomb and there He resuscitated. Accordingly, His appearances after three days in the tomb were merely perceived to be resurrection appearances. There are several reasons why this theory is invalid and can be easily proven as false, and there were at least three different persons or groups involved in Jesus' crucifixion who were all satisfied concerning the fact of His death on the cross. They are the Roman guards, Pilate, and the Sanhedrin.

The Roman Guards - There were two separate groups of Roman soldiers given the task of ensuring the death of Jesus: the executioners and the tomb guards. The soldiers in charge of execution were specialists in capital punishment, and crucifixion was one of the most brutal forms of execution in history. Jesus was nailed to a cross after enduring horrible beatings at the hands of these professional death merchants, and every person put to death by way of crucifixion was dealt with by these soldiers. Their job was to ensure the task was completed. Jesus could not have survived crucifixion, and these soldiers made certain that Jesus was dead before His body was allowed to be taken from the cross. They were completely satisfied that Jesus was truly dead. The second group of soldiers was given the task of guarding the tomb of Jesus because of the request made to Pilate by the Sanhedrin. Matthew 27:62-66 tells us "On the next day, which followed the Day of Preparation, the chief priests and Pharisees gathered together to Pilate, saying, 'Sir, we remember, while He was still alive, how that deceiver said, "After three days I will rise." Therefore command that the tomb be made secure until the third day, lest His disciples come by night and steal Him away, and say to the people, "He has risen from the dead." So the last deception will be worse than the first.' Pilate said to them, 'You have a guard; go your way, make it as secure as you know how.' So they went and made the tomb secure, sealing the stone and setting the guard" (NKJV). These guards ensured that the tomb was secure, and their lives depended upon completion of their mission. Only the resurrection of the Son of God could have stayed them from their task.

Pilate - Pilate gave the order for Jesus to be crucified and entrusted this task to be carried out by a Roman centurion, a trusted and proven commander of 100 Roman soldiers. After the crucifixion, a request for the body of Jesus was made by Joseph of Arimathea, in order that His body could be placed in a tomb. Only after confirmation was given to him by his centurion did Pilate release the body into the care of Joseph. Mark 15:42-45: "Now when evening had come, because it was the Preparation Day, that is, the day before the Sabbath, Joseph of Arimathea, a prominent council member, who was himself waiting for the kingdom of God, coming and taking courage, went in to Pilate and asked for the body of Jesus. Pilate marveled that He was already dead; and summoning the centurion, he asked him if He had been dead for some time. And when he found out from the centurion, he granted the body to Joseph" (NKJV). Pilate was completely satisfied that Jesus was truly dead.

The Sanhedrin - The Sanhedrin was the ruling council of the Jewish people, and they requested that the bodies of those crucified, including Jesus, be taken down from the cross after their death because of the ensuing Sabbath day. John 19:31-37: "Therefore, because it was the Preparation Day, that the bodies should not remain on the cross on the Sabbath (for that Sabbath was a high day), the Jews asked Pilate that their legs might be broken, and that they might be taken away. Then the soldiers came and broke the legs of the first and of the other who was crucified with Him. But when they came to Jesus and saw that He was already dead, they did not break His legs. But one of the soldiers pierced His side with a spear, and immediately blood and water came out. And he who has seen has testified, and his testimony is true; and he knows that he is telling the truth, so that you may believe. For these things were done that the Scripture should be fulfilled, 'Not one of His bones shall be broken.' And again another Scripture says, 'They shall look on Him whom they pierced.'" These Jews who demanded that Jesus be crucified, and even going so far as to suggest an insurrection had He not been crucified, would never have allowed Jesus' body to be removed from the cross were He not already dead. These men were completely satisfied that Jesus was truly dead.

There is other evidence that the Swoon Theory is invalid, such as the condition of Jesus' body after the resurrection. At every appearance, Jesus' body was shown to be in a glorified state, and the only marks remaining as proof of His crucifixion were the nail prints He asked Thomas to touch as proof of who He was. Anyone who had experienced what Jesus experienced would have needed months to recover physically. Jesus' body bore only the marks of the nails in His hands and feet. The way in which Jesus' body was prepared after the crucifixion is further evidence to refute the theory. Had Jesus only been unconscious, the linens He was wrapped in would have been impossible for Him to escape from, had He been merely a man. The way in which the women attended to Jesus' body is further evidence of his death. They came to the tomb on the first day of the week to further anoint His body with embalming ointments as they had little time to prepare His body prior to the beginning of the Sabbath after His crucifixion. Had He been merely unconscious as the theory supposes, they would have brought medicinal tools to help in His resuscitation.

The purpose for the Swoon Theory is not to dispute His death, but rather, it seeks to disprove His resurrection. If Jesus didn't resurrect, then He's not God. If Jesus truly died and rose from the dead, His power over death proves that He is the Son of God. The evidence demands the verdict: Jesus truly died on the cross, and Jesus truly rose from the dead.

Recommended Resource: Jesus: The Greatest Life of All by Charles Swindoll

Used with Permission from GotQuestions
https://www.gotquestions.org/why-believe-resurrection.html

Made in United States
Troutdale, OR
06/02/2024